The Persians

The Persians

from the earliest days to the ·
twentieth century

Alessandro Bausani

translated from the Italian by J. B. Donne

4792

Elek Books Limited
54-58 Caledonian Road London N1 9RN

Printed in England by
Weatherby Woolnough

Contents

Illustrations

Maps

Preface

This book is not intended to replace the existing histories of Persia. In particular the *Cambridge History of Iran*, of which two volumes out of a projected eight have appeared to date, will supply the reader interested in the political and cultural history of Iran with ample and detailed information. My aim has been to give a bird's-eye view of the development of the Persian nation from its origins to the present day. By concentrating on the *Persian* nation, I have automatically excluded the pre-Aryan civilizations of the Iranian plateau (e.g. the Elamites and others). Being personally much more interested in literary, religious and cultural history, rather than in political history, I have been able to approach Iran's political development from inside, as it were. My personal interpretation of Persian history is—as the reader will soon notice—rather anti-nationalistic and anti-romantic. This point of view will not perhaps be greatly appreciated by many Iranians.

The history of modern Persia epitomizes clearly the crisis that all modern so-called 'developing countries' are facing. Emerging from a 'feudal' culture in the space age, these nations seem to be compelled by destiny to jump over such precious experiences as those that we call 'the Reformation', 'the Renaissance', 'Illuminism' and the 'French Revolution', to confront modern international ideologies, and an economy rapidly developing in the context of a world-wide organization. This confrontation is not without reactions: Iran, like other nations in Asia and Africa chose nationalism not as a result of an autonomous social maturation in which its masses took part, but rather as a consequence of a sort of self-colonialism led by its extremely Europeanized elite. One of the best students of modern Persia, Professor Ann K. Lambton—whom nobody can suspect of being ideologically extreme—wrote in her remarkable book *Landlord and Peasant in Persia* (Oxford University Press, 1953, p. 395): '. . . it is futile to suppose a movement of reform can be brought about by an act of legislature alone. Its successful accomplishment presupposes changes so great as to amount to a social revolution'.

9

Can these changes, this social revolution, be brought about by resorting to a romantic nationalism that dreams of a supposed Achaemenian perfection, or by a liberalism taken from Europe and imposed on a population of which more than seventy percent are illiterate, or by a Marxism methodically ignoring any possibility of a religious reformation? One of the aims of this book is to show how a negative answer to this question is the logical outcome of a study of Persian history.

Just because I am myself a historian of religion and literature I have tried to counteract my natural tendency to emphasize purely cultural history, by devoting several pages of each chapter to the economic aspects of Iranian history. For this I am greatly indebted to the works of Soviet scholars, and especially the *History of Iran* written in collaboration by the Soviet orientalists Pigulevskaya, Yakubovskii, Petrushevskii, Stroevska and Belenitskii (see Bibliography).

The English edition contains only minor corrections and changes when compared to the Italian original. The most important difference is the omission of the last chapter which appeared in the Italian edition containing chiefly my personal (and perhaps slightly exaggerated) considerations on the present situation of Persian culture. This edition, without losing anything important, has become in this way more objectively historical.

The Bibliography has a double aim: first to give some guide to further reading; and secondly to give students of oriental history at least the chief sources (especially in Arabic and Persian) of the periods treated in each chapter. The subject is, however, so vast that omissions have been unavoidable.

Last but not least I feel it my pleasant duty to thank my translator Mr J. B. Donne for the fluent English form he has given to the translation, a rather difficult task, due to my proneness to long and complex sentences!

Rome, April 1970   A. Bausani

N.B. On the subject of transliteration of Persian names the following will be useful: The consonants sound more or less as in English, the vowels as in Italian. Long vowels are noted thus: $\bar{a}$, $\bar{\imath}$, $\bar{u}$, *Kh* is the *ch* of German *Nacht*. *Q* is articulated deeper than *k*, and in modern Persian is generally identical with *gh*.

CHAPTER I

The Aryans on the Iranian Plateau: The Achaemenian Empire

Geographically, the Iranian plateau lies like an immense crossroads between Central Asia (itself an extremely important meeting ground for the trade routes and various cultures of the Far East and Western Asia) and India, Mesopotamia and Asia Minor. Since about the eleventh century BC Indo-European tribes have been settled there; the name *Īrān* is derived from the ancient Iranian genitive plural *aryānām* = '[land] of the Aryans'. These two facts have had a decisive influence on the area's unusually long cultural history. The Indo-European peoples' proverbial capacity for assimilation, combined with their proximity to cultural centres of extraordinary importance for the ancient world, has made Persia both a cultural bridge and a melting-pot for a variety of civilizations which its inhabitants have succeeded in amalgamating. And this is true in both a chronological and a geographical sense. In ancient times Persia was considerably influenced by the Sumero-Akkadian civilizations of Mesopotamia, which subsequently fell under its domination. Chronologically, therefore, Persia forms a link between the archaeological world of the first millennia BC and the historical world which is so much more familiar to us. The latter followed upon what Jaspers has so rightly called the 'axial period' of human history from the eighth to fourth centuries BC, the period of the first 'individuals'—the Greek philosophers, Zoroaster, Buddha, and Confucius. And then geographically, the clarity of its thought and the constructiveness of its ideas seem to place Persian culture at an intermediary point between the world of India, with its tendency towards monism and naturalism, and that of the Near East, with its preference for polytheism and later for revealed religion. Ultimately, in the seventh century AD, the latter absorbed Persia in the great tidal wave of Islam, though vestiges of former times remained.

The Aryan invasion of the Iranian plateau can be dated to

about the eleventh century BC but it is not known for certain in what way the Aryans penetrated the region. As happened in other areas during periods of expansion of nomadic peoples, probably at first small groups infiltrated the plateau and were partly assimilated by the sedentary population, a non-Aryan people who, for want of a better term, are often referred to as 'Asianic', and whom certain scholars associate with the non-Aryan peoples to be found to-day in the Caucasus. Occasionally we come across references to areas with an Aryan aristocracy ruling over a non-Aryan population. Traces of such partial domination by Aryans who adopted the customs of the subject people are to be found in the names of kings and nobles among the Hittites, Mitanni and Kassites in Asia Minor, Upper Mesopotamia and Zagros (Western Iran). Subsequently, however, the situation altered, as Pagliaro has so clearly explained:

'Perhaps they were more numerous and united from the outset but, more probably because in time circumstances favoured a greater unity and a considerable increase in numbers, two groups of Aryans of a more recent migration succeeded in retaining, in the wide sense, their own distinctive linguistic, religious and cultural features, which at a certain moment led to the formation of a political organization. A large concentration of Indo-Europeans living on their own first developed a truly Aryan language (Indo-Iranian), and at the same time thrust their way into Upper Mesopotamia and the mountains of Zagros. Subsequently, they divided into two branches, one of which moved east and then south, reaching India, where it gave rise to the Indian peoples; while the other in part spread through the steppes to the west of the Caspian, and in part swept over the passes of the Caucasus or through the easy approaches from the north-east and reached the plateau which has received their name'. (*Civiltà dell' Oriente*, vol. I, Rome, 1956, pp. 389–90.)

Of the various groups that penetrated into the plateau two, the Medes and the Persians, are of major interest to us here. This short summary of the history of the Persians is too brief to permit us to deal with the archaeology of the civilizations which preceded the arrival of the Aryans on the Iranian plateau and the fascinating problems of prehistory and protohistory which the region poses.

The Assyrian annals written in the Akkadian language and in cuneiform script inform us that the Assyrian king Shalmaneser III (858–824 BC) invaded the territory of the *Parsua* to the west of Lake Urmia (Rezā'īyeh) and then thrust south-eastwards into the land of the *Māda*. This statement is extremely interesting, for it tells us that in the ninth century these two peoples, and in particular the Persians (the *Parsua* can definitely be identified as *Pārsa*, 'Persians'), were still at the stage of migration and displacement, and were at that time to be found in an area quite different from their historical centre—in the case of the Persians, Persis or Pārs. Later inscriptions and annals show that the Parsua continued to move further south-east, while the Māda remained in what came to be considered their historical home in the region of the modern Hamadān.

Towards the end of the eighth century BC, an inscription of Sargon II (722–705 BC) mentions the name of a Medean chief, Dayakku, almost certainly the same person as the Deioces of Herodotus. According to Herodotus, he was the founder of the Medean dynasty and of the capital, Ecbatana (in Medean, *Hangmātana*, 'meeting-place', perhaps an ancient military camp), where he built a palace surrounded by seven walls each, in imitation of the Babylonians, of a different hue, thus symbolizing the sun, the moon and planets. (It was the Babylonians who invented the seven-day week and the symbolism based on the number seven which was also to play such a large part in Persian art and letters.) Even in the sumptuous and majestic court ceremonial, the Medes closely followed the Babylonian and Assyrian forms. Deioces was perhaps succeeded by a Cyaxares I (*Uvakhshtra*), unknown to Herodotus but mentioned in 714 and again in 702 in the Assyrian sources. Then, according to Herodotus, came Phraortes or Khshathrita (a Medean form reconstructed from the Assyrian) who, again according to Herodotus, was the first to bring the Persians to submission, while from the Assyrian sources we know that he was the leader of anti-Assyrian coalitions. The 'challenge', to use Toynbee's word, which resulted in the formation of a great Medean power, was the invasion in the middle of the eighth century BC of the Scythians, wild nomads from 'Outer Iran' (Central Asia).

They were preceded by the Cimmerians who had come down from the passes of the Caucasus and penetrated south-eastwards into the Iranian plateau. After various vicissitudes, Cyaxares II, the son of Khshathrita, brought the Scythian rule on the plateau to an end in about 625 BC. While under Scythian domination, the peoples of Iran had adopted various of their practices, especially a method of fighting which employed archers on horseback, a speciality of the nomads of the steppes (in Mesopotamian texts the horse is the 'ass of the east', and in Hebrew *sūs*, derived from the name of the city of Susa), which was not the least of the reasons for their success in battle. There seem to be Scythian features in the famous Luristan bronzes, some of which date from this period and are to be seen in many museums in Europe and the East.

The vassal state to which the Pārsa (Persians) had been reduced by the Medean Khshathrita, the father of Cyaxares II, was probably somewhat relaxed under Scythian rule. Under Theispes (Pers. *Chishpish*), 'king of the city of Anshan' (north-west of Susa) son of Achaemenes (*Hakhamanish*), the Persians had extended their sovereignty ever further towards the south-east at the expense of the Elamites (a non-Aryan people who in the thirteenth to eighth centuries BC had created a powerful empire in the south-western region of present-day Iran). Eventually they made the ex-Elamite part of Persis (so-called from their tribal name) their stronghold. On his death in 640 BC, Theispes divided the kingdom between his sons Cyrus (*Kūrush*—640–615) and Ariaramnes (*Ariyaramna*—640–600). The former, who held the title of 'great king, king of Anshan', received Parsumash and Anshan (north-west of Persis), while the latter, with the title of 'great king, king of kings, king of the land of the Persians', received the south-eastern region of the territory, Persis proper. In these royal titles (still influenced by analogous titles from Mesopotamia) we find the first forms of the title *shāhinshāh* of the Persian sovereigns of to-day, familiar to everyone through the popular press. Here the ancient Persian form *khshayāthiyānām khshayāthiya* (*regorum rex*) has given, through middle Persian *shāhān-shāh*, the modern Persian form of *shāhinshāh*.

The two kingdoms went through periods of rebellion against and submission to the Assyrians and Medes, until *ca* 600

Cyaxares reunited them again under his vassal Cambyses I (*Kambūjiya*—600–599), the son of Cyrus I. With the aid of the Babylonians, who were in revolt, Cyaxares succeeded in defeating the Assyrian empire, destroying Nineveh for ever in 612. He thus extended his rule over the mountainous regions to the north and north-west, which had formerly been held by the Assyrians, while his Babylonian allies were enabled to maintain their sovereignty over the Mesopotamian part together with Elam (Nebuchadrezzar—605–562). On the plateau, Cyaxares' empire extended as far as Rhages (near present-day Teheran), but it was a long struggle before the Cadusii, non-Aryan inhabitants of the region between the Elburz Mountains and the Caspian, were forced to submit to Medean rule. It is interesting to note in passing that for geographical reasons—difficulty of access to the area which, unlike the rest of Iran, is thickly forested—this region and the people who inhabit it have always proved a thorn in the flesh for almost all those who have tried to govern it throughout the history of pre- and post-Islamic Persia. About 590 the Medes subjugated the Armenians in the mountains and highlands in the north and north-west and the authority of the Medes was extended as far as the Halys (present-day Kīzīl Irmak in Turkey), beyond which lay the powerful warrior kingdom of the Lydians. The Medean empire lasted, however, for only a short time. During the relatively peaceful reign of Astyages (*Ishtumegu*), (584–550), the successor of Cyaxares, the Medes seized Elam from Babylon, where there had been serious unrest following the death of Nebuchadrezzar in 562. Power became more and more centralized, almost inevitable in a conglomeration of vassal states of different race and culture held together only by force. In fact, it does not appear that the Medes had a strong culture of their own since, in the monumental inscriptions of the Persian kings after the unification of the states of Medea and Persia, it was found necessary to use the Elamite and Babylonian languages but not Medean, which therefore probably did not possess a script and furthermore was not too dissimilar from Persian. Also the customs of the Medean kings seem to have been modelled on those of the Babylonians and Assyrians.

The sudden rise and assertion of power of the Persians

under Cyrus II, or Cyrus the Great (558–528 BC), is one of those astonishing but not infrequent phenomena in the history of Asia past or present. It shows how a tiny state can, for no apparent reason, trigger off an explosion like that of a new star, widely extending its boundaries to include many peoples of various races and then, often after only a brief spell of power, come to an end as rapidly and with as little apparent reason as it had begun. We have already seen an example of this process in the rise and expansion of the Medean empire. The Persian empire lasted longer, but nevertheless we shall see that it fell to pieces like a house of cards after an existence of barely two centuries. The reasons for this recurrent phenomenon are probably to be found in the fact that the ordinary people played hardly any part in historical events, which were activated almost entirely by an aristocratic elite. When considering the ancient history of Asia (and only too often that of modern times as well) one should always bear in mind that expressions such as 'the Persian people', 'the Medeans', or 'the Babylonians' are only conventions which really mean 'the few thousand people forming the ruling class of the states termed Persian, Medean, Babylonian, etc.'. Of these few thousand people, and only these, we are familiar with the religion, language, art, philosophy, and aspirations. We know next to nothing of the religion, language, art, philosophy and aspirations of the other classes of these 'states'—subject classes, sometimes even racially distinct from the ruling elite, classes which could pass indifferently from subjugation by one elite to that of another, with hardly any alteration in their basic conditions. If we forget this fundamental point we shall continue to misinterpret the history of the ancient kingdoms of Asia, which will remain one-sided and incomplete until we succeed in uncovering the history of all levels of society—and often we lack the necessary documentary evidence to achieve this familiarity. On the other hand, the kind of history we are limited to is extremely easy to write—as easy as it was for the ruler of an ancient Asiatic empire to rise and to fall. Few were the men who counted and any of them could die in single combat, yet the outcome could change the map of an entire sub-continent.

From certain points of view, however, it can be said—

1. Figure of Darius on the relief of Behistūn, his foot placed on the body of Gaumāta. *N. Luscey.*

2. The palace of Darius at Persepolis. *Wim Swaan.*

3. The colossal bull's head capital among the ruins at Persepolis. *Wim Swaan.*

though with reservations—that the Persian empire was an exception to this state of affairs. Indeed, compared with the other ancient empires of Asia, it does reveal a certain modicum of humanity and moderation, examples of which we shall give shortly.

Cyrus II was the son of the Medean vassal, Cambyses I, already mentioned, and of the daughter of the Medean king Astyages. Shortly after he had ascended to the subject throne of Persis and Anshan (558), he built, as a symbol of his desire for internal unity and freedom from external interference, the new capital of Pasargadae (to the *Pasargadae* belonged the royal clan and thus they were the most important of the twelve Persian tribes), whose impressive ruins lie some 45 miles north-east of the far more extensive remains of Persepolis (some 100 miles from the modern Shīrāz). The origins of Cyrus' revolt against his Medean overlords are shrouded in the mists of legend (well-known is Herodotus' account in his *History*, I, 107–31). There were a number of factors in his favour: the discontent of many of the nobles at the Medean court, the usual inertia and the chronic unrest of the subject population and, last but not least, the determination of the king of Babylonia, Nabonidus (556–539), to turn on his former Medean friends. We shall merely outline the principal steps in the series of events that led up to the foundation of the Persian empire which the present-day Persians who, rightly or wrongly, consider themselves the descendants of Cyrus, are planning to celebrate as the '2,500th anniversary of the foundation of the Persian Monarchy'.

The rebellion against Astyages broke out in 553 and he was finally defeated in 550, when his capital of Ecbatana was seized. The Medean empire had come to an end after an existence of less than a century. Astyages—and the case is quite exceptional in the history of ancient Asia—was not killed but merely imprisoned. Ecbatana became, after Pasargadae, a second capital, and Medea the second satrapy of the empire. With his west flank (Mesopotamia) secure, since his ally Nabonidus was engaged in wars of conquest in Arabia, Cyrus turned his attention to consolidating his empire, now known as that of the Medes and Persians, and expanding his frontiers to the north. In 547, he attacked Croesus, king of Lydia, who had crossed the Halys and in a short time he had conquered Lydia and much of Asia Minor. Only the Ionian colonies on the coast were able to resist him. In the years 545–539, Cyrus consolidated and extended his eastern frontiers in order to create a *cordon sanitaire* against the nomads of Outer Iran. He conquered Hyrcania, Parthia, Areia, Drangiana, Arachosia, Sogdiana, the region lying between the Oxus and the Iaxartes, and Chorasmia, and established the eastern frontier on the river Iaxartes (modern Syr Darya), while on his return journey he tightened his control over Margiana and Bactria (cf. map p192). But Cyrus did not merely subjugate the peoples he came in contact with: he also set up irrigation systems in the areas of arid grazing grounds in the east, introduced a knowledge of agriculture, and strengthened his rule by building fortress-cities, only one of which we shall mention, *Marakanda*, known to-day as Samarkand.

Having reinforced his eastern boundaries as a result of this expedition on a grand scale, he now turned his attention to his former ally, Nabonidus of Babylonia. Babel was captured in 539, and Cyrus ingratiated himself with the population (or rather, the powerful local priestly elite) by having himself invested as sovereign in the name of the god Marduk (Bel), whom the conservative Nabonidus had held in contempt. Cyrus also freed the Jews in exile and ordered that the temple of Jerusalem, which had been destroyed, should be rebuilt. The downfall of the Babylonian empire meant that the Persians had now annexed the whole of Mesopotamia, together with Syria, Phoenicia and Palestine. Cyrus died in 529 on an expedition undertaken in order to put down disturbances on the eastern frontiers. He had already charged his son Cambyses with raising a further gigantic force for the conquest of Egypt which, after Babylonia, was the strongest power in the ancient Near East. His religious tolerance, the moderation with which he treated the defeated, his skilful policy of conciliating local divinities, and his considerable ability as an army leader, explain the universal praise that was accorded Cyrus the Great even by Babylonians and Greeks. He did not leave a number of Persian inscriptions vaunting his deeds. His official title inscribed on a Babylonian cylinder-seal by priests of the god Marduk grateful to the tolerant foreign ruler is 'Cyrus, king of all, the great king, the powerful king, the king of Babylonia, king of Sumer and Akkad, king of the four regions of the world, son of Cambyses the great king, grandson of Cyrus the great king . . . great grandson of Theispes the great king . . . king of the city of Anshan . . .'. His simple but imposing tomb at Pasargadae in what is now an expanse of desert is one of the most beautiful sights that Persis has to offer the traveller.

Cyrus' great work of conquest was continued by his son Cambyses (*Kambūjiya*), who had already played an active part in government for eight years and had been his father's representative in Babylonia, while his other son, Bardiya, had been made governor of the eastern regions. Cambyses, whom aristocratic tradition presents to us as having a much harsher and more cruel character than his father, considered that his brother Bardiya was a serious menace to his own supremacy and had him put to death. He was then free to attack Egypt, which he did in 525. The pharaoh, Psammetichus III, son of Amasis, was defeated in the same year and Memphis was taken. Cambyses' campaigns in the territories bordering on Egypt were less successful. He turned the local population (that is to say, the priestly elite) against him by slaying the sacred Apis-bull, profaning the tomb of Amasis, and carrying out acts of cruelty. Nevertheless, Egypt as far south as Elephantine, where frontier garrisons were stationed, with a population consisting partly of Jews who were both grateful and faithful to the Persians, became a Persian satrapy with the name of *Mudrāya* (cf. Heb. *Miṣraim*, Arab. *Miṣr*). In Syria, on his way back to his own country, Cambyses received news that a Medean mage named Gaumāta was claiming to be Bardiya and had usurped the throne. In 522, shortly after hearing this news, Cambyses died 'by his own hand' (*uvamarshiyus*, as Darius' inscription at Behistūn says). According to Herodotus he accidentally wounded himself with his own sword; according to some modern authorities he committed suicide.

The task of removing the usurper was undertaken by Darius (*Dārayavaush*), who belonged to a younger branch of the Achaemenian royal family, since he was the grandson of Ariaramnes (640–600), the vassal king of the Medes in Persis, and a brother of Cyrus I. Darius, helped by other nobles, was one of the first 'restorers of the rightful succession' who often appear in the history of Persia, in which the principle of the 'divine right of kings', personified in the sacred disk of the 'victorious glory' (*xvarena* or *farr*), plays an extremely important part. On the other hand, there is some evidence that Gaumāta, the Medean magus or mage, was a social and religious reformer who failed and, despite the lack of reliable information, it is not impossible that he had found the support of some of the lower classes of society in a struggle against the nobles. For instance, one should bear in mind that the counter-revolutionaries, of whom Darius was *primus inter pares*, were all drawn from the nobility. We also know that Gaumāta remitted the taxes for three years and abolished military service, both extremely burdensome in the Asiatic empires of ancient and modern times, and thus ingratiated himself with certain levels of society, while the Behistūn inscription confirms that he had deprived the 'people' (i.e. the nobles) of their possessions. The fact that, in another line of the inscription, he is referred to as a magus, member of the Medean tribe who supported the religious reforms of Zoroaster, and that Darius declares in his inscriptions that he had had to rebuild temples destroyed by Gaumāta, suggest that the latter was intolerant of the ancient and local pantheons. More than this, unfortunately, we do not know, but perhaps Gaumāta was the first in the long line of religious reformers with social and economic ideals which stretches down to the nineteenth century. Another extremely interesting and singular feature of all these movements, begun by the ancient and nebulous Gaumāta, is the messianic element, the declaration 'I am Such a one'. In the present case it is 'I am Bardiya whom you believed dead', in later cases, as we shall see, it is 'I am this or that sacred person risen again', or 'reincarnated', or, in the post-Islamic period, 'I am the promised Messiah', or 'a prophet', and so forth. The enormous following that Gaumāta-Bardiya attracted to himself is revealed by the fact that only a very few satrapies— a few provinces in the extreme eastern parts of the land— remained faithful to the 'legitimate' government. Even after the usurper's death, Darius found himself having to deal with other upstarts who employed a similar form of appeal. In Babylonia one proclaimed himself a second Nebuchadrezzar, a second incarnation of Bardiya appeared in Persis itself, in Medea a Fravartish (Phraortes) said to be Khshathrita, and so forth, but the scarcity of detailed information in the sources does not allow us to pursue the matter further. The series of revolts was finally brought to an end in 521, and in 520 Darius had an account carved in three languages (Babylonian, Elamite and ancient Persian, all in cuneiform script) on a lofty inaccessible part of the rock-face of *Bagasthāna*, the 'seat of the gods', to-day Behistūn-Bisutūn, near Kirmānshāh. The very position of the inscription where it cannot be read by the human eye (and furthermore, the fact that very few of his subjects were able to read the difficult writing employed), shows that the king's declaration was addressed to the supreme god Ahura Mazdā, from whom he claimed to be invested with royal authority and whom he 'informs' of the defeat of the usurpers.

Once the rebel areas had been pacified, Darius decided it was time for him to visit Egypt, where he had spent three years during the reign of Cambyses, in order to put right the shortcomings of the Persian satrap and win back the sympathy of the offended priests. The expedition, which took place in 519–518, was a complete success and considerably strengthened the Persian position in Egypt, partly due to the fact that Darius wisely reformed both the agricultural and the taxation systems. He then proceeded to overhaul the organization of the entire empire.

Herodotus tells us that Darius' immense empire was divided into twenty provinces or satrapies (from *satrapēs*, Gk. form of the ancient Pers. *Khsathrapāvan*, 'protector of the kingdom'). An exception was made of Persis, the dynasty's cradle and the centre of the empire, which enjoyed a privileged position and paid no taxes. The satrap had very wide civil powers (even where there still existed local rulers, religious or civil heads, whose positions were handed down from earlier times, these were entirely dependent on the Persian satraps), but he had no military authority. In fact, the military forces of each satrapy were under the orders of a commander completely independent of the satrap and directly responsible to the king himself. This ingenious arrangement enabled a mutual check to be kept on the civil and military authorities, both of which were directly responsible to the sovereign, who then employed his 'eyes and ears' in the guise of special inspectors, to visit the satrapies and see that no rebellions or separatist movements arose. Another ingenious feature was the fact that there were not as many military commanders as satraps, since each of the former commanded the military forces of four or five satrapies. The ordinary soldiers were recruited from the local population (the 'Persian' army included Greeks, Nubians, Babylonians, Egyptians, etc.), but the officers of the executive, the fundamental establishment, were drawn from the Medes and Persians, who were to be found, though in a relatively small proportion, in every detachment. One of the satrap's most important functions was the collection of tribute. Before Darius came to the throne, the various provinces of the empire had offered the court 'gifts', the amount of which had not been fixed. In the reorganization of the empire the rate of taxation for every satrapy was carefully laid down according to its relative wealth. The heaviest taxes were paid by the rich provinces of Babylonia and Egypt (the former paid 1,000 talents, the latter 700). The annual income raised in this way from the various satrapies reached a figure of 14,500 talents (a talent was worth about £200). Furthermore, each province also sent in tribute in kind (grain, horses, slaves, ivory, cattle, etc.).

Standardization of the taxation system was made possible only through the use of coinage, which had been known in Lydia. The royal currency consisted of a gold coin which circulated throughout the East for centuries and was called the 'daric', from Darius, or, according to another view, from the middle Persian *zarîk*, 'golden'. The satrapies had the right to issue silver coins and in some of the less important areas copper coins were current. The introduction of coinage brought about a great development in trade with the neighbouring peoples and states. For commercial and strategic reasons, it was necessary to maintain good roads and assure the safety of travellers. Herodotus mentions the excellent royal road which linked the Aegean with Susa, one of the capitals of Darius' empire where he built a magnificent palace, his other favourite residences being Ecbatana and Persepolis. The distance from Sardis to Susa was divided into one hundred and eleven post-stations, and the journey could be made in about ninety days. The route was patrolled by military detachments who saw that it was perfectly safe, while special couriers maintained a swift postal service—only for the benefit of the king, not of private individuals. Moreover, during Darius' reign, nearly two and a half thousand years before De Lesseps, a canal (already begun by the pharaohs) was completed from the lower Nile to the Red Sea, thus linking the Mediterranean with the Indian Ocean and the Persian Gulf. On its two banks an inscription in Egyptian hieroglyphics and Persian cuneiform recorded the immense undertaking of the Achaemenid king.

All power was concentrated in the hands of the Persian aristocracy and the priesthood. There were, especially in Babylonia, really 'great commercial houses', wealthy families, some of whose names have come down to us on cuneiform tablets. Their riches benefited from the security of the trade routes and also from the system, convenient for the central government but often ruinous for the provinces, of giving entire provinces in appanage to this or that family of wealthy merchants or nobles. Thus, the Babylonian house of Murashu held the province of Nippur in appanage, and every year had to pay into Darius' coffers a fixed sum in silver as tribute. The house's slaves and dependants naturally not only collected the tribute but also plundered the people to their own advantage. Fifth-century documents tell us that the complaints of a government official led to the house of 'Murashu and Sons' being threatened with legal proceedings, but that the Murashus succeeded in successfully bribing the officials, on this occasion with a large number of measures of barley and wheat, barrels of wine, and many head of cattle. As to the priesthood (not only that of the Persian religion which is difficult to define in this period, but also of the other religions which received a considerable degree of tolerance under the Achaemenids), Darius, realizing their power over the people, managed to win them over by protecting the financial interests of the temples. Thus, for example, we know that he rebuked a satrap in Asia Minor for having collected tolls from farmers dedicated to Apollo.

The Persians themselves did not pay taxes. The sole duty and honour of the free Persians (i.e. nobles) was to bear arms and devote themselves to farming and cattle-breeding. They formed the backbone of the military establishment and of the garrisons stationed throughout the various satrapies, and from them were recruited the officials of the civil administration. The work of the farmer alternated with the duties of the soldier, and any one person would be called upon to be one or the other according to circumstances. In view of the slave type of economy, forced labour was the norm. Building work, for example, was not carried out by Persians, though we know from an inscription that the work on the imperial palace at Susa was done by people from all over the empire—Egyptians, Greeks, Babylonians, Syrians, Lydians, and even Medes. Only Persians are not listed in the inscription: they probably acted as overseers. The king, backed by the army, enjoyed unlimited power: all the people, even the nobles, were the king's 'slaves' (*bandaka*). He was surrounded by great pomp and an involved ritual, largely borrowed from that of the Babylonians and Egyptians. He was protected by a bodyguard of ten thousand, the famous 'immortals' (Herodotus' interpretation is probably based on popular etymology). He wore a purple mantle interwoven with gold, while on his head he bore a magnificent tiara incrusted with gems and he sat on a magnificent throne. Everyone was obliged to prostrate himself at full length before the king. But, following the ancient Persian religious tradition which considered agriculture of sacred importance, he did not disdain carrying out simple farm work, and at the end of the fifth century BC Cyrus the Younger proudly showed the Spartan Lysander the garden which he cultivated himself.

One of the favourite pastimes of the king and nobles was to go hunting in the vast parks surrounded by walls which were called paradises (ancient Pers. *paridaiza*, 'enclosure', from which, through Greek, comes our word 'paradise'). The typical Persian gardens (even to-day surrounded by walls to protect them from the extreme climate of the plateau), are rectangular enclosures through which flow four streams in the form of a cross. It was certainly a Persian garden that inspired the author of *Genesis* to describe the earthly paradise as containing four rivers. The creation and enjoyment of these gardens are a regular feature of Iranian civilization. Even to-day gardening is one of the arts which the Persians cultivate with the greatest seriousness and devotion.

The material culture of the empire had reached a very high level. The building of the terrace at Persepolis (it is not known what the place was really called at this time, perhaps simply *Pārsa*), carried out first by Darius and then his successors, is one of the architectural wonders of the ancient world. The great halls, with their roofs supported on innumerable columns with capitals bearing animal motifs evolved by the Persians themselves, are decorated with bas-reliefs, some of which are realistic (there are the famous portrayals of the fight between the lion and the bull, probably representing symbolically the king and his enemy, and of the sovereign hunting with the army, etc.), while others are fantastic (winged bulls, figures incorporating both human and animal features, etc.). Those who are familiar with the even older art of Mesopotamia and Egypt will immediately feel that Achaemenian art has borrowed from various sources. Its originality indeed does not lie in the subject or form, but in the fact that these are handled in a more simple and lively manner. Moreover, it is well known (Darius himself mentions the fact in his inscriptions), that the reliefs of the royal palace at Susa were carried out by Greek workmen from Asia Minor. The Persians took their writing from Babylonia—a cuneiform simplified to the maximum extent and reduced to a quasi-alphabetic script at the time of Cyrus, possibly under the influence of Aramaic writing.

The problem of the religion of the Achaemenids, and in particular of Darius himself, from whose time we have the largest number of inscriptions, is a very difficult one and is far from being solved. The inscriptions leave us in no doubt that Darius and the Achaemenian race were worshippers of Ahura Mazdā, the 'wise lord' or, according to an interesting interpretation of Pagliaro's, the 'thinking lord'. Ahura Mazdā was also the supreme god of Zarathustra (most probably fl. *ca* 588). But while on the one hand the oldest, probably Zoroastrian, portion of the *Avesta*, the *Gāthās*, shows no knowledge of the existence of a vast centralized empire and is mainly acquainted with the extreme east of the Iranian territory, the inscriptions of Persis on the other hand show no knowledge of

25

Zarathustra. Scholars have put forward various theories to explain this situation. Zarathustra may have lived prior to the formation of the Achaemenian empire. *Vishtāspa* (Hystaspes), who protected Zarathustra, may be the same Hystaspes who was Darius' father. Ahura Mazdā may not have been a creation of Zarathustra, but preceded him and been the family god of the Achaemenides. The Magi, who, according to Herodotus, were a Medean tribe, may in fact have been the followers of another type of religious tradition who at a certain moment adopted the religion of the prophet Zarathustra (who never mentions them by name), and so forth. There is no doubt that many of the inscriptions of Darius are inspired by that sense of ethics, of the struggle and the choice between good and evil (=falsehood), which are typical of Zoroastrianism as we know it from later texts. But it is equally true that Zoroastrianism as revealed in the more precise form of priests' accounts is clearly opposed to certain Achaemenian practices (tolerance of foreign gods and tomb-burial instead of the exposure of corpses to birds, etc.). The problem may well remain unresolved for a long time yet. A solution may be found in the theory that the Medeans and Persians had three distinct religions for the different ranks of society: the religion of the king, to which the Achaemenian inscriptions bear witness; that of the people, of which Herodotus tells us; and that of the Magi, described in the *Gāthās* of the *Avesta*. Furthermore, the religious culture of Iran is far from being an original one, and reflects many features of ancient Mesopotamian origin. The portraits of the winged Ahura Mazdā which appear in Achaemenian bas-reliefs are Mesopotamian, while the Mazdaean idea of 'heavenly models' of things and the opposition between light and darkness are probably even Sumerian, and so forth. What is new is the introduction into an archaic cosmology of a sense of ethics, of moral choice. It is quite inconceivable that anyone in Assyria or Babylonia would ever have been able to express the magnificent thoughts recorded in an almost Biblical style in the inscription on Darius' tomb at Naqsh-i Rustam (inscription *b*), which we reproduce according to Pagliaro's interpretation: 'A great god is Ahura Mazdā who created this excellent work which you see, who created peace for mankind, who endowed Darius the King with wisdom and strength. Saith Darius the King: By the desire of AhuraMazdā this is my nature: to that which is just I am a friend, to that which is unjust I am no friend. I do not wish that the weak should suffer harm at the hands of the powerful, nor that the powerful should suffer harm at the hands of the weak. Whatever is just, that is my desire. The follower after falsehood do I detest. I am not vindictive. If anything raises up anger within me, I restrain myself with reason; I am master of my emotions. Who works for me I reward according to his work. Who does ill I punish according to the ill he has done ... If one man speaks ill of another, I do not give him credence until he has provided proof. If a man acts to the best of his ability, I am satisfied ... If you wish to see and hear what I have achieved, seek for it in the home and in the army. These are my qualities of thought and understanding'.

We remember from our school-days that Darius was concerned in the first Persian War with the Greeks, which we regard as one of the most important events in ancient history. Seen from the Persian point of view these wars do not have the same significance that we rightly attribute to them. Though it would be an exaggeration to regard them simply as frontier skirmishes, it is certainly true that they represent another attempt of the Persians to extend their immense empire further to the west, an attempt which was a failure but which had no serious consequences as far as the empire itself was concerned. The downfall of the Ionian cities had opened the way to the Aegean. Towards the end of his reign, Darius had taken possession of some of the Aegean islands which had been held by the Greeks. For a time the balance was broken by the revolt of the Greek cities in Asia Minor, which were supported by Athens, but the Persians subdued them and then turned on Athens herself, making an unfamiliar approach by sea. As is well known, the decisive battle was fought at Marathon (490). The Persian defeat led to uprisings not only in Asia Minor but also in Egypt. The last years of Darius' reign and the first years of his son's, Xerxes (*Khshāyarsha*) (486–465 BC) were spent in putting down these rebellions. Then Xerxes made preparations for the second great expedition against Athens, recruiting an immense army from different provinces; the

Persians themselves accounted for only one tenth of the entire force. In 480, Xerxes' army crossed the Hellespont, succeeded in forcing the passes of Thessaly and, despite the heroic resistance of the Spartans at Thermopylae, marched on Athens. The fate of the West (but not that of Persia) was decided at Salamis on 28 September 480, and at Plataea (479). Thus ended Persia's attempts at expansion towards the west.

Artaxerxes I (*Artakhshathra*: 465–424 BC) came to the throne over the dead body of his father, whom he had assassinated. The court intrigues of Artabanus together with internal dissensions had weakened Persian rule in Egypt, but Artaxerxes quickly succeeded in reasserting his authority. The king had also to crush a revolt in Syria. At the same time he kept the Jews on friendly terms. After his death there was a struggle for the throne between his son, Xerxes II, and another member of the royal family. The latter won the day and reigned as Darius II. Meantime the revolts continued, one breaking out in Lydia (410 BC). In 411 another uprising occurred in Egypt, as we are told in the Elephantine papyri, but it subsided after Darius' death in the same year. Faced with a rebellion, the king usually sent an armed expedition under one of his generals to put it down. However, in 405 when the warlike tribe of the Cadusii or Carduchii, who inhabited the mountainous region between Assyria, Medea, and Armenia, revolted the king himself set out to fight them, but on the way he fell ill and died in Babylonia (404 BC). His son, Artaxerxes II, had to defend his throne against Cyrus, his younger brother, Cyrus the Younger of the Greek sources. Cyrus assembled part of the Persian army together with some Greek contingents at Sardis, but fell himself in the battle of Cunaxa (401 BC). The story of the Greeks' return journey to the coast of the Black Sea is largely told in Xenophon's *Anabasis*. The part that Sparta had played in Cyrus the Younger's revolt decided Artaxerxes, who dreamed of restoring the empire to its former greatness in the days of Darius, to break with the Spartans, who had become the leading people in Greece after the Peloponnes an War. His satraps began the fight in Asia Minor, and in 394 the Athenian general Conon, who was in the service of the Persians, defeated the Spartans at Cnidos. As a result of the King's Peace or peace of Antalcidas (387 BC), which was highly favourable to the Persians, the Greek cities of Asia Minor and the island of Cyprus once again became tributaries of Persia. However, Artaxerxes II failed to subdue Egypt, which had rebelled for the umpteenth time, and the last years of his life were tormented by court intrigues.

Fearing the usual struggles for the succession, Artaxerxes III, surnamed Ochus (359–338 BC), first secured his position on the throne, and only then, nine months later, announced the death of his father. He led his first campaign against the Cadusii, who were in a permanent state of unrest. Then he turned his attention to Egypt, which for the past sixty years had to all intents and purposes been an independent state. Egypt, Phoenicia and Cyprus formed a coalition, and in 351–350 Phoenicia broke out in open rebellion. Artaxerxes set out from Babylonia at the head of his army. Seeing that it was about to be overrun by the Persians, the wealthy Phoenician city of Sidon decided on self-destruction. The inhabitants shut themselves in their houses and set fire to them, they themselves perishing in the flames. Out of sheer terror Phoenicia surrendered to the Persians, and Cyprus quickly followed suit. At the same time the 'Persian' general, Mentor of Rhodes, put down a revolt of the satraps in Asia Minor. Another general, Bagoas, maintained the Jews of Jerusalem in a state of complete subjection to the Persians by playing off the chief priests against one another. A further Persian army, directly under the command of Artaxerxes himself, moved against Egypt, whose forces were strengthened by the inclusion of Greek mercenaries. The Persians gained a victory at Pelusium and in 343 Egypt once more fell under their sway and suffered severe reprisals. Thus the Persian empire had once again attained the enormous size that it had had under the first glorious Achaemenid kings. The Greeks tried to ingratiate themselves with Artaxerxes. Philip of Macedon formed an alliance with him, while at the same time making secret preparations to attack him. Artaxerxes III died by poison administered to him by Bagoas. He was succeeded by his son Arses, who in due course was also killed by the all-powerful Bagoas. His successor, Darius III would have met the same fate had he not succeeded in making Bagoas drink the poison that was intended for himself.

Darius III (335–330) was the last of the Achaemenid kings. He lived to see his throne and the empire collapse beneath the blows of Alexander the Great, son of Philip of Macedon (359–336), who succeeded in injecting into Greek civilization, still highly refined but almost completely exhausted, the youthful energy of a semi-barbarous people. The various stages of Alexander's conquests are too well known to need repeating here. Let me merely remind the reader that he crossed the Hellespont in 334 at the head of 40,000 men, encountering practically no resistance. The Greek colonies were declared liberated. After passing through Cappadocia Alexander descended to the plains of Cilicia, and, following the coast, met the Persian army near Issus. Here he won a victory which opened up Syria to him. Egypt welcomed him as her deliverer, and accorded him divine honours. After founding the city of Alexandria, he set out from Memphis in the spring of 331, and as a result of the battle of Gaugamela he gained Babylonia together with Susa and Persepolis—the heart of the empire. Darius was forced to flee to the east, and Persepolis, the most truly Persian of the capital cities, was destroyed by fire. While Darius was planning to make a last stand in Medea, he was killed by two satraps, Bessus and Barzaentes, in July 330. He was succeeded by Bessus, a short-lived and quite powerless king, who took the name of Artaxerxes IV. Alexander marched northwards as far as the Iaxartes, and founded another Alexandria, the modern Leninabad or Khojand. In 327 he married a member of the Persian nobility called Roxana (the name means 'luminous') in Bactria, and then he marched down the valley of the Indus as far as the river Sutlej, subjugating the local Indian princes along his path. The land army returned after heavy losses passing through both Arachosia and Khorāsān and through Gedrosia (Baluchistan?), while the fleet, commanded by Nearchus, made its way back along the coast in the autumn of 325. Hardly had Alexander reached Babylon in 323, worn out by his superhuman exertions, than he died of a fever at the age of 32 in the palace that had once belonged to Nebuchadrezzar. His embalmed body was taken to Alexandria in Egypt. Alexander's campaign (like many of the conquests of Asia, including the the Islamic conquest of Persia discussed in Chapter IV) has something miraculous about it, and his personality has remained, even in the eastern versions of the legend built up in the west in the romanticized history of the pseudo-Callisthenes of the second century AD, that of a semi-divine hero, of a prophet. The only dissident opinions were in the artificial reaction of the Sassanid aristocracy, according to the traditions of the Mazdaean priests in which Alexander was represented as a manifestation of the principle of evil, and his rule a 'misrule' *par excellence*.

Even if Macedonian Hellenism differed in many respects from the Athenian democracy of the golden age (though one should not forget the element of simple military comradeship among Alexander's Macedonian 'companions', some of whom failed to keep up with the rapid orientalization of Alexander and his entourage), one of the reasons for the fantastically sudden collapse of the colossal Persian empire remains that expressed a century and a half earlier in the dialogue between Atossa, Xerxes' mother, and the Chorus in Aeschylus' immortal tragedy, *The Persians* (11. 231–242):

Atossa: But tell me, where by men's report, is Athens built?

Chorus: Far westward, where the sun-god sinks his fainting fires.

Atossa: But why should my son yearn to make this town his prey?

Chorus: Athens once conquered, he is master of all Hellas.

Atossa: Have they such rich supply of fighting men?

Chorus: They have;
Soldiers who once struck Persian arms a fearful blow.

Atossa: Besides their men, have they good store of wealth at home?

Chorus: They have a spring of silver treasured in their soil.

Atossa: And are they skilled in archery?

Chorus: No, not at all:
They carry stout shields, and fight hand-to-hand with spears.

Atossa: Who shepherds them? What master do their ranks obey?

Chorus: Master? They are not called servants to any man.[1]

---

1 Aeschylus: *Prometheus and Other Plays*, translated with an introduction by Philip Vellacott, Harmondsworth, 1961.

The extreme individuality of the Greeks, so well expressed by Aeschylus, but dangerous in that it could easily lead to internal dissension and fragmentation, had found its counter-balance in the centralized power of Macedonian Greece. On the other hand, the stifling despotism of the last Achae-menids and the Persian people's absolute inexperience of the sea, which is still to be found to this day and which Aeschylus had already foreseen as another reason for the Persians' inability to advance beyond the Aegean (*The Persians*, 102–114), had turned the great empire into a colossus with feet of clay. And it is extraordinary that, centuries later, Muslim tradition was to produce a dialogue between the first free Beduin of the 'democratic' caliph Omar and the Sassanid general Rustam at the beginning of the second astonishing downfall of the restored empire of Iran, which is in many ways similar to that between Atossa and the Chorus in Aeschylus' play. In both cases a people who were racially unified and inspired by a religious ideal (Pagliaro has emphasized the importance of the religious and mythical aspect in Alexander's achievement in his recent penetrating work on him) easily overcame a conglomeration of racially diverse groups, held together only by their unwanted slavery to a single powerful ruler repre-senting one socially dominant race.

The Achaemenian civilization, though the most 'modern' in the whole of the ancient world of Asia (to the phrases from Darius' testament quoted on p. 28 should be added the beauti-ful words of the other inscription at Naqsh-i Rustam—inscription *a*—'If you would now think, "How many are the lands that Darius the King possessed?", gaze on the figures that adorn the throne and you will see and you will come to know how far the lance of the Persian Man penetrated . . .', which shows a sense of *national* rather than merely royal pride), this civilization had the singular fate to be almost completely forgotten by the time of the Parthians. If history is above all a matter of memory, what is most lacking in the passing of centuries and dynasties in Iran is indeed an alert sense of *memory*. For this reason, Iran never achieved a Renaissance comparable with that of European history. The equivalent of the Hellenic and Roman spirit could have been sought to a certain degree in Achaemenian or Zoroastrian ethical pride,

4. Bas reliefs in the Apadana (royal audience hall) at Persepolis.   *Wim Swaan.*

5. The tomb of Cyrus at Pasargadae from Sir Robert Ker Porter's *Travels in Georgia*, 1817–20.   *British Museum, London.*

6. *Below* The dome of the Madrasa Chahar Bagh at Isfahān. *Wim Swaan.*

7. The Chahar Bagh in the nineteenth century from *Voyage en Perse* by
E. Flandin and P. Coste, 1851. *British Museum, London.*

and yet this was simply forgotten. What were the reasons for this? Certainly, they were very complex, but let us at least consider two important points, which are to a certain extent connected: the great limitations to the spread of knowledge of writing, and the very small number of individuals whose word counted. Paradoxically enough, it might be said that the killing of a few hundred people as a result of invasion could have led to a whole period of history being forgotten.

CHAPTER II

The period influenced by Hellenism: Seleucids and Parthians

Greek civilization is often described as the civilization of the *polis* and it was the Greek conquest that gave rise to the first real cities in Iran. Alexander and his successors seldom built cities in areas that had previously been completely deserted; they preferred to develop places that were already inhabited, enclosing them within walls, within which they put up imposing new buildings. The centre now had legal standing, it was granted the rights of a *polis*, and took on a new name, given it by its founder. Thus, the future capital of the Parthian kings had two names—Ctesiphon and Seleucia. The ancient town of Dura on the Euphrates was converted into a fortress and 'the Greeks called this city Europos'. The social organization of these cities was completely novel to Persia, for all the citizens were free people, as in Greece. The organization on the lines of the *polis* was run by a Greek population and a Macedonian Greek colony, and neither foreigners nor slaves had any part in it. For example, at Seleucia the Greek section of the population controlled both the Council of the Three Hundred and the Gherousia—the characteristic institutions of the Greek cities. The Persians and Syrians were independent of the *polis* and formed their own particular corporations. Seleucia, the centre of a satrapy, had its *strategus* and *epistates*, who were in command of the garrison.

An extremely important factor, from both a cultural and a political point of view, was the distribution of military colonies throughout the eastern territories. The Greek and Macedonian military colonies in Asia Minor, the *katoikiai*, had their own plots of land, each known as a *kleros*, which were subject to tax, and which together made up the *kleruchii*. The *kleros* was quite distinct from land considered royal property, but if for some reason its ownership lapsed, then it once again became part of the royal or state demesne. The *katoikia* might be attached to a city, and in certain cases it was granted the rights of a *polis*.

There is a record of a Macedonian *katoikia* at Harrān in Upper Mesopotamia in 312 BC, and Greek military colonies are known to have existed at Edessa (Syria), Taxila (India), Ecbatana (Medea), etc.

The development of cities also became a means of Hellenizing new areas and of assimilating and colonizing them, and for the king an excellent way of strengthening his economic control and political authority. Each city paid taxes to the king, who owned the land granted to the city as a concession. Alexander and his successors populated distant cities with prisoners of war—care was taken to see that they were sent far away from their homeland—while the wounded and the sick were integrated into the Greek colonies already in existence. The population of the cities was predominantly oriental—in those beyond the Tigris mainly Persian. Mixed marriages between Greeks and the local inhabitants speeded up the process of cultural exchange. As early as 324, Alexander had openly encouraged his Macedonian troops to contract marriages with Persian women in Susa, and he himself had already set an example. While Greek was the dominant language of the cities, in the provinces and the countryside Persian, Aramaic (in Syria and Mesopotamia) and other vernaculars were spoken as in the past, and the old traditions were maintained. In Mesopotamia and the western parts of Iran, wealth was based on the possession of slaves. Babylonian tablets dating from the end of the fourth century record that slaves and prisoners of war were employed to build walls, fortresses and palaces.

The unification of the immense territory stretching from the Mediterranean as far as Syr Daria and the Indus was of great cultural importance. Seleucia-Ctesiphon, the new centre of the empire, was the meeting-point of numerous routes which linked Central Asia with the Mediterranean, and the Caucasus with the shores of the Persian Gulf. The ancient royal road running from eastern Iran to Seleucia and from there on to Sardis and Antioch remained open, enabling commercial relations to be developed, and all kinds of goods to be produced and exchanged. The cult of the sun-god Mithra gained an important position in Asia Minor, while the Greek pantheon became well known in Bactria—it appears that the earliest

Buddha images were the work of Greek craftsmen. Of great interest is the coinage, based on Greek prototypes even in areas that were definitely Iranian—for example, in the Graeco-Bactrian kingdom—and it had an influence for many centuries on the coinage of Central Asia. The symbolism of the Greek divinities and of the Iranian cults were here combined in an extraordinary way. The Hellenization of the Iranian areas went hand in hand with a parallel orientalization of the Macedonian Greek peoples who had come in contact with eastern, particularly Persian, civilization. The expansion of Iran towards the west in the time of Cambyses and Darius and the expansion of the Greeks towards the east under Alexander influenced both sides and affected every aspect of government and cultural life in the Near East. This had incalculable consequences for the history not only of Asia but also of Europe, for instance in the importance of Mithraism under the Roman Empire and the history of early Christianity itself.

The struggle for the succession after the death of Alexander was temporarily solved in 323, when Ptolemy ascended the throne of Egypt and Seleucia became a satrapy of Babylonia. This position was maintained until 316 BC. In 312, Seleucus Nicator founded the Seleucid dynasty, and this date was for many centuries employed as the base for the chronology of the Near East. The capital of the Seleucid state was first Babylon, then Seleucia on the Tigris, and finally Antioch on the Orontes, in Syria. Seleucus himself died in 281, after uniting Syria, Mesopotamia and Iran, the greatest and most important parts of the old Achaemenid empire.

The rivalry between the Seleucids and the Ptolemies of Egypt—which was a prolongation under rulers of a different race of the ancient enmity between, first, the Egyptian and Assyro-Babylonian empires, and then between Egypt and Persia—continued until the Ptolemies were defeated by the Romans. This struggle made the Seleucids concentrate their attention on the western frontiers and neglect internal affairs. At home, the Persian opposition increased its strength, and the Parthians began to build up their power. Antiochus Soter (281–261 BC) was forced to war against Pergamus, which had risen against him but which he succeeded in overcoming. He was also attacked by Ptolemaeus Philadelphus (285–247 BC). By the third century BC it had become impossible to govern distant provinces, such as Bactria and Sogdiana, from Antioch. Sogdiana, which from about 250 was governed by Diodotus, one of the generals of Antioch, enjoyed almost complete independence, and down to 227 it was ruled by his son who took the title Diodotus II. New forces now began to appear in Iran. Arshak (Arsaces), chief of one of the nomad tribes of eastern Iran generally known as the Dahae or Dai, started the process of uniting Parthia and managed to destroy Androgoros who commanded the Seleucid forces in the area. At the same time Arshak's brother Tiridates succeeded in gaining control of Hyrcania (Gurgān) and Parthia. Thus the Parthian state and the Arsacid dynasty (250 BC–AD 224) were born. Seleucus II raised an army in Babylonia, but his intended expedition against Tiridates in 228 had to be called off because of the news of a rising in Antioch. Tiridates retained his authority over the territory on the shores of the Caspian up to the time of his death in 211. During the reign of his son Artabanus I (d. 191 BC), the Seleucids made continued attempts to destroy the Parthian power, but without success. Under Mithridates (171–138 BC), Parthia became one of the most powerful states in Western Asia, which not even Antiochus IV, under whom there was a renewed Hellenization of the eastern regions, could in any way unsettle. At the end of the third and beginning of the second century BC, the Macedonian Greeks, who were in a privileged position, had the upper hand, but little by little the east began to gain in influence even in the economic field. Antiochus' policy of Hellenization was an attempt to regain lost ground and to strengthen the economic position of western traders. But Parthia was strong: Mithridates gradually gained control of Gedrosia, Drangiana (modern Sīstān), and Areia (the territory of Herāt), while the conquest of Elymais and Medea opened the way to Mesopotamia. Babylon fell to Mithridates in 142, and in July 141 he occupied Seleucia on the Tigris. By 140 the ancient Achaemenid royal title had been revived and the Babylonian cuneiform inscriptions refer to the Parthian sovereign as the 'king of kings'.

With the conquest of Mesopotamia the conflict with the

west became even more acute. Antiochus VII, surnamed Sidetes (139–129 BC), defeated the Parthian army, which was reinforced with Saka mercenaries, on three occasions, reoccupied Seleucia and the satrapy of Babylonia (130 BC), spent the winter at Ecbatana, but was driven out by Phraates II, son of Mithridates. Meanwhile, however, the Sakas had invaded the north-eastern provinces of the Parthian empire, Phraates' armies were defeated, and the king himself fell in battle in 129. His successor, Artabanus II, was also killed in 124, in a fight with the Saka invaders, who had occupied Areia and Drangiana. The latter henceforth took the name of *Sakastāna* ('land of the Sakas', modern Persian *Sīstān*) by which it is still known to-day. Artabanus had appointed a certain Himer as satrap of Mesopotamia, but his cruel rule caused discontent in Seleucia and other cities. We know that he sold the inhabitants of Babylon into slavery in Medea in punishment for their rebelling.

Near the Persian Gulf there arose, after 129, the Arab kingdom of Characene and we know from the evidence of coins that its ruler Hispation even occupied Seleucia and Babylon in the years 128 and 127. But Himer reconquered the lost territory and himself assumed the title of king, an achievement due partly to the particularly grave situation in the other Parthian provinces, which were being threatened by the Sakas. Then Mithridates II, the son of Artabanus, overcame Characene and once more brought Babylon within his rule (122–121 BC) and in about 115 the Parthians succeeded in conquering the Massagetae. Thus they were masters of the territory stretching as far as the Oxus.

Parthia was now firmly established across the trade routes which led to India and China, and the Silk Road passed through the Parthian domains. Mithridates had received embassies from the Chinese emperor Wu Ti of the Han Dynasty who wished to strengthen his relations with Parthia in order to be able to trade with the West without interference and the importance of Parthia's position was also recognized by Rome. Mithridates sent an embassy to Sulla to improve his relations there. He also subdued the Arab tribes which were stirring up trouble in Mesopotamia with the support of Antiochus IX, and organized them into three principalities.

Adiabene and Gordyene, both occupied by the ever rebellious Cadusii, had already become independent at the time of the general weakening of the Seleucid state. In 132 the little principality of Osrhoene was formed by the Seleucid governor of Iranian origin called Osrhoes (*Khusrau*, Chosroes); thereafter it was ruled by Arabs until it came under Roman suzerainty. We do not know the extent of Mithridates II's kingdom but he certainly held the west bank of the Euphrates. Most of our information on the subject is derived from coins. For example, we know from the lists of official titles (written in Greek until the time of Vologases I, AD 51–77) that in 108 BC Mithridates bore the title of 'king of kings'. Nevertheless, in 89 Gotarzes I considered himself 'king of Babylon'. After Mithridates' death, in 88–87 BC the Armenian king Tigranes occupied Adiabene and Gordyene. In about the year 80 BC, the king of Babylon was Orodes I, while from 64 onwards this title was held by the Arsacid king Phraates III, who regarded Babylon as his capital. The struggle between the Armenian Tigranes and the Arsacid Phraates for the possession of northern Mesopotamia was settled by Pompey, who assigned Gordyene and Nisibis to the former and Adiabene to the latter. Phraates lost the Caspian provinces and his authority over the Massagetae, but he retained Merv. The Oxus formed the frontier between the Central Asian Sakas and the Parthians. Sakastān and Arachosia in the basin of the Helmand River in modern Afghanistan were lost, and out of them arose the Indo-Scythian kingdom well known even to Chinese writers of the first century BC. Phraates was killed in 58–57 by his sons, Mithridates III and Orodes, who proceeded to fight one another for the throne. For a time Mithridates had the support of the Consul of Syria, Gabinius, but Orodes drove him out of Iran and had him killed when he took refuge in Babylon.

Parthia was now confronted by a new and powerful enemy, the Romans. It was during Orodes' reign that the Roman triumvir Crassus, consul of Syria, was defeated by the Parthians in the famous battle of Carrhae (Harrān) in 53 BC. At the suggestion of Abgar II, surnamed Ariamnes, prince of Osrhoene and a vassal of the Parthians, Crassus plunged into the plains of Mesopotamia where the famous Parthian cavalry were able to move to their full advantage. More than twenty thousand Romans were left on the field of battle and ten thousand prisoners were taken to Merv in Central Asia, while the victorious Parthian general, Sūrēn (Surena), held a mock Roman triumph in Seleucia. It appears that Orodes chose Seleucia on the Tigris as his capital, and it remained the seat of government even under the Sassanids. Armenia itself made an alliance with Persia, whose prestige had greatly risen as a result of the victory. The northern districts of Mesopotamia with Nisibis and Gordyene were again annexed to the empire. Nevertheless, Iran's attack on Syria in 52–51 was not crowned with success. Orodes had considered that Sūrēn was becoming too successful a general and had had him put to death and his son, Pacorus, was merely able to send his cavalry on raids into Cilicia and along the frontiers of Cappadocia, but before the walls and fortifications of Antioch he was powerless. It is also possible that the campaign had no other purpose than to make brief incursions into enemy territory in order to loot and pillage. In 50 BC the Parthian cavalry recrossed the Euphrates. In 38–37, Orodes was killed by his own son, Phraates IV, whom he had shortly before nominated as his successor.

The position of Mark Antony, the Roman triumvir who had undertaken the task of establishing Roman power in the East was a somewhat difficult one. His plan to seize Babylon from the Parthians failed. In the spring of 36, he abandoned Zeugma and turned his steps northwards along the banks of the Euphrates, passing through Melitene on the way to Carina (Erzerum). From Carina he turned eastwards, but he found it difficult to protect the immense baggage-train which he insisted on accompanying him, and he was attacked by the Parthians who seized many valuable cartloads of supplies. Antony remained in the city of Phraaspa until October, and then began the intense cold and an inglorious retreat—it was only with great difficulty that the Romans reached Armenia. More than 8,000 of his legionaries had died from cold and exhaustion. From Armenia Antony appealed to Cleopatra in Egypt for assistance. In due course supplies and heavy clothing arrived from Egypt, but this help could not make up for the rout of the Roman armies.

In 30 BC Augustus arrived in Syria and developed Rome's eastern policy along new lines. His plan was basically to strengthen the border with Parthia, at the same time pushing it as far east as possible. It was easy to interfere in the internal affairs of Armenia and Parthia, since the great noble families were always quarrelling among each other and sometimes formed states within the state. Armenia was ever a cause of discontent between Rome and Parthia, for it was nominally a vassal of the Parthians, but had rebelled under the energetic leadership of king Tigranes. Since it was virtually impossible for the Romans to realize their dream of controlling the trade routes with Bactria and India, the struggle with Parthia during the following centuries was restricted to conflicts for control of the frontier along the Euphrates. All the Roman attempts to cross the Tigris failed, although from time to time the Roman legions penetrated into areas that were strictly Parthian.

In AD 58 the Roman legions under the command of Corbulo Domitius started out on a long-planned campaign against Armenia. The Parthian armies assembled in Hyrcania failed to come to the aid of the Armenian troops in time. Artaxata (Artashat), the ancient Armenian capital, was occupied and its walls were destroyed. By AD 60 the whole of Armenia had been conquered. A new treaty regarding Armenia was concluded between Rome and the Parthians in AD 63. An Arsacid related to the Parthian dynasty was made puppet king and was crowned by Nero in Rome. Armenia thus came to be ruled by a branch of the Arsacid dynasty for the long period lasting from 63 to 428. During this time it acted as a buffer state between the Roman empire and Persia. Other branches of the Arsacid dynasty governed Caucasian Iberia (Western Georgia) and Albania (Northern Azerbaijān). The Parthians therefore had to protect their western frontier and in addition had to keep watch all the time on the north and north-east because of the continual threat of the nomadic tribes from that direction. In 72, aided by the 'king' of Hyrcania, the Alani, who were a tribe of Iranian Scytho-Sarmatian stock from Outer Iran (their present descendants are the Ossetes of the Caucasus), passed through the Iron Gates in the Caucasus and laid waste Atropatene. Rome

turned a deaf ear to the appeals for help from Vologases I
(*Valkash*, AD 51–77). The campaigns of Trajan, the future
emperor, in Armenia and Osrhoene resulted in the latter
becoming a Roman province and helped considerably to
strengthen the frontier. In 115, Trajan, now emperor, descended the Tigris in a fleet of boats and, using siege engines,
succeeded in taking Seleucia-Ctesiphon. The Parthian king
Osrhoes (*Khusrau*) fled, allowing his daughter and the famous
golden throne to fall into the hands of the Romans. Trajan
was thus able to claim the title of 'Particus' in 116. The
throne of Parthia became a plaything in the hands of the
Roman diplomatists; but in eastern and north-eastern Iran,
so often in history the scene of unrest and rebellion, the
adversaries of Rome regrouped and in due course brought
such pressure to bear that the Roman legions were forced to
withdraw further west. In August 117 Trajan died.

Vologases II (128/9–147) tried to maintain good relations
with Rome. The Alani attacked Parthia (136) but were thrown
back. Under Vologases III the Parthians once more gathered
together their strength and advanced westwards, taking Edessa
on their way. A little further south they crossed the Euphrates
and entered Syria, where they expected an uprising against
the Roman overlords to break out. Rome had foreseen this
possibility and had sent the western legions to Syria. The
emperor, Lucius Verus, made Antioch the centre of opera-
tions, reorganized the army, and in 163 conquered Artashat
in Armenia. The Romans fought off the Parthian attack,
turned westwards, and in 165 retook Seleucia, but an epidemic
broke out and they were forced to withdraw. The Parthians
gathered the strength to make a counter attack, but they were
again thrown back (166). The result of this campaign was that
the provinces west of the River Khabur were ceded to Rome
and the Romans gained political control of Edessa and Harrān
(Carrhae). The feebleness of the royal authority in Parthia
and the continual struggles over the succession to the throne
weakened resistance to Rome. It was this that enabled the
emperor Septimius Severus to mount a further Parthian
campaign in 196. Meanwhile, two members of the Arsacid
family, both named Vologases, one of whom (Vologases IV)
was established in Seleucia, were fighting for the throne.

A revolt broke out in the north-eastern provinces but was put down by Vologases, who, after a long pursuit, drove the rebels towards the Caspian. Then, in order to punish him for not having come to his assistance, Vologases attacked and routed Narsetes, king of Adiabene. Yet another Roman campaign in 199 led to Ctesiphon and Babylon being taken once again, but Septimius Severus failed to capture Hatra.

Finally, in 211, the emperor Caracalla conquered Osrhoene, the kingdom around Edessa ruled by Abgar IX, and made it a Roman province. Taking advantage of the dissension between the two brothers, Vologases V in Seleucia and Artabanus V in Ecbatana, Caracalla succeeded in occupying Mesopotamia, Arbela, and part of Medea. Artabanus V collected together the Parthian armies and fled across the Tigris (217). The Romans and Parthians met at Nisibis, which Septimius Severus had already made his main arsenal in the area. The Romans were twice defeated, and had to buy peace at a considerable price.

Meanwhile critical events were occurring in Iran. The Persians—the people of Pārs and southern Iran—were trying to shake off the Parthian domination. Ardashīr, son of Pāpak, who was a member of the noble family of the Sassanians (descendants of Sāsān, who in turn was supposed to be a descendant of the Achaemenids) played a prominent part in a rebellion that took place in 212. Pāpak himself had united various territories under his control, had received from Artabanus the title of 'king of Pārs', and had requested the Parthian king to accord the same title to his son Sapor (Shāhpūr). On the latter's death the throne was occupied by Ardashīr. The authority of the Arsacid dynasty had become weaker and weaker. Vologases V was killed in 222–3. Artabanus V fell in battle against the new Sassanid pretender in 224, and his son Artavazd succeeded in putting up a resistance for only a short time. With Ardashīr, son of the Sassanid Pāpak, a new and very important period of Iranian history begins—that of the Sassanid dynasty.

For a number of reasons the Parthian period is one of the most interesting in the history of Iran. It saw the amalgamation of all the factors which were to shape the future of Persia, thus revealing that ability to assimilate without becoming servile which is one of the basic features of the Persians. Unfortunately, we know too little about the Parthian period, and many of the problems of its history and culture remain unsolved. The administration of the state was still based on the system of satrapies as in the past, except that they were subdivided into 'eparchies' controlled by civil or military governors. Greek sources inform us that these were further split up into even smaller districts for the purpose of land control and taxation. Also, a form of feudal government began to appear. Beside the Arsacid king of kings (*shāhān-shāh*) there existed local aristocracies, small dynasties which ruled over various provinces, often in a way that showed they were quite independent. The centre of the state was Medea, and the summer residence of the *shāhān-shāh* was Ecbatana, though the king usually spent the winter in the warmer city of Babylon. The king of kings was surrounded by a large number of courtiers, the heads of the great aristocratic families (seven in number), and his bodyguard. He was advised by a council of nobles and another council consisting of wise men and magi, that is to say, Parthian priests who exercised considerable authority. Some titled positions, it seems, were completely hereditary and limited to certain noble families, such as the Sūrēn and Karēn. The army, and in particular the famous cavalry, was made up of Parthian nobles and freemen, and in addition the kings and vassal princes had their own armies which took part in the imperial campaigns under their command. The Parthians were noted for their archers. Their foot-soldiers and horsemen wore coats of mail, as can be seen from some of the wall-paintings at Dura-Europos. The army auxiliaries consisted almost certainly of slaves. Though it was not as highly developed as in the Roman empire, slavery was fundamental to the economy. As we have seen, Himer sold the Babylonians into slavery.

In the eastern part of the empire the chief occupation was cattle-rearing, whilst in the west this was combined with farming, particularly in Mesopotamia. Also important were the market gardens, orchards and vineyards. The most widely grown cereals were barley and wheat. Mesopotamia was essential to the economy, culture, and trade of the empire, and again and again in the long history of Persia it became an appendage of the Iranian highlands. Mesopotamia was situated at the crossroads of many trade routes linking east and west. The situation was somewhat different only at the end of the second and beginning of the first century BC when continuous political disorder meant that the trade routes could no longer be protected from the Arab nomads (Beduin), who regularly attacked and plundered the caravans. As a result the use of the sea routes connecting the Persian Gulf with the Indian coast revived to a certain extent. The Seleucids, having lost Asia Minor, had brought commercial life back to the coast of Phoenicia and had opened up trade relations directly with Greece. One of the most important trade routes ran from the Persian Gulf along the Tigris to Seleucia, from there on to Dura-Europos and thence to other Syrian commercial centres. Navigation on the Caspian and the Black Sea began to develop only during the Roman period. Parthia jealously guarded its control of the Central Asian trade routes, and the struggle with the Romans, which lasted for centuries, was in large part due to the latters' desire to appropriate this monopoly. The path that these trade routes followed, particularly during the second and first centuries BC, is fairly well known. They ran through Chinese Turkestan as far as Merv, and then passed through Hecatompylae (the modern Dāmghān) to reach Seleucia and Ecbatana (the modern Hamadān). In Mesopotamia there was a brisk trade along another route running north of Seleucia and connecting Hatra with Nisibis and Zeugma. The extent of these trade relations is shown by the existence of Chinese silk in Syria and Egypt, the flow of Syrian textiles into Mongolia, and the fact that coins of Mithridates II have been found in Turkestan.

The Chinese traveller Chang Ch'ien, who was sent by the Han emperor Wu Ti in about 128 BC to form an alliance with the Yüeh-chih (Sakas) against their common enemy, the Huns, introduced into China the vine (Chinese *p'u-t'ao* < *bu-daw*, according to Laufer, from middle Pers. *bādak*, modern Pers. *bādè* = wine), and lucerne or purple medick (*mu-su* < *muk-suk*, from an unknown Persian term). The pomegranate was known in China as the 'Parthian fruit' (*an-shih-liu*: *an-shih* in ancient times was prounounced *an-shek* or *ar-shek*, from *arshak*, the Arsacid dynasty). And vice versa, peaches and apricots were introduced into Iran from China and then brought to the West, as is revealed by Lat. *persicum* and *Prunus Armeniaca*. Besides silk, the Parthians highly valued a special Chinese steel, then known even outside Iran as 'Merv steel', which indicates the importance of Merv on the Silk Road. Ostriches were brought from Babylon to China, where they were known as 'Parthian birds'.

The Mesopotamian cities played a very important part in this trade. On the one hand, the road from Persepolis through Carmania to Sīstān linked Iran with India; on the other, the sea route across the Persian Gulf connected the Euphrates directly with the Indus. The city of Babylon still retained its importance as a multilingual and cosmopolitan trading and cultural centre. Furthermore, the Hellenization of the city had led to Greeks learning the Babylonian language, and later Aramaic, while the local inhabitants knew Greek. Greek remained the language employed on Parthian coins up to the time of Vologases I (AD 51–77). Clay tablets were replaced by parchment (and even papyrus), and the difficult cuneiform script by the Aramaic alphabet. Astronomy and the system of of dating, both of which had originated in Babylon, continued to develop. It is even thought that the Chinese took their names for the constellations from the Babylonians, while the Greeks based their mathematical speculations partly on Babylonian learning. During the Seleucid and Parthian period the Persian language developed from its ancient form to one approaching its medieval form with the almost complete loss of inflections. Our knowledge of the Parthian form (or *pahlavīk*, from *parthavik*) of middle Persian is limited to a few inscriptions and certain Manichaean texts discovered at the beginning of this century in Turfan, which are dated after the fall of the Parthian kingdom. Over two thousand *ostraka* discovered from 1948 onwards in the ancient Parthian capital of Nysa (in modern Soviet Turkmenistan) are now being studied by Russian scholars. They appear to date from the first century BC and are written in Aramaic script (it is not yet clear whether this is Aramaic containing Parthian loan-words or Parthian with Aramaic ideograms). This script had astonished Chang-Ch'ien, who noticed that it ran from right to left. The strong Aramaic influence during the Parthian period, which continued under the Sassanids, resulted in a strange type of writing in which many words were written in Aramaic ideograms but read in Persian. This probably arose because the majority of the nobles were illiterate and writing was left to Aramaic scribes, who looked at an Aramaic text and read it out aloud in Persian translation.

Little has come down to us of Parthian art. There are a few architectural remains, including the palace at Hatra, and sarcophagi and sculptures, which reflect the eclecticism of the period and many features which foreshadow the Sassanid style. This eclecticism is also to be found in the religion. The pantheon of the Mesopotamian cities during this period included not only the ancient local deities but also Greek and Egyptian gods. The Parthian kings were Mazdaeans, at least in theory, but their Mazdaism appears to have incorporated many features of other local and foreign cults, while in Pārs, the cradle of the Sassanid dynasty, it seems to have retained a purer form. Under Vologases I there seems to have been a revival of 'Iranism'; during this period some Iranian divinities and forms of worship spread beyond the frontiers to Pontus, Commagena, Cilicia and Armenia. At Hierapolis, Membij and Dura-Europos, there were temples dedicated to Atargatis, the 'mother of the gods', an ancient Aramaic divinity. At Dura, Adad, Nanaia and even Artemis were worshipped. At Uruk, in the heart of Parthia, there was a temple of the Babylonian god Abu, while at Ecbatana, Palmyra, and in Cappadocia, the Mesopotamian Bel was worshipped. During the first century AD, the Iranian god Mithra began to find followers in the West, as a result of Pompey's Middle Eastern campaigns.

The existence of so many different gods and cults was one of the results of the intermingling of Iranian, Babylonian, Syrian and Greek populations. Mesopotamia in particular was the centre of these syncretic beliefs. With the coming of Christianity, which occurred during the Parthian period, Christian features were also introduced. It is therefore impossible to underestimate the importance of this melting-pot of cultures in the history of the subsequent centuries.

CHAPTER III

The Sassanid period

Ardashīr (archaic form *Artakhshēr* from ancient Pers. *Artakhshathra* = Artaxerxes) conquered Babylon and then made a triumphal entry into Ctesiphon. At his subsequent coronation in 226 he took the traditional title of *shāhān-shāh*. A well-known rock relief at Naqsh-i Rustam near Persepolis shows king Ardashīr on horseback receiving the investiture from Ahura Mazdā. Ardashīr tramples underfoot the deposed Parthian king Artabanus, while Ahura Mazdā similarly treats Ahriman, the principle of evil. It is possible that the actual ceremony took place at *Stākhr* (Istakhr) nearby. It was here that Ardashīr's ancestor Sāsān had served as priest in the temple of the goddess of the waters *Anāhita*, a fertility goddess of Mesopotamian origin who had long found a place in the Mazdaean pantheon. According to tradition, Ardashīr married a relative of Artabanus, probably his daughter, in order to strengthen his position. He then proceeded to rebuild the ancient empire, subduing the various provinces one by one. On his death in 241, the Persian empire had regained almost all the territory held by the ancient Achaemenids, apart from Egypt, Syria and Asia Minor. Stakhr replaced Persepolis as the spiritual centre. But in the eyes of the Sassanids, the Achaemenid period of greatness appeared more as a legendary golden age than as a historical fact. Alexander's conquest and the subsequent Hellenization had had the effect of making a sharp break with the past, as is shown by the fact that the Persians knew extremely little about the Achaemenid period. It is no exaggeration to say that the reconstruction and reassessment of Achaemenid history are almost entirely due to Western archaeologists. There were survivals of Hellenism: for example, the inscription on the king's horse on the rock relief at Naqsh-i Rustam is in three languages, Greek (Ōhrmazd—the form the Medes and Persians gave to Ahura Mazdā—is translated as *Zeus*), Parthian and *Pārsīk* (sometimes called Arsacid or Sassanid Pahlavi). Sassanid *Pārsīk* borrowed heavily from Parthian, and these borrowings are still to be found in modern Persian.

Ardashīr built, or rebuilt, a number of cities which nearly all bear his name, e.g., *Ardashīr-khvarreh*, 'Glory of Ardashīr', the modern Fīrūzābād; *Vēh-Ardashīr*, 'The Good of Ardashīr', the new Seleucia which replaced the city destroyed by the Romans in 165; *Nēv Ardashīr, Rām Ardashīr*, etc. Persis once again became the heartland of the empire, and Seleucia-Ctesiphon the administrative capital. Ardashīr soon became something of a legend. Indeed, in the Pahlavi *Legend of Ardashīr, Son of Pāpak* he is sometimes accorded the attributes of Cyrus, and even of the Babylonian god Marduk, slayer of monsters and dragons. Besides reuniting the shattered Arsacid state, Ardashīr also succeeded in reorganizing the administration of the empire, which was to remain largely unchanged to the end of the Sassanid period.

After absorbing or rejecting the many Greek features, the Sassanid empire took on the appearance of a restoration of an earlier period. The lack of a sense of history, however, prevented the development of any kind of renaissance. The two outstanding features of the Sassanid state consist of a marked centralization (as opposed to the Arsacid feudalism) and the creation of a state religion (as opposed to the eclecticism and syncretism of the previous period). But in fact, both the feudal system and religious syncretism remained deep-rooted, overlaid by a conscious determination to achieve unity at all costs.

Sassanid society was divided into four professional and four social classes, whose interrelations are little understood to-day. The former consisted of the priests (*asravān*), warriors (*artēshtārān*), the administrators (*dipīrān*), and the common people (*vastryōshān*, farmers, and *hutūkhshān*, artisans). These are very similar to the old Aryan and Achaemenid social divisions. The chief difference lies in the addition of the scribes (*dipīrān*), who were unknown to the Aryans and who were of Mesopotamian origin, as is revealed by the word itself (from the ancient Sumerian root *dip-/dup-* to engrave, write). The other subdivision was clearly inherited from the Arsacids, and consisted of the princes (*shāhrdārān*), heads or perhaps members of the great families (*vaspūhrān*), the grandees (*vuzurgān*), and the nobles (*āzādān*). The *shāhrdārān* included not only the vassal princes but also the rulers of the border provinces (*marzbān*, from *marz*, frontier), the four greatest of whom resided at the four cardinal points, and the governors of the large provinces belonging to the royal family, who often bore the title of *shāh* or king (this is why the Sassanid king was *shāhān-shāh*, 'king of kings'). The *vaspūhrān* consisted of the heads and members of the seven great families (the Kārēns, the Aspahbads, etc., were still powerful under the Sassanids), wealthy landowners, some of whom held hereditary positions which were more honorific than anything else. The *vuzurgān* were probably the senior government officials (ministers and administrative heads), while the *āzādān* (those born into the nobility and therefore freemen) belonged to the petty nobility who were responsible for provincial administration. The latter included the *dehkānān* or village headmen (or better still, owners of villages) and *katak-khvatāyān*, hereditary heads of the small local administrative centres, the backbone of the Iranian social system even in the immediate post-Islamic period.

After the king, the most important person in the central government was the grand vizier (the modern form is not accidental, for the administrative system of the Arab Abbasid caliphate was largely modelled on that of the Sassanids). He was sometimes known as *hazārpat* or chiliarch (originally the commander of the guard of 1,000 men), but more often *vuzurg-framādār*, grand commander. In view of the king's omnipotence, his power resided in the fact that he was the royal coadjutor. Religious administration, which was of immense importance on account of the revival of orthodoxy, was in the hands of the head of the magi, the Zoroastrian pope, who was nevertheless appointed by the king. He bore the title of *mōbadān-mōbad*, *mōbad* of the *mōbads*, a form modelled on that of *shāhān-shāh*. Below the *mōbad* (*mogh-bad*, head mage) came the ordinary magi, the *mōghān*. The *dastevār* or *dastūr* were like ecclesiastical judges. While the royal family vaunted its Achaemenid ancestry, the priestly families (for the magi were a 'tribe') claimed to go back to the mythical times of the ancient *Manushchīhar* and the beginning of the world. (This sense of aristocratic ancestry was very much alive in ancient Persia.) There was also a number of lower orders of specialist priests, for Zoroastrianism was much concerned with ritual.

The official responsible for the collection of the land-tax (*vastryōshbad*, 'head of the farmers', and also *hutūkhshbad*, 'head of the artisans') acted as minister of finance. The state's revenue came largely from the land-tax (*kharāg*, from which is derived the Arabic *kharāj*: another example of Arab imitation of Sassanid administration). This consisted of from a sixth to a third of the harvest, depending on the fertility of the land (occasionally it rose to a half, according to some authorities), and or a personal tax (*gēzīt*, giving the Arabic *jizya*), which was particularly burdensome for the artisans. The remaining sources of revenue consisted of extraordinary taxes, special gifts (*āyēn*), and customs duties on merchandize.

Industry, commerce, and the trade routes continued more or less the same as during the Parthian period. Iran remained the crossroads between Central Asia and China on the one hand and the Graeco-Roman world on the other. A strong army was required in order to defend such a vast empire. Ardashīr's title of *argabad* (fortress commander) was hereditary. The army was commanded by an *ērān-spāhbad* (commander-in-chief of Iran), who also acted as minister of war and negotiated peace treaties. He had the right to make his entry into camp to the sound of trumpets. There was also the king's bodyguard. The navy, consisting partly of Arabs from the Persian Gulf, was as always of little consequence. On account of the highly centralized organization of the Sassanid state, the scribes (*dipīr*) held an extremely important position, and had to be familiar with the very difficult system of Aramaic-cum-Iranian ideogrammatic writing. At their head was the *ērān-dipīrbad* or *dipīrān-mahist*, who was assisted by a number of other officials concerned with the law, the postal system, finance, etc. Provincial governors (*marzbān*) replaced the former satraps: the most important of them were those who were in charge of the frontier provinces. The number of provinces appears to have varied, and the king sent a *marzbān* to this or that province as and when required. The provinces were further subdivided into districts (*istān*), and these into sub-districts and villages governed by landowners from the small local aristocracy.

The problem of the religion of the Sassanids is, as usual, extremely complex, though, in contrast to the previous periods, we do possess a large corpus of theological texts and writings on ecclesiastical law in Pahlavi (Sassanid middle Persian), and a number of references in the Greek, Armenian, Syriac and other sources. Unfortunately, the non-Iranian sources give us a picture of the Sassanid religion which fails to tally with that furnished by the Pahlavi texts. Even if we take into account the possibility that foreign observers may have misunderstood the facts or interpreted them in terms of their own religious ideas, some basic differences remain. These may be explained either by difference between the religion of the people and the religion of the elite, or between that of the warrior caste and that of the priestly caste, or else by the possibility that even the earliest Pahlavi sources (nearly all of which date from after the Arab conquest) are very late. One cannot escape the impression that Zoroastrianism must have undergone considerable reforms immediately following the Arab conquest and that, though this may appear strange, the Pahlavi texts that we possess have been influenced by monotheism and an Islamic simplification. The Sassanid religion must have retained many more mythical features and elements of nature worship from the earlier periods of eclecticism than did post-Islamic Zoroastrianism. For example, the foreign sources speak of the preponderant part played by sun worship, which is completely absent from the Pahlavi sources. It was only in the Sassanid period that fragments from the Parthian period were gathered together in the *Avesta*, which was a canonical text in twenty-one symbolic books. (The very idea of books and holy scripture was foreign to Aryanism, and was borrowed from the Semites.) It is almost certain that some parts of the *Avesta* existed first in Pahlavi, and were then translated into the older, ancient Iranian language. This obviously does not rule out the existence of an oral tradition of the original text, nor the possibility that certain parts of the *Avesta* (the noun *apastāk* means 'basic text', as opposed to *zand*, the Pahlavi 'commentary') are of considerable antiquity.

During the Sassanid period, the theological school, or at most the heresy (though some scholars consider it an actual religion itself), of Zurvān developed considerably. This gave supremacy to 'Infinite Time', over and above the gods Ōhrmazd and Ahriman, the principles of Good and Evil,

Light and Darkness. There is no doubt that during this period, as is shown by the birth of such heresies and religions as Manichaeism and Mazdakism, Zoroastrian theology must have been very fluid and its relations with the popular religion, of which we are almost completely ignorant, very close. Fire worship, the *shibboleth* of Mazdaism, is known to have existed from the temples where it was laid down that the priests should officiate five times each day, and from the large number of fire altars (often represented on Sassanid coins), which are to be found throughout the whole of Iran. (It would be most interesting to make a study of the sites of these holy places, comparing them with those of the numerous post-Islamic sanctuaries of mystics and *imāms*.) In fact, there were even various 'fires' that were held sacred locally, rather like Madonnas. The three most important of these fires (*ādur*) were the *ādur-farnbāgh*, the protective fire of the priests, in the district of Kabul, the *ādur-gushnāsp*, the royal fire, between Urmia and Hamadan (*Takht-i Sulaimān*), and the *ādur-burzēn-mihr*, the fire of the farmers in the Rēvand mountains, north-east of Nīshāpūr.

The Zoroastrian calendar consisted of twelve months of thirty days with five intercalary days. The names of the months survived the Islamic invasion and are still in use in Iran to-day. They recall the most important genii of the Zoroastrian pantheon: *fravardīn* (the *fravashi*, men's guardian angels); *urdvahisht* (the archangel *Asha*, 'upright law'); *khvardād* ('integrity', another of the *ameshaspenta* or 'immortal holy ones'); *tīr* (*Tishtrya*, Sirius, the dog-star); *amurdād* ('immortality', another of the *ameshaspenta*); *shahrēvar* (the archangel of the 'kingdom'); *mihr* (Mithra); *ābān* (the 'waters', represented by the goddess *Anāhita*, of whom the Sassanid kings were hereditary priests); *ādur* (fire); *dadhv* (the Creator, that is to say, Ōhrmazd); *vahman* ('good thought', one of the most important of the *ameshaspenta*); and *spandarmad* ('holy submission', a protective archangel symbolizing the earth). There were numerous festivals, some of the oldest of which are still held to this day. The most popular and joyful of these was (and still is) *Naurūz*, the celebration of the New Year (21 March), which now lasts thirteen days, though in Sassanid times it may have extended over only six. Others include

The Sassanid period

Mihrgān ('feast of Mithra'), held on the 16th day of the month bearing his name, which was the former autumnal New Year; and *Sadak* (mod. Pers. *Sadè*), which was above all a fire festival, commemorating the discovery of fire by a mythical king of earliest times. But the precarious position of the magi's authority and of the revival of orthodoxy is revealed by the sudden appearance, immediately after the foundation of the dynasty, of Mani and of his extremely dangerous heresy, Manichaeism, which rapidly spread through wide areas of the civilised world.

Ardashīr was succeeded in 241 by Shāhpūr I (the name means 'king's son'), who might have become the first ruler of a Manichaean Iran. Mani's parents were of Iranian stock and belonged to the small Arsacid nobility, who had emigrated from Medea to settle in Babylon. His father, Patik, joined a baptist sect, one of many that sprang up in Babylonia during the Parthian period. Mani was brought up in the doctrines of this religious group, but he also studied Christianity, Mazdaism, and the teachings of Bardaisan and Marcion, and probably also Buddhism. An angel, whom he called 'the Companion', or 'the Twin', revealed to him the divine truths, and he proclaimed himself the last of a line of prophets who had founded religions. These included Buddha, Zoroaster, and Jesus, representing India, Persia, and the West. Mani, however, had come 'from the land of Babel to raise a resounding cry throughout the entire world'. It is impossible to go into the content of this 'cry' in any detail. Basically, it consists of a gnostic doctrine which is inherently pessimistic. Human souls, which come from the world of Light, are imprisoned in the loathsome world of matter, which is the work of Evil. Birth, physical existence, nature, death, and marriage are all works of the devil. The Manichaean texts, full of eschatological and salvation myths, are written in many languages. Mani himself wrote largely in Aramaic, but the Manichaeans encouraged the making of translations, at which they were expert, and these have given us an understanding of a number of Asiatic languages that would otherwise have remained almost unknown.

Christianity strongly influenced this mixture of religious ideas, while Buddhism supplied the concept of reincarnation. Though the Manichaean cosmology and eschatology were extremely complex, the rites were very simple and were accompanied by hymns and chants, while Manichaean books are often illustrated with delightful miniatures. It is not difficult to explain the initial success of Mani's preaching, nor the extremely severe persecutions that Mani himself and his followers suffered. It appears Mani began his preaching during the reign of Ardashīr, found favour with the heir to the throne, and also converted two of the king's brothers. King Shāhpūr himself wanted to meet Mani, who impressed him favourably. Mani tells us in his work, the *Kephalaia*: 'I appeared before king Shāhpūr, and he received me with great honours. He granted me permission to travel throughout his kingdom and to preach the word of Life. I spent several years . . . in his retinue, many years in Iran, in the land of the Parthians as far as Adib [Adiabene?] and the countries bordering on the Roman empire'. One of Mani's books in Persian takes its title, *Shāhpūragān*, from the name of the king. According to one tradition, at a certain point Shāhpūr withdrew his support, according to another, even after Shāhpūr's death in 272, Mani continued to be well treated by his son and successor Hormizd I (272-3). It appears that it was in fact Hormizd I's brother and successor, Vahrām I (273-6), who allowed Mani to fall into the hands of the magi, who put him to death after torturing him at length. (There are various traditions concerning 'the passion of Mani', which was celebrated by his followers at the feast of the *Bēma* or 'tribune', the empty throne indicating the spiritual presence of the founder.) The majority of Mani's numerous works, most of which have disappeared, were written in Aramaic and the *Shāhpūragān* in middle Persian. The *Kephalaia*, of which we now possess a good part in a Coptic version of a Greek translation, contains the master's instructions which were gathered together after his death. There also exist a number of Mani's letters, some of them known now in Coptic translation, addressed to Manichaean communities in Ctesiphon, Babylon, Mesene, Edessa, Susiana, Armenia, India, and elsewhere, which shows how widespread Manichaeanism had become during the founder's own lifetime. Manichaeanism spread throughout Iran, and from the third to the twelfth century, the date of its final disappearance, Manichaeans could be found throughout the civilized world, while Manichaean states arose among the Turks of Central Asia and there were numerous followers of Mani in China and India.

From the point of view of the Mazdaeans, Manichaeanism was utter heresy, and this appears to have been the attitude of members of all the other religions with which it came in contact, and they did not hesitate in joining forces in order to eradicate it. (The persecuted Christians in Iran made common cause with their persecutors against the heretic; after the Arab conquest, the Moslems and Zoroastrians combined in persecuting the Manichees; the German *Ketzer*, meaning 'heretic', comes from 'Cathar', a member of a religion with Manichaean tendencies in the Middle Ages, and so forth.) The reason for this ferocity on the part of the ruling classes of the period is fairly obvious: the utter pessimism, the denial of the goodness of nature and of all that visibly exists, and the idea that it was Satan rather than God who created the vile visible world, were regarded as blasphemy. If one thinks of the rock relief of Ardashīr at Naqsh-i Rustam, which shows the king corresponding exactly to Ōhrmazd the Creator God, each trampling under his feet the vanquished, illegitimate rival (the king's enemy is thus equated with Satan), it is quite natural to think that the Manichaeans' identification of Satan with the Creator might—despite Mani's initial friendship with the highest members of the aristocracy and with the king himself—easily be interpreted by the oppressed masses as the portent and symbol of the overthrow of authority. One should also bear in mind the element of individualism in Mani's teaching. The Manichaean myth is one long hymn to the possibility of *personal* salvation from the evil of the world, and it was the individual person that the despotic regimes ignored. If to this we add the fascination of Mani himself, who replaced the king and the priests in the people's veneration, and the probable re-emergence of certain tendencies in Persian popular religion about which we know little, one soon realizes that it would have been impossible for the aristocracy not to have fought Manichaeanism. Shāhpūr's and perhaps Hormizd's initial acceptance of Mani can be explained by an incipient jealousy and divergence of interests between throne and altar, between the royal warrior caste and the priestly caste. The priests triumphed, and were always to do so up to the time of

8. The Khwaju bridge at Isfahān built in the mid-seventeenth century by 'Abbas II. *Wim Swaan.*

9. The 'Ali Gāpu or 'Sublime Porte' created by 'Abbas the Great at Isfahān. *Wim Swaan.*

10. *Left* Entrance portal to the Masjid-i-Shāh or Royal Mosque, built at Isfahān by 'Abbas the Great and completed in 1616. *Wim Swaan.*

11. *Top* A youth with a narcissus. Miniature of the Isfahān school painted in the seventeenth century. *Treasury, Topkapi Palace Museum, Istanbul.*

12. *Bottom* The shrine at Mashhad, seat of pilgrimage since the ninth century. *By courtesy of the Imperial Iranian embassy.*

13. *Top* The Shāhristan bridge near Isfahān, whose stone piers probably date from the Sassanian period of rule during the third to the seventh centuries. *By courtesy of the Imperial Iranian embassy.*

14. *Bottom* The Safid Rūd dam, the highest buttressed dam in the world, completed in 1963. *By courtesy of the Imperial Iranian embassy.*

the Arab conquest. It is interesting to note that wherever Manichaeanism was allowed to develop freely and even become the state religion, there, paradoxically enough considering the doctrine's inherent pessimism, the figurative arts, poetry and national languages flourished. (The Manichaeans, like the Christians, had no sacred language.) Despite its absolute otherworldliness, which could easily have sapped any sense of protest, Manichaeanism appears from a social point of view to have represented one of the first attempts to overcome the despotism of the early rulers of Iran. However, it was a premature attempt, and it was not till the coming of Islam that success was achieved.

Under the early Sassanids, Armenia, which was really too small to serve as an efficient buffer state between the Roman and Persian empires, continued to be an apple of discord between them. The war against Rome which Ardashīr I had initiated was brought to a close by Shāhpūr. Little was gained, though the Roman emperor, Philip the Arab, ceded Armenia to the Persians. Shāhpūr also had to fight the usual rebels in the Caspian area and in the eastern part of Iran. In Khorāsān he founded *Nēv-Shāhpūr*, 'Good Shāhpūr', modern Nīshāpūr.

In 260, Shāhpūr succeeded in defeating a Roman expedition and took prisoner no less a person than the emperor Valerian himself, who died in captivity. Many of the Roman prisoners, whose ability as civil engineers was much appreciated, were settled at Gundēshāhpūr, a city Shāhpūr had founded in Susiana, and at Shushtar. The triumph over Valerian is recorded in a number of reliefs, the most famous of which is one that can still be seen on the historic wall of Naqsh-i Rustam, beside the tombs of the Achaemenids, which every Persian guide is particularly proud of pointing out to European visitors. Valerian is shown kneeling before Shāhpūr's horse and begging for mercy.

Shāhpūr now ravaged Syria and Cappadocia, but the king who had been able to overcome the Romans now suffered a severe defeat at the hands of the Arab ruler of Palmyra, a Roman vassal and the husband of the famous queen Zeinab (Zenobia), who reigned after his death. The Persians kept up the war with Palmyra without success until 265. The appearance of a number of small Arab states on the borders between the Roman and Persian empires, vassals now of the one, now of the other, dates from the beginning of the Sassanid period.

Shāhpūr died in 272. Virtually nothing is known of the events during the reigns of his two sons, Hormizd I (272–3) and Vahrām I (273–6). War with Rome broke out again under Vahrām II (276–93), Vahrām I's son and successor. After a series of brilliant successes—the emperor Carus penetrated as far as Ctesiphon—the Romans retired, but at the peace treaty of 283 the Persians were obliged to yield Armenia and Mesopotamia because of the threat of invasion by the Sakas of Outer Iran (Scyths from Khorāsān and Central Asia).

On the death of Vahrām II in 293, Vahrām III came to the throne but after only four months his great-uncle Narsah (*Narsēh*), a son of Shāhpūr I, rebelled against him. Narsah was not very successful in his Roman campaigns which were brought to an end in 298 by yet another peace, though this time it endured for some forty years. The reign of Narsah's son, Hormizd II (302–9), was followed by internal struggles until the notables put on the throne Shāhpūr II, a young boy who was to reign for nearly seventy years (310–379) and to become one of the most important Sassanid sovereigns. Little is known of the first thirty years of his reign (at first under the regency of his mother and the notables), except that he fought fiercely against the frontier Arab tribes, for which he was nicknamed 'the wrencher of shoulders' after a cruel custom of the day. (It should be noticed in passing that there is frequent mention of the Arabs in Sassanid history and it is therefore quite wrong to think of the Moslem invasion as the first occasion on which there was contact between Arabs and Persians.)

During Shāhpūr II's reign an event of fundamental importance took place in Rome: Constantine embraced the Christian faith. From this moment on, the traditional struggle with Rome is intimately linked with the state of affairs of the Christians in the Iranian empire. Christianity had reached Iran in the first and second centuries, and in the early days the Christians were regarded with sympathy since they were being persecuted by the common enemy, pagan Rome. Hostilities with

Rome were re-opened by the *shāh* sending a flowery but firm letter to the emperor Constantine. It is interesting to note the official Sassanid title given by the latin historian Ammianus Marcellinus, 'king of kings, companion of the stars, brother of the sun and the moon' which corresponds closely with that found in other Sassanid inscriptions: 'worshipper of Mazdā, the divine, king of kings of Iran and non-Iran, descendant of the gods'. The Persians captured Amida (modern Diyarbekir) in 359, and then, after the death of Constantius in 361, the war was continued by his nephew, Julian the Apostate, who was an unsuccessful general and indeed lost his life in the field in 363. Peace was concluded with his successor, the emperor Jovian, and as a result the Persians gained Nisibis, Singara (Sinjar), and parts of Armenia. When Valentinian became emperor he tried to maintain a pro-Roman puppet on the throne of Armenia. Shāhpūr, who had meantime become involved in struggles with the Chionites of Bactriana, now had to fight for control of Armenia, where rivalry between the pro-Roman and pro-Iranian parties was raging, while at the same time also protecting himself against the pro-Roman intrigues of the Christians at home. It was for largely political reasons that Shāhpūr, who, according to some sources, appears not to have shown any hatred for Christians as such, was forced to launch the first large-scale persecution of the Christians in Iran, which lasted from 339 to the time of his death.

Shāhpūr II was succeeded first by his brother, Ardashīr II (379–83), and then by his sons Shahpūr III (383–8) and Vahrām IV (388–99), who was succeeded by a Chosroes, whose rule, however, extended over only the eastern part of Iran. Ardashīr II and his successors—as distinct from the early Sassanids—chose as a place to build monuments or commission carvings to commemorate their deeds an area now known as *Tāq-i Bustān* ('the garden arch'), north-east of Kirmānshāh, where there may well have been an ancient sanctuary dedicated to Anāhita (here still to-day springs gush from the rocks to form a beautiful pool). The princes were weak, and the nobles, often allying themselves with the Mazdaean priests, succeeded in gaining, or rather, regaining considerable power. The position of the Christians improved after the death of Ardashīr II, and particularly under Yazdagird I (399–421), whom the Christian sources praise highly—in contrast with the Iranian sources which accuse him of having been both wicked and deceitful! This improvement was made possible by the fact that Yazdagird had to keep the peace between Rome and Iran in order to be free to strengthen his own position at home. (He even acted as guardian to the Roman emperor Theodosius II during his minority.) But the Christians responded with further intrigues and acts of violence (they even went so far as to destroy some of the fire temples), so that towards the end of Yazdagird's reign their relations with the emperor had become strained. Yazdagird died in 421 in mysterious circumstances, probably put to death by the nobles who hated him. They attempted to supplant his sons with their own candidate, a member of a collateral branch of the Sassanid lineage. But the young prince Vahrām, who had been brought up at the small Arab court of Hīra and was despised by the nobles on account of his Arab ways, succeeded in overthrowing the usurper with the help of his guardian, the Lakhmid king Mundhir, who placed at his disposal an army commanded by his son Nu'mān. Vahrām, who reigned until 438 or 439, was one of the most popular Sassanid kings and many tales and legends evolved around his name even after the Islamic conquest. The most beautiful epic poem about him is Nizāmī's *Haft Paikar* (twelfth century), one of the masterpieces of Persian literature. On coming to the throne he assured the nobles that he would mend his ways, but it does not appear that he kept his promise too faithfully. He was a hunter, a pleasure-seeker and a lover of music (he summoned bands of *Luti*, the ancestors of the gypsies, all the way from India), who became the prototype of the chivalrous king in later legends, and earned himself the cordial dislike of the Zoroastrian priesthood. Nevertheless, it was a devout Zoroastrian, Mihr Narsēh, a man of great influence in the days of Yazdagird, who held the important position of grand vizier at Vahrām's court. He was a resolute persecutor of Christians, who fled in large numbers to Byzantine territory during this period. For this and other reasons war once more broke out between Iran and Byzantium in 421. (In the Pahlavi and later in the post-Islamic texts, 'Roman' and 'Byzantine' are synonymous.) It was conducted by Mihr Narsēh, but resulted in a Persian defeat in 422 and the promise on the part of the king of kings to permit the Persian Christians freedom of worship. Meanwhile, however, the Christians were torn by internal struggles, and in 424 the Synod of Markabta declared the Christian Church of Iran independent of that of Byzantium. Vahrām also warred against the Chionite and Hephthalite barbarians who were pressing down on the eastern frontier and had invaded Bactriana, and against the vassal king of Armenia. Even Vahrām's death was turned into legend: he was said to have disappeared into a cavern while out hunting onagers. *Gūr*, onager (wild ass), was in fact one of the names applied to the king, but probably not so much on account of his love of hunting as a reference to his personal character.

Yazdagird II succeeded his father in 438 or 439. He would have liked to take up the struggle with the Romans (i.e. Byzantines) once more, but he was unable to do so on account of the continual infiltration of White Huns (Hephthalites and Chionites) into Bactriana. He also attempted in vain to convert the Armenians (who had invented a script of their own) to Zoroastrianism in order the better to assimilate them with the Persians. It was during his reign that Mihr Narsēh published his refutation of the Christians, to which the bishops responded violently. The Armenian leaders rebelled, but the revolt was put down in 451 and many of the ecclesiastics were killed. The Christians of Syria and Babylonia—the two regions with the largest Christian population after Armenia—were also persecuted. Nevertheless, in Armenia the *marzbān* tried to mitigate the oppression, and after Yazdagird's death religious freedom was re-established. Yazdagird II was succeeded in 457 by his son Hormizd III, but he had to contend with his brother Pērōz, who did not hesitate to seek support from the barbarian Hephthalites. Pērōz was victorious, and in 459 he killed Hormizd. His lengthy reign of twenty-five years was not a happy one, for there was a very severe long-drawn-out famine which forced him to reduce the level of taxation and make a partial distribution of the nobles' holdings. At the same time the barbarians continued to pour in from the east. Indeed, Pērōz lost his life in a campaign against the Hephthalites in 484, and for several years the empire had to pay tribute to the barbarians. An interesting feature of Pērōz's religious policy was his support of the Nestorians. In 475, the Monophysites gained control of the theological school in Edessa, Syria, where the Persian Christian clergy were trained, and the Nestorians were expelled. Many of them sought refuge in Persia, and many more came after they had been banished from the Byzantine empire by Zeno the Isaurian. The king of kings welcomed the Nestorian influence on Persian Christianity, for it served as a useful means to break the chains that linked the Christian minorities of Persia with the Christian forces in enemy territory across the frontier. At this time, a Nestorian theological school was founded at Nisibis, in Persian territory, and this helped to give Persian Christianity a national Nestorian character.

When Pērōz died, Zarmihr, a general and a remarkable soldier who had fought against the Armenian rebels, placed Pērōz's brother Valāsh on the throne, but there was little he could do, for the treasury was empty and the victorious Hephthalites were demanding tribute. With a small army gathered at his own expense, Zarmihr succeeded in forcing the Hephthalite king to make peace, forgo the tribute, and release the hostages that had been taken, amongst whom was Pērōz's son Kavādh. His uncle was deposed, and Kavādh ascended the throne in 488.

As Christensen has remarked, racial purity and land ownership were the foundations of Persian society. From the time of the ancient inscriptions of Darius ('I am Persian, son of a Persian, Aryan, of Aryan stock', *aryacithra*), there was this insistence on Iranian race: free and noble were synonyms of 'born of pure blood' (*āzāt*, modern Pers. *āzād*). In order to maintain this purity, Mazdaeism favoured *khvētūkdās* (Avestan *khvaēthvadātha*), marriage between close relatives, even between brothers and sisters. Contrary to the early Christians, the Mazdaeans regarded wealth as morally good, and ownership was firmly protected by the religious and civil laws. But by the end of the fifth century, for various reasons not least of which was the general weakening of institutions during Pērōz's unfortunate reign, Iranian society was severely shaken by the Mazdakite movement. One of the many accounts of Mazdakism, that of Firdausī, which was derived from a more ancient source, the *Khvatāināmak*, relates that in the reign of Kavādh (Arabic and modern Pers. Qubād), there appeared a man called Mazdak. During a period of famine, he succeeded in convincing the king, through his eloquence and moral fables, that the origin of all the injustice in the world was the covetousness induced by the private ownership of women and chattels. 'The rich and powerful are the same as the empty-handed poor. It is unjust that anyone should have super-fluous wealth, the rich are the weft and the poor the woof . . . Women and possessions should therefore be held in common, if you do not wish the Good Religion to be impaired, for from these two things come Envy and Avarice and Want, which secretly unite in Anger and Hatred, and then the devil perverts the body of the sages . . .' It is an extraordinary fact, but all the sources agree, that Kavādh accepted this doctrine and began to apply it, to the horror of the priesthood and nobility, who, however—on account of the sovereign's sacred authority —did not dare at first to contradict him openly. Mazdak's fiercest opponent at court was Kavādh's son, Chosroes. The reformer's arrogance reached the point where he suggested that the king should alter the intended succession (in general, it was the sovereign who nominated his successor, who was not necessarily his eldest son), and proposed that another son, the Mazdakite Kāūs, should replace his enemy Chosroes. The prophet even went so far as to treat Chosroes with insolent familiarity. This was too radical an application of Mazdakite principles—it sounds revolutionary enough to our ears, but to Persian society of the fifth century it must have appeared simply insane—and the king himself now lost his patience. Kavādh had probably been using Mazdak to break the arrogance of the nobles and priests, and also in order to fill the empty coffers of the state at the expense of the rich, so in-gratiating himself with the lower classes.

Mazdakism certainly contained strong social elements, though the idea of holding women in common is doubtless exaggerated in the sources; this probably reflects a desire to break down the rigid racial system by means of completely exogamous, mixed marriages. But one must not forget that Mazdakism—and it could not be otherwise during this period —was above all a religious doctrine, with a clearly Manichaean origin. Mazdak's father was called Bāmdād (a common name among Manichaeans), and the heresiarch himself was born in the Babylonian city of Madaraya on the banks of the Tigris. It appears then that Mazdak was not the founder of the movement (which the Mazdakists probably called *drist dēn*, the 'upright religion'), but was himself a follower of the doctrines of a certain Zaradusht who lived some two hundred years before him. According to recent research carried out by Klíma, the movement came to an end in 524, and not in 528–9, as had previously been supposed. Mazdak's downfall was brought about by Chosroes' party, who used the very simple stratagem of organizing a theological debate. This was attended not only by the finest orators from among the magi but also by the Christian bishop Bazanes. (The Christians and Jews, who now held large possessions in Iran, did not hesitate to make common cause with the Mazdaean persecutors on this and other occasions when their own interests were nearly involved.) As to the manner in which Mazdak met his death, the sources fail to agree. Probably, as soon as his theological defeat was officially proclaimed, the soldiers of the guard fell on him and killed him then and there, while at the same time his followers were massacred. It also appears that all their religious books were burnt, for all we know of their doctrines is derived from hostile sources.

Mazdakism differs from Manichaeanism in its insistence on the chance nature of liberation and illumination, which anyone, even a plebeian, could obtain, and perhaps even the ascetic Manichaean aristocracy felt this doctrine to be dangerous. The cosmological and moral principles of Good and Evil seem therefore to have been understood in a more materialistic manner, and their intermixture in a more fortuitous way. Believers were expected to avoid certain kinds of food, and one passage, of doubtful interpretation however, suggests that they were even recommended to commit suicide. Mazdakism is important not only for the effect that it had on Sassanid society, but also because it continued to survive in widely dispersed and little-known centres even after the Islamic conquest.

The political events of Kavādh's reign can be summarized as follows: in 497, Kavādh was deposed by the nobles, who were exasperated by his Mazdakite reforms, and shut up in the castle of Gelgard or Andmishn in Susiana, a sort of

Sassanid Bastille. It was known as *Anūshbard*, 'the castle of oblivion', for it was strictly forbidden to mention the name of any of its prisoners or even of the castle itself. However, with the help of some of his friends, Kavādh succeeded in escaping and took refuge with the king of the Hephthalites. With his assistance, he succeeded in 499 in regaining the throne, which had meanwhile been occupied by his brother Zhāmāsp. He probably had to reassure the nobles that he would moderate his support of the Mazdakites, but they remained extremely powerful at court up to the time of the catastrophe of 524. It is significant that the contemporary sources and the Arab and Persian chroniclers make no mention of any actual social movements or of any efforts of the new government to put down rebellions. The fact, however, that Kavādh spared his brother's life and did not even have him blinded, as was the usual custom in these situations, suggests that he was acting with Mazdakite moderation. On the external front, there were the usual outbreaks of fighting with the Byzantines in the west and the Huns and other nomads of Iranian stock in the east. Towards the end of the reign, the Byzantine general Belisarius fought the Persian armies, and was defeated at Callinicum in 531, the year of Kavādh's death. Chosroes, the principal architect of the downfall of the Mazdakites, ascended the throne after some opposition from his brother, the Mazdakite Kāūs.

Chosroes I, who was to receive the name *anōshak-ruvān*, 'having an immortal soul' (modern Pers. and Arabic *nūshirwān*), is the most famous of the Sassanid sovereigns, even in Muslim tradition, and one of the most brilliant. The much-criticized reign of Kavādh had achieved some good results: the power of the nobles was broken, and that of the priesthood received a rude shock. Chosroes was to rule with absolute authority over priests and nobles alike. On the other hand, the wars with the Hephthalites and the internal disorders had undermined the economic and financial structure of the state. One of Chosroes I's most important achievements was the reform of the system of taxation, already begun under Kavādh. All cultivated land was carefully surveyed and taxed accordingly. The land tax was fixed at one drachma per year for every 1.7 acres under wheat or barley, eight drachmae for the same area of vines, seven for lucerne or purple medick, five/six for rice, and one drachma for every four Persian palm trees or six Aramean palm trees or every six olive trees. All other produce of land as well as free-growing date palms were exempt from tax. The head-tax was also revised. It had to be paid by all men between the ages of twenty and fifty, with the exception of the 'nobles and grandees, soldiers, priests, scribes, and other persons in the king's service'. Taxpayers were divided into various categories according to the census: some paid twelve drachmae, others eight or six, and the great majority four drachmae a head. The taxes were collected regularly every quarter. Chosroes also set up a system of legal inspection to see that no injustice was committed and that no unproductive land, plants or trees were taxed. The organization of the army also underwent reform. The lesser nobles, who formed the backbone of the army and up to now had been obliged to provide their services free and equip themselves at their own expense, received financial assistance towards their equipment together with regular pay. Special importance was attached to the cavalry, and groups of barbarian prisoners of war were injected into the army in order to reinforce the very weak infantry, which until then had been made up of discontented peasants who were ready to flee at the first opportunity. The position of *ērān-spāhbad* was abolished, and the army was placed under the supreme command of the king and was led by four *spāhbad*, one for each of the cardinal points: East (Khorāsān, Sakastān and Kirmān), South (Persis and Susiana), West (Irak, the frontier of the Byzantine empire), and North (Great Medea and Azerbaijān). All the sources speak of the strict discipline and justice of the time of Chosroes, whose fame reached as far as Arabia and who was referred to in the Islamic world as 'the Just'.

Chosroes made peace between the Byzantine and Persian empires in 532, but this was again broken a few years later due to a quarrel between two Arab states, Ghassān, a vassal of Byzantium, and Hīra, a vassal of Iran. In 540, Chosroes seized and destroyed Antioch. Fighting and skirmishing broke out as far afield as the Caucasus, with now one side, now the other having the upper hand, until the peace of 561 which more or less re-established the *status quo*. It was laid down that there should be freedom of trade and religion, but in their respective territories the Christians and Mazdaeans were forbidden to proselytize. Between 558 and 561, Chosroes finally succeeded in destroying the kingdom of the Hephthalites, to whom for a time tribute had had to be paid (an inheritance from the reigns of Pērōz and Kavādh). The defeat of the Hephthalites had been achieved because they were under attack from Turkish tribes who had emigrated from the east and the north-east and had invaded Central Asia. Thus arose a very serious threat in Central Asia, the 'Turkish peril', which was to affect the history of Iran for centuries. For a long time, the Oxus (the modern Amu Darya) was to form the frontier between the Turkish *khāgān* and Iran. In the south, Chosroes extended his domains as far as the Yemen, which had formerly been a vassal of Ethiopia: after 570, therefore, even distant Arabia Felix was a Persian province. At about the same time, frontier incidents led to the renewal of hostilities with Byzantium, but once again neither side achieved a clear victory. Chosroes died in 579, while peace negotiations were taking place.

We have stressed the importance of Chosroes' administrative reforms, but also from a cultural and artistic point of view his reign represents the last vigorous flourish of the Sassanid empire before its final collapse. The king fortified and embellished his capital of Ctesiphon (*Tēspōn* in Pahlavi), which was formed out of several neighbouring towns (in Arabic it was known as *al-Madā'in*, 'the cities'), one of them being the ancient Seleucia. The great ruins of 'Chosroes' arch' (*tāq-i kisrā* in Arabic) are still to be seen on the ancient site of the city, beside the banks of the Tigris. The palaces were decorated with mosaics and stucco-work, and contained magnificent gardens. During Chosroes' reign many books were brought from India and translated into Pahlavi, and thence, during the Islamic period, their contents were made known throughout the civilized world and served in particular to enrich our store of fables (examples include *Kalīla and Dimna* and *The Book of Sindbād*). It was during this period too that the *Psalms* were translated into Pahlavi. The game of chess was introduced, and also, according to some authorities, *nard*, or backgammon. The administrative system and court etiquette strongly influenced the future Muslim states and even had an effect on Byzantine ceremonial. Iran provided a meeting-ground for Greek and Indian ideas, with the result that there was a great development in medicine and the other sciences, especially astrology. Chosroes himself was interested in philosophical discussion, while the people relied on the practical philosophy of the *andarz*, books containing maxims and advice expressed in exemplary tales—a type of literature which is still fashionable to-day. However, few names of learned men and scholars with a marked personality of their own have come down to us from pre-Islamic times. An exception is the famous physician Burzōē, whose short autobiography reached us through an Arabic translation by the eighth century Persian convert Ibn al-Muqaffa'. The legendary minister Vuzurgmihr, who is mentioned in the late accounts of Chosroes' reign, is probably to be identified with him.

In 579, Chosroes was succeeded by his son Hormizd IV, who maintained his father's policies but failed to carry them out with the same discretion and authority. The war with Byzantium continued, though without much success, and there were occasional campaigns against the Turks in the east. Then one of Hormizd's generals, Vahrām, called *Chōbēn* ('man of wood'?), rebelled, and with the support of other nobles he dethroned and blinded the king and in 590 put in his place the latter's young son, Chosroes called *Aparvēz* (mod. Persian *Parvīz* = 'the victorious'). Shortly afterwards, Hormizd was put to death, either at his son's instigation or at least with his approval. Vahrām, however, was not prepared to play second fiddle to the king. The Mihrān family, to which he belonged, boasted of its Arsacid ancestry, and this can be the only explanation for Vahrām insolently proclaiming himself king, despite the opposition of many of the nobles. Such an act was completely unheard of in Persia, where the indisputable legitimacy of the royal line was rigorously insisted upon up to the Islamic conquest, and to a certain extent even afterwards. But Vahrām's reign was short-lived. Chosroes sought protection from the Byzantine emperor Maurice, who helped him to regain his throne in exchange for certain territorial concessions. (The Persian king also married a Byzantine princess, Maria.) Vahrām fled to 'the land of the Turks' but was assassinated, and Chosroes II ascended a secure throne. Nevertheless, Vahrām Chōbēn's picturesque adventures left a considerable impression on the minds of the people which is reflected in a Pahlavi romance (the text is lost but the story can be reconstructed from other sources) and repeated references in post-Islamic literature. Chosroes had brought back with him from Byzantium certain 'Christian superstitions' which his favourite Christian concubine Shīrīn, an Armenian, tried to strengthen, and as a result he had difficulties with the magi and the nobles, including those who had helped him to win back the throne. After Maurice's death in 602, hostilities with Byzantium broke out once more, and during the reigns of the emperors Phocas and Heraclius, the Persians achieved some striking successes. A large part of Asia Minor was conquered, including Edessa, Damascus and Jerusalem, whence the True Cross was borne to Ctesiphon, as well as Alexandria and parts of Egypt. Then Heraclius succeeded in halting the Persian advance; he won back much of the lost territory, and in 623 brought the war into Iran itself, while the Khazars in the Caucasus pushed down from the north. Heraclius laid siege to Ctesiphon, Chosroes fled and was killed in a palace revolt backed by his son Shērōē (628). Despite the idealization of his love for Shīrīn, which appears in some of the famous post-Islamic ballads, Chosroes II was in fact avaricious and cruel, though he left behind him a tradition of splendour and ostentation which are admirably described in a long twelfth-century poem by Nizāmī. There are accounts of his store of jewels, his love of perfumes, the extraordinary wonders of his court and its gardens, his feasts and, above all, his love of music. We know the names of two famous musicians at his court, Bārbad, who is supposed to have invented the Persian musical system, and Sarkash.

Shērōē, who reigned as Kavādh II, had ruled for hardly six months when he died in suspicious circumstances. He was succeeded by his young son Ardashir III, who was a minor. There followed a period of internal struggles with the nobles in open revolt. In the space of four years (628–32), Iran had some ten kings (and even possibly a queen, Bōrān, daughter of Chosroes II), but each ruled over only a few provinces. Reunification was achieved under Yazdagird III, another of

Chosroes II's sons, who was supported by the nobles and was, in fact, dominated by them. He was the last of the Sassanid kings. Indeed, in 636 the battle of Qādisiyya (not far from Hīra) was fought between the Arab general Sa'd ben Abī Waqqās and general Rustam, son of the *spāhbad* Farrukh-Hormizd who had been executed for having rebelled against the king. At the end of three days, the Persians had to admit defeat. Rustam himself lost his life, and the Persian standard, the *drafsh-i kāvyānī*—which, according to tradition, was the leather apron of the legendary smith Kāvagh (mod. Persian *Kāvè*) who helped the mythical king Frēdōn (Ferīdūn) to win back his throne from the dragon Azhi-Dahāk—fell into the hands of the Arabs. The road to the capital lay open, and in 637 Seleucia (with the Sassanid name *Vēh-Ardashēr*) was occupied. Ctesiphon proper, on the left bank of the Tigris, attempted to resist, but fell the following year. King Yazdagird fled into Medea. A bloody battle at Jalūla opened the way to the passes through the mountains of Zagros, and thus enabled the Arabs, after the battle of Nihāvand (between Behistūn and Burūjird), to penetrate the plateau and the heart of Iran. The Persian army was shattered. At a few places the *marzbāns* with their own troops put up a fierce resistance. One after another Hamadān (the ancient Ecbatana), Rayy (Rhages 'the Zoroastrian'), Azerbaijān and Armenia fell, while Yazdagird retreated to Isfahān. But Isfahān and then Stakhr (Persepolis) also surrendered, and in a short time Persis, the cradle of the dynasty and of Iranism, was conquered. Rather than accept the hospitality of the *spāhbad* of the mountainous and inaccessible Tabaristān on the southern banks of the Caspian, where resistance to the Arabs was maintained long after the conquest, the king decided to flee to Sīstān and Khorāsān, but the local chiefs refused to fight. Finally he sought refuge in Merv, where the *marzbān*, who saw that resistance was useless and therefore wished to rid himself of the embarrassment of the king, formed an alliance with a Turkish chief. The latter tried to seize the king, but he fled in time, and then, according to tradition, was killed in his sleep by a miller, with whom he had taken refuge, and who, without recognizing him but seeing the valuables he had with him, had decided to rob him. This was in the year 651 or 652.

CHAPTER IV

The early centuries of Arab domination and the first independent dynasties

The extraordinary success of the Islamic invasion is difficult to explain and still astonishes scholars to this day. At the battle of Qādisiyya, some seven to eight thousand Arabs opposed forty thousand Persians. Between the years 636 and 651, an army inferior in weapons had succeeded in breaking and subduing one of the most powerful empires of the day, while at the same time seizing large provinces from its Byzantine rival. The conquest and subsequent Islamization of Persia are unique, in that never before had such a complex and highly developed tradition been so quickly abandoned in favour of another religion which almost completely obliterated its predecessor. The Roman Empire's conversion to Christianity is hardly comparable: Christianity was only slowly accepted, and at first at least the means employed for conversion were peaceful. And apart from the return of pagan elements (the cult of the saints, etc.) one must bear in mind that the tradition of Roman law remained intact. In Persia, the situation was different. Islam, with its egalitarianism and straightforward doctrine, certainly accepted Persian features, but it was a case of Islam assimilating and dominating Persian culture, and not the other way round, so that these features, so proudly insisted on by many Persian nationalists to-day, have little connection one with another when considered apart from their Islamic setting. Indeed it was only *after* Persia and Mesopotamia and Syria and Egypt had been conquered, and *after* Hellenistic influences had taken effect through Syriac translations, that Islam became a historical force that was to endure for centuries. So it is just as incorrect to associate everything good in Islam with Iranism as it is to identify Islam with Arabism. Islam is a firmly monotheistic religion, and also a complex eclectic culture, *one* of whose fundamental features is the Iranian element. It is quite unreal to equate the Arabs with Islam and the Persians with

71

non-Islam. The Persian conquest marked a vital stage in the development of Islam as we know it to-day. The religious system created by Muhammad merely provided the seed of Islam; with the conquest of Persia and also of the Near East it developed into Islam itself. Moreover it is quite incorrect—though many have been led astray by the fact that the Muslim chroniclers themselves speak of the conquest as a miracle—to consider that the Arabs were an unknown quantity to the Persians, that they were ignorant barbarians who emerged from the unknown desert and took the civilized Persians by surprise. The Persians were well aware of the Arab strength: Shāhpūr I had been defeated by the Arabs of Palmyra, and over the centuries the Persian kings had had to counter the extremely dangerous incursions of the frontier Arabs. In addition there had been more peaceful associations. Vahrām V (reigned 421–*ca* 438) had been brought up at the Arab court of Hīra and had adopted some Arab ways, while the continual contacts between the Persian governors and the Arab vassal states, which had long been influenced by both Hellenistic and Iranian culture, show that it would be unwise to exaggerate the cultural contrasts between the two peoples.

It is true that the Arabs were much more sophisticated than their own traditions suggest, but in Iran the cultural tradition which some modern scholars attribute vaguely to the 'Persian people', was limited to a very small elite. The majority of the people, of whose culture and religious life we know so little, certainly lived at no higher cultural level than the Arabs themselves. It is, in fact, an over-simplification to speak of a Semitic (Arab) mentality in contrast to an Aryan (Persian) mentality. Indeed, if we must talk of an Aryan culture, we should not forget that it had long been subject to Semitic influences. The diplomatic language of the Achaemenid empire was Aramaic and its scribes Aramaeans. Ancient Iran had been strongly influenced by the partly Semitic world of Mesopotamia. The Parthians and Sassanids had assimilated Gnostic, Christian and Manichaean features, which were partly Semitic in origin. The concept of a purely Aryan Iran is therefore an illusion, and the Islamization of Iran was neither so strange nor so miraculous as has been thought in the past. Moreover, the religion of Islam, with its dislike of metaphysics and traditionalism, its insistence on moral values, its voluntaryism, and its social egalitarianism, presented a comparatively modern and democratic outlook to the traditional archaism of Iran. Like Christianity, Islam shattered the caste structure of the ancient traditional society: to Islam, the servant and the master, the wise man and the unenlightened, are all the same before God. It is easy to understand, therefore, how the mass of the Persians might have regarded the conquest as an actual liberation. Furthermore, historians are agreed that force of arms was not an overriding factor in the conversion to Islam. One of the strongest motives was an economic one: since non-converts had to pay higher taxes, many of the great landowners became Muslims. We should also avoid applying our own nineteenth-century notions of nationhood to Asia of the seventh century AD! Though, for example, the Arabs met with strong resistance in Tabaristān, Dailam and Gīlān (in the mountainous regions on the southern shores of the Caspian) this cannot be regarded as Iranian nationalism defending itself against the Semitic invaders. In the same way, the Cadusii, who inhabited this area, had obstinately resisted the Achaemenids, as later the Dailamites resisted successive empires. These were mountain tribes who refused to submit to a central power, be it Muslim or Zoroastrian, Semite or Aryan.

In Sīstān and Tokhāristān (in the region of Balkh) opposition to the Arabs also continued until the beginning of the eighth century. In 661, the *dihqān* or small landed nobility of Tokhāristān put on the throne for a short period Yazdagird III's son, Pērōz, though in 674 he fled to China, from which country his father had also hoped to receive support, but he could achieve little on account of its being so distant. Likewise Pērōz's son, Narsēh, was forced to seek refuge among the Chinese. He had taken a last stand against the Arabs, but resistance was finally broken with the capture of Balkh in 707.

The Arabs were unprepared for governing such a large empire. Of necessity they had to adopt many of the Sassanid institutions, such as the administrative structure and the system of taxation. There is therefore another strong Iranian element in the development of Islam. Some of the basic technical terms of Islamic law, such as *kharāj* (land tax) and *jizya* (head tax) are of Iranian origin. At first these were used in a broad sense, and only afterwards received their strict meaning under the Abbasids. In the early days of the conquest, there was naturally a great deal of plundering. Immense booty was seized and then distributed among the conquerors roughly according to the Koranic laws for the division of spoil as well as the personal decisions of the caliph Omar (634–44). Taxes were at first higher than they had been under Chosroes I. At the time of the calpih 'Alī (656–61), Iran paid into the caliph's coffers the large sum of almost 120 million silver drachmae, either in coin, which was then very scarce, or in kind. By the time of the last Omayyads (661–750) this amount had decreased, following a huge rise under the cruel and avaricious Omayyad governor al-Hajjāj (691–713). According to Islamic law, the *jizya* was to be paid only by non-Muslim subjects. Immediately after the conquest, even the *kharāj* was paid in full only by Zoroastrians, Christians and Jews, while Muslim landowners paid a tenth part (*'ushr*). In 700, al-Hajjāj decreed that even non-Arab converts should pay the full *kharāj*, and this caused a great deal of discontent, particularly among wealthy Persian landowners who had embraced Islam merely in order to reduce their taxation. Thus Islamic law, which was fairly elastic and on the whole designed to fulfil the needs of a semi-nomad and rather more democratic society, was applied only in part in Iran. The development of feudalism, begun under the Sassanids, continued under the Arabs, who found that they had to adapt their ideas of religious law to the new conditions. The lands of the *dihqān* who had fought against the Arabs, a large part of the royal domains of the former kings and other members of the Sassanid dynasty, and the estates owned by the Zoroastrian temples were declared the property of the Muslim community (*fai'*). Ultimately, this meant that they were sequestrated by the Omayyad central government and exploited for the benefit of the Arabs themselves, who thus found themselves forming part of the feudal system. There still remained personal estates (*mulk*) held by Arabs, as well as Persian *dihqān*, which could be inherited.

The Arabs garrisoned the conquered cities, and at first welcomed the influx of other Arabs. For example, in 671–2, under the Omayyad caliph Mu'āwiya, the governor of Iraq, who resided in Kūfa—a garrison town founded near the ruins of Babylon in about 638—sent 50,000 Arab soldiers and their families to settle in Nīshāpūr, Merv, Balkh and other cities in the far eastern districts over which he ruled. These new arrivals gradually merged with the local inhabitants, with whom they now shared a common religion. As a result, Persians and Arabs found themselves on the same side in uprisings, such as 'Abd ar-Rahmān ibn al-Ash'ath's revolt against al-Hajjāj in 701–2. On the other hand, the former royal domains were sometimes held in fief or even in outright possession by Arabs who thus allied themselves with the ancient Persian landowning aristocracy. For example, Yazīd I (680–3) granted a large amount of land to the governor of Nihāvand, while Tabarī tells us that the rich Arab governor of Khorāsān, Asad ibn 'Abdallah, celebrated the pre-Islamic feast of *Mihragān* by inviting the local Persian *dihqān* and Arab generals to a sumptuous reception, at which the *dihqān* offered Asad the traditional gifts which used to be presented to the local feudal lord in Sassanid times. One must bear in mind, however, that in the early years of the conquest, Persian converts often attached themselves to Arab families as *mawālī* (clients or dependants, plur. of the Arab *maulā*), and sometimes took their name, so that an Arab name is not always a sure indication of origin. The *mawālī*, who were generally better educated than the Arabs themselves, played an important part in the administration. For example, one of them, Sulaimān ibn Abīu's-Sārī, helped to organize a postal service in Khorāsān and Transoxiana during the time of Omar II (717–20). Along the roads used by the service there were stages where horses could be changed, and also the *khān* or caravanserais.

There is little detailed information about the political and cultural life of the Persians themselves under the Omayyad caliphate (661–750). It is often impossible to be sure to what extent the occasional uprisings represented Persian national feelings, or resulted from the economic and social aspirations of combined Persians and Arabs alike. During this period, the word 'nation' has the sense of 'a community ruled by common religious laws', since religion entered into every aspect of life in the ancient East. By the end of the Omayyad caliphate conversion had led to the virtual loss of individual identity of the

Arabs and the Persians. The Persians adopted the Arabic script, though continuing mainly to speak in their own vernacular, and from now on produced a number of great figures in Arab literature, such as Avicenna and Ghazzālī, the stylist Hamadānī and the grammarian Sībawaih. This is not so surprising when one remembers that before the conquest only a limited number of scribes were familiar with the Persian written language, and that the new difference between the written language (now Arabic) and spoken Persian can have made hardly any impression on the great mass of illiterates, especially if we bear in mind that even to-day the number of illiterates in many eastern countries exceeds 90% of the population.

Towards the end of the Omayyad period and the beginning of the Abbasid (750), revolts of a political and religious nature occurred which appear to have been quite different in character to those of the earlier period. The anti-Omayyad propaganda of the supporters of the Abbasids, who considered themselves the heirs of the great caliph 'Alī, while the Omayyads were comparative newcomers and converted at a later date, was extremely intelligently organized. The Abbasids' supporters took advantage of every dissatisfaction with the Omayyad government, whether it was religious, economic or political.

The most capable of these leaders was a Persian, Abū Muslim. Under his guidance the Abbasid *dāʿī* (propagandists) in Khorāsān and Transoxiana made capital out of the peasants' grievances, promising them full representation in the future government, and even encouraging the activities of the Mazdakites, who had never died out in these parts but had turned themselves into semi-secret sects such as the Khurramites (*Khorrāmdīnān*), whose leader Khidāsh caused the local governors a great deal of trouble. When the Omayyads were finally overcome, the new dynasty took over the government of the immense Arab empire—or rather Muslim empire—in 750, largely thanks to Abū Muslim. The first two Abbasid caliphs, as-Saffāh (750–4) and al-Mansūr (754–75), partly succeeded in fulfilling the promises made by their supporters. The new capital of Baghdād, which was situated within the frontiers of the old Sassanid empire and took its name from the Persian for 'gift of God', was founded by al-Mansūr in 762, replacing the Omayyad and Arab capital of Damascus. From the beginning of Abbasid rule, representatives from Khorāsān and Transoxiana began to enter government circles in Baghdād.

In 755, al-Mansūr had the over-influential and perhaps over-honest former leader Abū Muslim killed. This was badly received, and revenge for Abū Muslim's death became one of the common features of a number of different revolutionary movements. The Abbasids were unable to keep the promises made by their supporters, particularly to the peasants, the Mazdakites and the Shi'ite extremists who considered that the only legitimate heirs of the Prophet were descended through his cousin and son-in-law, 'Alī. Thus there arose various movements of dissatisfaction which had first appeared around Kūfa in Omayyad times (Mukhtār, 684–6, Mughīra, ca 737, 'Abdallāh ibn Mu'āwiya, 745, Abū'l-Khattāb, 755–6). At Nīshāpūr there arose the para-Zoroastrian movement of Bihāfrīd (745–50), who was overthrown as a result of the opposition of his fellow Zoroastrians, who regarded him as a heretic, and by Abū Muslim. In Khorāsān and Rayy, there appeared a certain Sindbād, the Magian (756), who claimed that Abū Muslim was dead only in appearance and that in fact he was in the company of Mahdī, the future saviour of Muslim belief, and of Mazdak in a mysterious castle, and that all three would return to triumph on the earth. Other heretical movements in Khorāsān included that of Ustād-sīs (767–8), whom some call a Zoroastrian but who was probably a Zoroastrian heretic who employed features of the popular religion, and of al-Muqanna', the 'veiled prophet of Khorāsān' (780), who clearly declared himself to be God. But the most powerful of all was that of Pāpak or Bābak, which lasted some twenty years (817–38), putting the Abbasid administration to a severe test. This was the only one of the revolts to originate in the western regions (Azerbaijān and Mesopotamia).

There has been a great deal of disagreement among scholars as to the explanation for these revolts. Some see, beneath a veil of religion, attempts by the Persian feudal landowners, deprived of their property, to reassert themselves as representatives of the former elite; others regard them as uprisings of the people, who had as their common enemy both the Persian feudal lords and the Abbasid authorities (now allied with the former) who had broken their promises. The religious aspects of the revolts are distorted by the sources. In some cases it is stated that the defeated Zoroastrians were reacting against Islam, but it is much more likely that these movements represent an outburst of popular belief in the incarnation of God in a particular individual, who disappears in order to return again as a Messiah at the end of the world, as well as other beliefs which do not belong to orthodox Zoroastrianism. In certain cases, such as that of Bihāfrīd, the Zoroastrians allied themselves with the Muslim authorities in order to put down a revolt of heretics. It appears more probable, therefore, that here we are dealing with movements which were genuinely popular in origin and which, if we were better informed, would throw a very interesting light on the popular beliefs of ancient Persia.

While these popular uprisings were occurring, the upper classes were eagerly discussing the respective virtues of the Arabs and Persians. The *shu'ūbiyya* movement (from *shu'ūb*, 'peoples'), which laid claim to Persian superiority, or at least equality between non-Arabs (particularly Persians) and Arabs before God, probably served to revive old memories. But one must not equate the *shu'ūbiyya* with modern nationalists, for in this literary-philosophical dispute there were Persian supporters of the Arabs and Arab supporters of the Persians. Moreover, these debates were held between the learned men of an elite, and in Arabic, the language of the elite. The first literary use of the Persian language, now written in Arabic script, must be placed later, when the Abbasid caliphate began to break up in the ninth and tenth centuries and when the first semi-independent dynasties appeared, as yet in Khorāsān and Transoxiana in the extreme eastern part of the empire.

The first of these minor principalities began with the dynasty of the Tahirids in Khorāsān (820–72). The name is derived from that of Tāhir the Ambidextrous who had been granted the governorship of Khorāsān by the caliph of Baghdād in 820, and who passed on the post to his successors, without concerning himself overmuch with the caliph's intentions, though he later confirmed them in their governorships. The Tahirids made Nīshāpūr their capital and succeeded in extending their authority as far as Rayy and Kīrmān. They were deprived of their power by the Saffarids (867–903), also of Arab origin, or at least Arab in name, the founder of the family being Ya'qūb ibn Laith as-Saffār ('the Copper-smith'), who had fought in distant Sīstān against the Khārijite rebels, Montanists of Islam. Though they made dangerous thrusts towards the west, the Saffarids really ruled over the Khorāsān area, the present-day Afghanistan, part of Central Asia, and Sind in modern Pakistan. The last great Saffarid, 'Amr, Ya'qūb's brother, was defeated by the troops of another local dynasty, the Samanids, discreetly encouraged by the caliph of Baghdād, who was afraid of further Saffarid expansion. 'Amr was put to death in Baghdād in 902.

In contrast to the Tāhirids, the Samanid dynasty was purely Iranian in its origin. Its founder, Sāmān-khudāt, chief of the village of Sāmān in the district of Balkh, was a member of the Iranian landed nobility, and appears to have been descended from the Sassanid sovereign Bahrām Chūbīn (Pahlavi Vahrām Chōbēn). A Zoroastrian, he embraced Islam after he had learned to appreciate the protection of the Arab governor of Khorāsān, Asad ibn 'Abdullāh. His grandsons had distinguished careers in the service of the Abbasid caliph al-Ma'mūn (813–33), who was most friendly towards the Persians and granted these warriors the governorships of Samarkand, Farghāna, Shāsh and Herāt. As the result of further honours and conquests, the Samanids gradually built up an empire which stretched as far as the borders of India and Turkestan, and almost reached Baghdād. The Samanids' centre of power, however, always remained Transoxiana. Bukhārā and Samarkand became brilliant centres of Islamic culture, even rivalling Baghdād, and they served as the springboard for the new Persian literature. The dynasty endured for nine generations, but after the death of the third ruler, Nasr ibn Ahmad (942), internal struggles, the increasing power of the Buyid dynasty in the west, and the attacks of the Ilek Khān or Karakhanid Turks in the north-east gradually reduced the power of the Samanids. Soon they controlled little beyond Transoxiana and Khorāsān, and the exercise of power fell more and more into the hands of the Turkish slaves who had filled the court. One of these slaves, Alp-Tigīn, founded the dynasty of the Ghaznavids, who replaced the Samanids in the regions south of the Oxus. Meanwhile, the İlek Khān Turks, who were the overlords of the Turanian tribes from Farghāna to China, invaded Transoxiana and took Bukhārā in 990, thus bringing to an end the sovereignty of the Samanids. The Turkish infiltration of the Iranian regions of Central Asia thereafter continued apace.

The names, and sometimes isolated verses in Persian, of poets who lived during the period when the two dynasties of the Tahi ridsand Saffarids were in power have been preserved in documents. But it was only under the Samanids that Persian poetry began to flourish, dominated by the great names of Rūdagī and Daqīqī, who both enjoyed the protection of the Samanid princes. Other learned men, such as ar-Rāzī and Avicenna, both of Persian origin, also added lustre to the Samanid court. But it must be realized that the Iranian literary renaissance was centred on the courts, and once again the literary tradition gives us no idea of the feelings of the ordinary people in Persia. The Persian poetry that has come down to us—despite various imaginative attempts, mostly due to Soviet scholars, to trace its origins to popular sources which must have existed and which may well have influenced men of letters—arose as a sophisticated form of art in sophisticated circles familiar with Arabic. It was never completely autochthonous, but even at the outset was influenced by Arabic poetry though much of this too had been composed by Persians.

Another centre of Iranian culture during this period was Tabaristān, a mountainous area difficult of access, which runs along the southern shores of the Caspian and the home of the Shi'ite dynasty of the Ziyarids (828–1077). This region had been only superficially converted to Islam at the conquest, and pockets of Zoroastrianism were to be found here even in the ninth century. Here the Alids, believers in the legitimacy of 'Alī as the political successor to the Prophet as head of the Islamic community—a belief that later developed into a complex body of religious thought—found refuge and followers. A local prince with the typically Iranian name of Mardāvīj, whose father, Ziyār, gave his name to the Ziyarid dynasty, achieved independance in 928 and seized Qazvīn, the district of Rayy, and then Gurgān or Jurjān (the ancient Hyrcania) and the surrounding areas. His vassals were the three sons of Buvaih or Būyè, the first Buyids, who later founded a dynasty of their own. The policy of Mardāvīj's successors, the most remarkable of whom was Vushmgīr, was to maintain a balance between the Samanids, their powerful neighbours to the east, and the even more dangerous Buyids to the south-west. As the Samanid power declined—at one time the Ziyarids had been their vassals—so the Buyids took over their lands. And then Mahmūd of Ghazna forced the fifth Ziyarid, Manūchihr, patron of the poet Manūchihrī, to become his vassal. The last three Ziyarids suffered the attacks of the Seljuks, until the Seljuk Malikshāh put an end to their dynasty (1077). The Ziyarids produced a famous prince and writer, Qābūs, son of Vushmgīr (976–1012), while one of his descendants, Kai-Kā'us, was the author of an extremely popular moral treatise (a sort of 'Mirror for Princes') written in 1082–3 in clear Persian prose.

Buvaih or Būyè was a soldier from the mountainous region of Dailam, south of the Caspian, who led his Shi'ite compatriots in the service of both the Ziyarids and the Samanids. His sons succeeded in becoming independent of their Ziyarid overlords, took over large stretches of land, and then in 945 one of them, Ahmad, advanced towards the west and entered Baghdād, where the Abbasid caliph granted him and his brothers such grandiloquent titles as 'fortifier of the state', 'pillar of the state', and so forth. The most important Buyid sovereign was 'Azudu'd-Daula ('Arm of the State'), who was the son of one of the three brothers. He died in 983, after succeeding in uniting the whole of Iraq and Persia under his rule. A great builder and patron of the arts, Arabic literature flourished particularly during his reign. At his death, internal struggles as well as attacks from beyond the frontiers brought an end to the Buyid state, which was finally destroyed by the Seljuks under Toghrul Beg in 1055.

In contrast to the Shi'ite dynasties in the west, the Sunnite (i.e. 'orthodox') dynasties of the east did much to develop Persian art and literature. This is particularly true of the Ghaznavids who were of Turkish origin. As in similar cases, instead of the revival of nationalism they were more interested in variations on a theme, the theme being the common Islamic culture, and the variations the different languages spoken throughout the Islamic world, which now for the first time were being used for poetic expression. This explains the facility with which so many authors were able to turn from their mother tongue and write with equal ease in one of the other languages within the Islamic area, as if they were merely performing a literary exercise within a common tradition.

Alp Tigīn, the first Ghaznavid, was the Turkish slave whom the Samanids had appointed governor of Khorāsān. He was deposed, and withdrew to Ghazna (modern Afghanistan) in 962, where he ruled with considerable independence. His son-in-law Subuktigin extended his authority into India and also regained the fiefdom of Khorāsān from the Samanids (994). After his death a period of internal struggle was brought to an end when Mahmūd seized power, to become the most important of the Ghaznavid sovereigns. He received formal recognition of his rule over Afghanistan, Khorāsān, and Sīstān directly from the Abbasid caliph of Baghdād, and thus finally made the dynasty independent of Samanid vassallage. 'After Prince Mahmūd had conquered Merv', wrote the historian Gardīzī in the middle of the eleventh century, 'and had made himself lord of Khorāsān, he came to Balkh, and was still at Balkh when an envoy from the caliph of Baghdād, al-Qādir bi'llāh (d 1031) arrived with the instrument of investiture ('ahd) as ruler of Khorāsān, with the standard (liwā), and splendid robes, and the crown. And al-Qādir gave him the official title (laqab) of "Right arm of the dynasty (Yamīn ad-daula), fiduciary of the [Islamic] community (Amīn al-milla), Abū 'l-Qāsim Mahmūd, representative (walī) of the Prince of the Believers". When the instrument of investiture and the standard arrived, Prince Mahmūd seated himself on the royal throne, put on the robes, placed the crown upon his head, and held court in the presence of the nobles and commoners in the month of dhū 'l-qa'da 389 [October 999].' One of the interesting points in this account is its brief reference to the ceremony of investiture by the caliph. On account of Mahmūd's title of Yamīn ad-daula, the Ghaznavids have also often been called Yaminids.

Mahmūd was above all a warrior king. He led many campaigns in India, as well as fighting against his neighbours in the west, the Īlek Khān, the Seljuks and the Buyids. At the time of his death (1030) his empire extended from Gujarat in India to Samarkand in Central Asia, and from Kashmir to the western limits of the Iranian plateau. As was so often the case, internal dissension and attacks from without (by the Seljuks, Ghurids, etc) slowly brought about the downfall of the Ghaznavids, especially after the reign of Mahmūd's son, Mas'ūd (1030–42), when their authority was limited to the Punjab, and even this came to an end in 1186. The closing years of the Ghaznavid period therefore belong more to Indian than Iranian history.

It is often stated that Mahmūd's court at Ghazna was a brilliant centre of Persian culture, but it would be better to speak of Islamic culture. We should not forget that the language of the court bureaucracy was Arabic. Shortly before his conquest of Khārizm (1017), an Iranian Muslim principality in Central Asia, Mahmūd, who has been called a 'kidnapper of literary men', requested the prince of Khārizm, Ma'mūn, to send him the learned men at his court. They included the great philosopher and physician Ibn-i Sīnā (Avicenna), the historian and man of science al-Bīrūnī, the philosopher Abū Sahl Masīhī, the physician Abū'l-Hasan Khammār, and the mathematician Abū Nasr 'Arāq. But Avicenna and Masīhī refused the invitation and fled. Those who agreed to join the court of the capricious Ghaznavid sovereign, including such famous Arabic poets as Abū'l-Fath al-Bustī, were subjected to all kinds of vicissitudes. For example, Firdausī, who with 'Unsurī (*maliku 'sh-shu'arā*, 'king of poets' or poet laureate), 'Asjadī, Asadī and Farrukhī was one of the great Persian poets at court, was a victim of Mahmūd's volatile nature. According to a famous semi-legendary account, jealous courtiers made various accusations against Firdausī which came to Mahmud's ears. Consequently he paid the great poet for his *Shāhnāmè* ('The Book of Kings') in silver instead of gold as promised. Firdausī scornfully divided the silver coins between a brewer of beer and the keeper of a public bath as a reward for their services, and then wrote a fierce satire on the sovereign. Tradition says that on hearing a magnificent verse of the *Shāhnāmè* recited aloud, Mahmūd repented of his cruel treatment of the poet. In recompense, he sent Firdausī a vast quantity of riches, but as the camels entered the poet's village from one end, from the other came forth his funeral cortège.

The rise of the first independent dynasties certainly resulted in considerable economic and social development in areas with a predominantly Iranian population, though of course it strengthened the feudal system and led to an increase in the number of local tyrants. Above all, the land revenue, most of which in the past had gone to fill the coffers in Damascus, now largely stayed within the Iranian domain.

The 'Arab' geographers such as Istakhrī, Mas'ūdī, Ibn Hauqal and Muqaddasī provide much important information on the social and economic conditions, farming, handicrafts and trade in Iran from the tenth to the middle of the eleventh century. Agriculture was considerably improved, largely due to the excellent system of irrigation, without which the Iranian and Central Asian plateau would be almost entirely unproductive. The *kārīz* or subterranean canals reached a depth of nearly 300 feet in some places, such as Kūhistān, and, as in the case of the Kirmān area, they could carry water for a distance of 80 miles from its source. Many new canals were constructed to tap the waters of the Kārūn, Helmand, Harī-Rūd, Zāyandeh-Rud and other rivers. Great wheels were built to raise water from one level to another, and specialists were employed in the search for underground springs and streams and in designing irrigation works. In the second half of the tenth century the Buyid 'Azudu'd-Daula constructed the famous dam across the river Kur in Fārs between Shīrāz and Istakhr, known as the Amir's or Prince's Dam, made out of blocks of stone reinforced with lead joints, so wide that two horsemen could ride along it abreast. There is still a large dam there to-day, and the local village, now quite tiny, is called Band-i Amir, or the Prince's Dam. The water formed an artificial lake, on the banks of which ten huge water-wheels were set up to provide power for mills and supply the canals with water. There were wind-mills, especially in Sīstān, as well as mills driven by animals. In order to keep in check the shifting sands tamarisks were planted, for example in the oasis of Yazd, while special embankments were employed in Sīstān.

The cultivation of traditional plants increased, and new species were introduced. Rice, which is still the basic food of Persia but which was very little grown in Sassanid times, was cultivated over a very wide area, but particularly in Khūzistān, in certain low-lying areas of Fārs and Khorāsān, and along the shores of the Caspian. Citrus fruits were introduced during this period and were grown in low-lying areas, such as southern Iran, on the shores of the Caspian, and in the oasis of Balkh. Wheat and barley were cultivated almost everywhere on the plateau up to an altitude of 8,000 feet and sometimes even above this level. Barley and millet were regarded as the poor man's food—this is often revealed in the poetry of this period —while clover and lucern were widely grown as cattle-fodder. The sources mention the development of cotton cultivation in Khorāsān, northern Iran, Fārs and southern Azerbaijān, and gradually it displaced flax as a textile fibre. Fruit trees were divided into two groups depending on whether they grew in *garmsīr*, that is hot regions lying below 3,250–4,000 feet, where the products were pistachio nuts, figs, olives, oranges, lemons and dates; or in *sardsīr*, above a level of 4,000–6,500 feet, where peaches, apricots, apples, cherries and so on were found. Cultivation of the date palm spread from southern Iran to other areas, such as Kirmān, where, according to Istakhrī, one could buy 100 *mann* of excellent dates for one *dirham* of silver. Elsewhere we are told that one *dirham* or drachma would purchase between 11 and 18 lbs of meat or honey, or up to 50 cakes of barley. Vines were cultivated everywhere up to an altitude of 6,500–7,500 feet. In some areas, such as Khorāsān, as many as a hundred different species of grape were to be found. Although prohibited by Muslim canon law, wine made from grapejuice or the sap of palm-trees was fairly widespread, and the wines of Shīrāz and Rayy were especially highly prized. As always in Persia, gardening was a widespread occupation, and flowers were also grown in many places for making perfume. Dried fruits—still popular to-day—are mentioned as forming an important part of provincial tribute paid in kind. Fārs sent to the treasury annually 30,000 bottles of rose-water and 20,000 *ritl* (1 Baghdād *ritl* = 14 ozs) of currants; Khūzistān sent 30,000 *ritl* of cane sugar; Kirmān 20,000 *ritl* of dried dates and 1,000 *ritl* of cumin. Livestock was largely the concern of various Iranian nomadic tribes such as the Lurs, often referred to as Kurds. The animals consisted almost entirely of sheep and goats, with a few camels and poor quality horses. Cattle were comparatively rare, as they are even to-day. The grasslands of the plateau over 5,000–6,500 feet served as summer grazing grounds.

The manufacture of textiles was the most important industry in Iran at this period. The tenth-century geographers tell us that silk-weaving and the making of gold and silver brocade were carried on in the towns. The cities of Fārs and Kāzerūn were famous for their linen, and material from Kāzerūn in particular was sold throughout the then Muslim world. Carpets from the cities of Fārs, especially Shīrāz, were renowned as were those of Khūzistān and Khorāsān. Other products included ceramics (at Kāshān, Rayy, etc), metalwork (in bronze, gold, silver, copper, etc), which was produced almost everywhere, perfumes and aromatic oils, sugar-cane, soap, and ink (Fārs). The tenth century saw considerable developments in the mining industry. The mines belonged to the state but were worked by contractors under licence, who had to pay a percentage of up to one third of the proceeds to the treasury. Deposits of silver, iron, copper, tin, lead, sulphur (near Mount Demavend), lapis lazuli (Badakhshān and Azerbaijān), rubies (for which Badakhshān was famous), and turquoise (near Nīshāpūr) were all mined. Marble was quarried in Khorāsān, Azerbaijān and elsewhere, and petroleum and bitumen deposits were exploited particularly in Fārs. These products were sold in the markets around the large cities and on the caravan routes. Overland and maritime trade developed considerably in the tenth century. The most important trading posts on the caravan routes were Hamadān, Rayy, Nīshāpūr, Herāt, Isfahān, Shīrāz and Ahwāz. Balkh and Kābul were important centres for trade with India, which had begun to come under Islamic influence as a result of Mahmūd's campaigns.

The principal ports on the Caspian were Amul and Sarī, which traded with Khārizm, Transcaucasia, the Khazar regions of the Volga, and with Russia. The most important port on the Persian Gulf was Sīrāf, whose merchants, often extremely rich, had the monopoly of all of Iran's sea trade.

Istakhrī mentions a highly successful merchant who was so actively involved in trading that in forty years he had hardly ever set foot on land. Of another he says that he had a personal fortune of four million *dīnār* (that is to say, forty million *dirham*). In order to appreciate the size of this sum—if Istakhrī is not exaggerating—one must bear in mind that it was approximately equivalent to the revenue of the entire province of Fārs over a period of eighteen months. It is interesting to note the change that overtook the role of the Persians in the Gulf with the introduction of Islam. Up to and during the Sassanid period there were hardly any Persian sailors, but now, according to Istakhrī, nearly all the sailors and merchants in the Gulf were Persians. The principal markets for Iran's exports were the Mediterranean countries, Arabia, India and China. They consisted in particular of cereals, cotton, linseed and sesame oil, fruit and dates (either dried or in the form of preserves), wine, honey, currants, dyes, sugar from Khūzistān, raw silk, perfume, medicaments, camels, and horses (which went mainly to India). Persian manufactures, especially brocades, silks, linen and cotton materials, metalwork in bronze, silver and gold, and pottery, were exported to Arabia and on to the Mediterranean. Sīrāf also served as a mart for goods from India and China. From India came aloes, amber, camphor, precious stones, bamboo, ivory, rare woods such as sandalwood, pepper and other spices, and substances with medicinal properties, all of which passed through Iran and into countries beyond. There was also a not inconsiderable trade in slaves, many obtained from the countries of eastern Europe, for the Slavs with their fair skin were particularly sought after (the word 'slave' ultimately derives from 'Slav'). Others came from the Turkish steppes, from India and especially from Africa. As evidence of the size of this trade, Istakhrī reports that during the summer trading season of 936 a Persian merchant residing on the shores of the Persian Gulf imported 12,000 slaves along with other goods in a fleet of 400 boats. It is true that much of this merchandize was in transit from the Turkish steppes and eastern Europe to the Arab countries, or from Africa and India to Central Asia. Only a small number of slaves remained in Iran. It seems that at this time, as compared with the period immediately following the Arab conquest, the number of slaves employed in agriculture and industry had greatly diminished. The slaves most commonly found in Persia were young Turks, who often formed a sort of Praetorian guard at local courts, and could acquire considerable political power, even founding dynasties of their own, as in the case of the Ghaznavids.

This decrease in the employment of slaves is closely connected with the decrease in the amount of land directly administered by the State. There developed instead the system of *iqtā'*, a system already known under the Omayyads but which became particularly widespread under the Abbasids, and which involved a form of limited feudal ownership, sometimes comparable with our own medieval benefices. At first it consisted in granting soldiers, during their period of service or even for life, the right to *kharāj* or other taxes from certain state lands in lieu of their pay. There were various forms of *iqtā'* and in only one (the *iqtā' tamlīk*) was the concession to collect the land-tax combined with the right to the land itself. The numbers of these benefices were continually increasing, as also were the lands belonging to the *vaqf*, or pious foundations enjoying certain exemptions. In Fārs before the tenth century the amount of land owned by the state was already exceeded by that in private hands, the best of which, according to Istakhrī, was owned by descendants of the Arab conquerors. The descendants of the tribe of Hanzala ibn Tamīm had possessions near Istakhr which, by the middle of the ninth century, produced a *kharāj* of ten million *dirham* per annum, almost a third of the entire *kharāj* for Fārs. In the same province there were still at that time many *dihqān* belonging to the old Persian lesser nobility who possessed as many as 5,000 castles with their attached lands held in *mulk* (privately). On the other hand, according to later local historians of Fārs, such as the twelfth-century Ibn al-Balkhī and fourteenth-century Ibn Zarkūb, after the Buyids had conquered the district the lands held in *mulk* were distributed in the form of *iqtā'* among the soldiers on whom the new invaders depended. In Khorāsān, too, the number of *iqtā'* increased continually during the century. Neither in the territories of the Buyids nor in the lands of the Ghaznavids were the *iqtā'* hereditary by law in the tenth century, but already we can see the beginnings of a process which resulted in the eleventh and twelfth centuries in the *iqtāʿ* ceasing to be merely a temporary benefice and becoming a feudal heritage.

Although the state lands were now reduced in size, their extent remained considerable. The government received from them the *kharāj*, sometimes in kind as a proportion of the harvest, elsewhere in coin according to the area of the territory and regardless of the size of the harvest. This latter system prevailed in areas near the large cities, where the harvest was sent to market. In Fārs, for example, the highest rate of the *kharāj* was collected from the state lands around Shīrāz, the most important commercial centre in the area. The annual tax due was based on the area under cultivation measured in large *jarīb* (the small *jarīb*—the Arabic form of the Persian *garīb*—was approximately three-quarters of an acre, the large *jarīb* about two acres), but varied according to the crop grown. For example, a large *jarīb* of wheat or barley paid 190 *dirham*; of broad beans or legumes, 192 *dirham*; of lucerne 237½ *dirham*; of cotton, 256¾ *dirham*; of vines, 1,425 *dirham*. In other districts the rates were considerably lower. In southern Iran every date palm was rated at between a half and 3 *dirham*. These taxes were higher than those laid down by Chosroes I during the Sassanid period (see p. 65), but there was now much greater prosperity, and in any case Chosroes' rates may have remained completely theoretical. The *kharāj* on land which lacked artificial irrigation was a third of that on land irrigated by canals, which was naturally more productive, and the rate of taxation on land irrigated by means of wells or water wheels bearing river water was two-thirds of that on land irrigated by canals. Land was considered to be irrigated if it received water by artificial means at least twice per season. The government also exploited some state lands by a system of share-cropping, while the *kharāj* of the *iqtāʿ* obviously passed straight into the hands of the beneficiaries. In some parts of Iran in the tenth century there were still untied farmers, either members of farming communities or very small landowners, whose lands were termed *mulk*, 'private property', as in the case of the large landowners. But from the end of the tenth century onwards these lands were progressively taken over either by force, or through the system of *iltijā'* (meaning 'to seek refuge') whereby the free farmer placed himself under the protection of a large landowner or feudal lord by registering his land in the latter's name (thus protecting himself from any more powerful usurper) while in fact retaining the ownership in person. The price of this form of protection was generally a quarter of the harvest.

The development of the feudal economy, and in particular the progressive differentiation between an 'industrial' and an agricultural economy (though this distinction was far less highly developed than in medieval western Europe), is reflected in the development of the city. Travellers in the Islamic countries of the East have often remarked on the comparative rarity of what westerners would call cities, and this had been attributed to the nomadic nature of Islamic culture, Muslim resignation in the face of destiny, the destruction wrought by never-ending wars, and so forth. The real reason for the difference between the Islamic city and the European city (even in medieval times) is to be found in the much slower development of feudalism in the East, and also in the fact that the merchant classes in the cities did not set themselves up, as in Europe, in opposition to the nobility but found themselves closely bound to it. During this period we find in many cities that the *shahristān* (Arab. *madīna*, the old part of the city containing the houses of the *dihqān* and of the Arab aristocracy) gradually disappeared and the commercial centre moved to the *birūn* (in Persian 'the outside', Arab. *rabad*), that is to say to the business suburbs where the artisans lived, the 'new city'. The largest of these cities had in some cases greater populations than their counterparts in medieval Europe, the number of inhabitants sometimes rising to hundreds of thousands. Nīshāpūr, Rayy, Isfahān and Shīrāz were the biggest cities, each with a population of over a hundred thousand at this time. Craftsmen and merchants formed guilds, the most important of which in Nīshāpūr, for example, were those of the hatters, cordwainers, and dealers in raw and woven silk. The ruling class, however, consisted of the great feudal vassals in the neighbourhood, Persian *dihqān* or Arab aristocrats. These gradually gave up living on their estates and moved to the city since they were closely involved with the large merchant houses and in wholesale, foreign and forwarding business. A large proportion of their farm produce was invested in these merchant houses, which repaid them in goods, mostly textiles. As a result of this alliance the craft guilds were considerably less powerful in Iran, and in the Islamic East in general, than was the case in medieval Europe. The city ruler, the *ra'īs* (a sort of governor), the *qāzī* (the cadi or judge under Islamic law, and head of the local clergy), the *imām* (the teacher or instructor of the congregation in the mosque or *masjid-i jāmi'*), the *muhtasib* (a kind of head of police who was also a vigilante, and overseer of the bazaar), the *asas* (head of the night guard), and others were all members of the upper class. This close alliance between the great feudal vassals and the city merchants meant that a free community of citizens did not arise in the Muslim East. At the same time, Islam did not favour the excessive development of an aristocracy by blood (as occurred in feudal Europe through Germanic influences), and so the Muslim 'merchant aristocrats' were somewhat different in kind from their European counterparts. However, the various wards of the city and the craft and trade guilds and ecclesiastical bodies enjoyed a certain amount of autonomy, and elected their own heads who were responsible to the *ra'īs*. The artisans, combined in their guilds (*sinf*, pl. *asnāf*) and graded as masters (*ustād*), assistant masters (*khalīfa*), and apprentices (*shāgird*), were freemen under the law, but in many cities they continued to pay a form of tax to the government or local feudal lord on the products of their labour (a similar situation had existed in the time of the Sassanids). The centre of the city's social life was the *bāzār*, or rather the several *bāzārs*—markets. The various streets running through this network of bazaars met in the middle to form the main crossroads called the *chārsū* ('meeting of four ways'), or in Arabic *murabba'a*, over which was erected a cupola. (Excellent examples of these *chārsū* are still to be found in various cities to this day.) Wholesale trade was carried on around the *chārsū* in special buildings and caravanserais (Pers. *kārvān-sarāy*, 'palace of the caravan'; synonymous with the Arabo-Greek *funduq*), which served at one and the same time as inns for merchants from other cities, warehouses, and exchange-houses for large transactions. The philosopher and traveller Nāsir-i Khusrau tells us that in Isfahān in the eleventh century there were some fifty large caravanserais in one street alone. Each merchant house usually had its own. Since it was somewhat dangerous to carry around large sums of money on account of the number of bandits on the roads ('bandit' in both Persian and Arabic is 'one who cuts the road', *rahzan* or *qāti' at-tarīq*), business deals were settled by means of cheques (the word is of Persian origin, as also is 'exchequer'). A merchant setting out on a journey deposited his money with a money-changer (*sarrāf*) in his own city and was given a cheque which was accepted as payment by the merchants in the city he was visiting. Small dealings in articles of local manufacture, however, were settled in cash. Such wares were sold in the workshops themselves, which had their own sales counters, and both were called *dukkān*.

On the whole, those employed in a particular profession all lived and worked in the same quarter, hence the quarter or the street (*kūy*) of the silk weavers, coppersmiths, dyers, armourers, jewellers, tanners, etc, a situation that still exists in some cities in the East to-day. Food products were brought to the city bazaars by peasant farmers from the surrounding areas (*rustāq*). During this period as many as a thousand sheep and a hundred oxen were sold daily in the bazaar in Isfahān, and about a thousand sheep were sold annually to be dried and preserved. These are valuable figures for they give us some idea of the city's population.

It was during the tenth century that the typical Muslim religious schools and colleges (*madrasa*) developed. The cities contained powerful bodies of theologians and *sayyids* (true or presumed descendants of the Prophet), who elected their own superiors. Mosques and madrasas possessed, in the form of pious foundations or *vaqf*, workshops and sometimes entire bazaars, and they received income from the craftsmen and merchants occupied in them.

Thus, in the tenth to twelfth centuries, the cities contained four main centres of social life: the old *shahristān* or *madīna*, the *chārsū*, the *madrasa* or mosque, and the craftsmen's quarter with its workshops and the bazaar for the small traders. The largest city seems to have been Nīshāpūr (the ancient Nēv-Shāhpūr, founded by the Sassanid ruler of that name) which covered an area of a square *parasang* (about ten square miles). According to Muqaddasī, Nīshāpūr consisted of forty-four wards, some of which were half as large as the whole city of Shīrāz. It had a larger population than Baghdād, whose inhabitants were numbered in hundreds of thousands. There were some fifty main streets running through the city. Even travellers in those days complain of the filth of these great medieval towns, and of the large number of outcasts (*sāsiyān*) and beggars, who sometimes formed themselves into guilds. We have no accurate figures for the populations of these cities at this time, but at the beginning of the twelfth century, Balkh, which was not one of the largest, contained some 200,000 inhabitants. Arragān, in Fārs, a city of secondary importance, had a population of upwards of 40,000 in the middle of the eleventh century. In many cases, cities then had a larger population than they do to-day. This is partly to be explained by the terrible devastation that occurred during the Mongol conquest, and in some cases by the sheer despotism of governors who, for the flimsiest of reasons, decided to move their capital elsewhere, which led to the emigration of entire populations.

From the point of view of the basic institutions, this period marks the beginning of the medieval economic life of Persia, and therefore shows signs of progress or development. From the cultural point of view, however, these early dynasties do not so much herald the coming of a new dawn (which is often the interpretation put forward by those with a nationalist axe to grind) but rather, because of the obvious slowing down of cultural development itself, represent, to a certain degree, the end of an era. They bring to a close the vigorous, forward-looking initial period of Islamic culture, which in the ninth and tenth centuries was immensely enriched by the innumerable translations from Greek and Syriac, through which Greek and Hellenistic thought was absorbed. At first in particular, this enrichment was attained through an avid desire for knowledge and a practical curiosity which are typical of the ancient Islamic world and are well illustrated by the saying attributed to the Prophet: 'Search after knowledge, even as far as China'. The theological discussions of the first Abbasid period, the study of the early Greek philosophers and, at the same time, of the Pythagorean and Neo-Platonist gnostics of the Hellenistic period, the discussions of the *shu'ūbiyya* and the careful and delicate experiments in the literary use of languages previously confined to speech (this is the period of the birth of Persian literature), are all aspects of the same great cultural development. But this is true of Islam in general, and not only of the world of the Persians. Almost everything said above can be applied, with minor variations in the particulars, to the entire, basically homogeneous cultural world that stretched from the Atlantic in the West to India in the East. Then a more introvert assimilation occurred: while on the one hand Islam began to crystallize into orthodox juridical and theological systems, on the other it became, and was to remain for centuries, fascinated by the gnostic elements in the Hellenistic heritage. The period that follows is marked by this combination of gnostic and orthodox features, which, in the field of political history, reveals itself in the struggle to the death between the Seljuks and the Assassins, or Ismailis, whom the Ghaznavids had already regarded as their greatest foe.

CHAPTER V

The Seljuk period

'With the Seljuks a new period in the history of Islam begins. The mosaic of restless, unstable, and mutually hostile minor states into which the caliphate was split up, is for a time replaced by a new political unity. The Muslim lands, from Syria in the west to Afghanistan in the east, fell into the orbit of a new dynasty. Their sovereigns were Sunnites, and therefore the *sunna* shone once again in all its glory after its partial eclipse by the numerous Shi'ite dynasties which had sprung up here and there.'

F. M. Pareja, *Islamologie* (French edition) p. 128-9.

The Seljuks were a branch of the Ghuzz, a people of Turkish origin (Seljuk derives from the name of their semi-legendary ancestor Seljuq or Selchūq). They formed one of the successive waves of Turko-Mongols that rolled across Central Asia towards the West. The first Seljuks to penetrate Iran were the brothers Toghrul-beg and Chaghrī-beg Dāūd. In 1037 Merv and Nīshāpūr fell to them after they had defeated the Ghaznavids. The battle of Dandānqān in 1040 marks the final downfall of the Ghaznavids and the beginning of the Seljuks' rapid conquest of their western and other lands. Tabaristān and Gurgān (1041), Khārizm (1042), and then the territory ruled over by the Buyids were conquered. In 1055 Toghrul-beg entered Baghdād and the caliph granted him the title of *sultān* (sovereign), which was handed down to his posterity. On his death (1063) the Turkish emirs acknowledged his nephew, Alp Arslān, son of Chaghrī-beg, as his successor. Both Alp Arslān and his son Malikshāh (1072-92) warred against the Byzantines and the Fatimids of Egypt and raised the Seljūk sultanate to its greatest splendour. In the time of Malikshāh an enormous area stretching from Kāshgar in Central Asia to Damascus in Syria was subservient to the Seljuk sultan, while for a time his authority extended to a varying degree throughout the Yemen and other parts of Arabia.

The Fatimids (909–1171), the heretical anti-caliphs of Egypt, were so called because they claimed descent from the Prophet's daughter Fatima and her husband, the Prophet's cousin, 'Alī, who is regarded as a demigod by certain Shi'ite sects. It was during the long reign of al-Mustansir (1035–94) that the Fatimid caliphate achieved its greatest glory. Its centre was Egypt, though the people of Egypt, largely Sunnites, took little interest in the religious attitude of their rulers. Nevertheless, the Fatimids were closely involved in the dissemination of the dangerously extreme ideas of the Shi'ites of the Ismaili sect throughout the whole of the Islamic world, and particularly the eastern parts.

The beliefs of the Ismailis formed a kind of Islamic gnosticism which combined penetrating philosophical and psychological insight with abstruse cabbalistic doctrines, ideas taken from the late Hellenist philosophers with the assumption that the hereditary leaders (*imāms*) were infallible manifestations of the divine, as well as being descendants in the flesh of the Prophet of Islam through his cousin and son-in-law 'Alī.

It is not clear to what extent Fatimid politics were involved in the dissemination of Ismaili ideas beyond the Egyptian frontiers, but it seems highly probable that up to 1094, when the pretender Nizār suffered a political defeat and Musta'li seized the Egyptian throne, the Fatimids used the more or less underground ramifications of the movement abroad for their own political ends. But the Ismaili danger was apparent before the arrival of the Seljuks. In the ninth century the movement had taken on a millenarian character, partly coloured by communist utopianism—its members at this time were known as Carmathians—and received support from the expropriated classes and, to some extent, the masses. The success of al-Mahdī's campaign in North Africa in 909 led to his assumption of the throne of Egypt, and this appears somewhat to have placated the extremists. There is some doubt about the precise relationship between the rulers of Fatimid Egypt and the Carmathians, who were based on the Arabian shore of the Persian Gulf particularly around el-Ahsā, and who in 930 sacked Mecca. The term Carmathian derives from the name of one of the preachers of the movement, the ninth-century Hamdān Qarmat, and should strictly be applied only to those Ismailis who refused to accept the idea of an uninterrupted line of peaceful *imāms* and awaited expectantly the imminent coming of the Promised One who would liberate the world and establish the Kingdom of God. The Ismailis took their name from Ismāʿīl, son of the *imām* Jaʿfar as-Sādiq, who appears for some reason to have appointed another of his sons, Mūsā, to continue the succession of the twelve *imāms* accepted by the moderate or 'imamite' Shiʿites. The anti-Ismaili sources make no distinction between the beliefs of the Ismaili in general and those of the Carmathians, the Batinis (the 'esoteric ones', from *bātin*, 'inner meaning'), and the Taʾlīmīs (from *taʾlīm*, 'teaching', for they blindly followed the infallible dictates of their leaders). The Ghaznavids struggled hard to combat the Carmathians, though at one point, as a result of Tahārtī's embassy of 1012–3, the Fatimids hoped to have the Ghaznavids as their allies against the caliphate. But the Ghaznavids, who were fanatically orthodox, valued highly the prestige that their friendship with and recognition by the Abassid caliphate gave them. In 1029, Mahmūd of Ghazna subdued the small Buyid court of Rayy, which had become pro-Ismaili, and at about the same time put down the Carmathians of Multān in the Punjab. These names alone suffice to indicate how widely this dangerous movement had spread (it was particularly powerful in Khorāsān). It derived its strength from a variety of economic and social factors, but it was always openly hostile to the Ghaznavids and Seljuks.

After Nizār's defeat in 1094 his followers in the eastern half of the Islamic world began to spread the *daʿwa jadīda*, 'the new propaganda'. Their leader was Hasan Sabbāh, who in 1090–1 had succeeded by means of a trick in gaining possession of the impregnable fortress of Alamūt ('Eagle's Nest' or 'Teaching of the Eagle') in the mountains south of the Caspian Sea. Thereafter a state within the state began slowly to develop within the Seljuk empire. From a chain of inaccessible fortresses, mainly in the Kūhistān area (Kāīn, Khūr, Khusf, Zauzan, Tūn), the Ismailis proceeded to threaten the welfare and security of the state not only through their subtle and intelligent use of propaganda (some of the original documents, written mostly in Arabic, have recently come to light), but also by means of lightning raids and political assassination. It appears that they had a rigidly organized hierarchy, at the head of which was the Great Propagandist (dā'ī ad-du'āt), known to those outside the sect as the shaikh al-jabal ('the master on the mountains'), which the Crusaders translated rather inaccurately as 'the old man of the mountain'. Hasan Sabbāh held this position up to the time of his death at a very advanced age (1124). Legend has it that he was a fellow student with Omar Khayyām, and in Marco Polo's Travels there is the tale of The Old Man of the Mountain. Below him in the hierarchy came what one might call the 'bishops' (hujjat, lit. 'Proofs'), and then the ordinary propagandists or preachers (dā'ī). These senior officials who were well acquainted with the esoteric philosophy of the sect, were followed by other ranks of adherents, descending finally to the utterly faithful fidā'ī (those 'ready for the sacrifice', the devotees) who provided the ordinary soldiers of this much-feared organization. The word 'assassin' seems to be derived from the Arabic hashshāshīn ('those who take hashīsh'), on the basis of Marco Polo's well-known account. Until fairly recently our knowledge of this sect was based almost entirely on hostile sources, which were naturally highly derogatory. The discovery of actual Ismaili texts has now thrown a more favourable light on the Assassins, who from certain points of view were neither so heterodox as had been made out nor so morally reprehensible as their Seljuk detractors pretended. (The Ismailis are frequently and ridiculously accused of holding their property and women in common, of immorality, etc; similar accusations had been made against the Mazdakites and those who joined the first anti-government movements in Khorāsān, remnants of which very probably still remained in the area and may well have attached themselves to the Ismailis.) The Ismaili movement was very attractive both to the intellectuals, such as the great Persian poet and philosopher Nāsir-i Khusrau (d. ca 1074), who became a member of the Ismaili community and wrote profound treatises on religious philosophy in which he tried to demonstrate the spiritual concordance between Greek philosophy and Ismaili gnostic theosophy, and to the masses, who as always were restive under the oppression of feudalism and lived in the hope of an apocalyptic reversal of fortune, which indeed was what the Ismaili dā'ī promised them.

The central concept of Ismaili theosophy, in fact, consists in the belief in a succession of prohetic cycles, the most recent of which, that of Muhammad, was due to end during this period, to be followed by the seventh and last cycle, that of *Qā'im al-Qiyāma*, the 'Operator of the Resurrection'. A solemn proclamation to this effect was made by a descendant of Hasan Sabbāh in 1164. Nevertheless, wherever the Ismailis exercised real political powers (for example, in the tiny fortress-state of Alamūt, particularly in its later stages), their rule was based on exactly the same class organization and social system as elsewhere. It is not too much to say, however, that from this period on, the whole of eastern Islam, *nolens volens*, felt the effects of the esoteric doctrines of the Ismailis, which were transmitted through channels that are often extremely difficult to define, such as art, poetry, and even the writings of their adversaries.

One of the most ruthless opponents of the Assassins was the faithful Seljuk minister Nizāmu'l-Mulk, vizier to Alp Arslān and then to his son Malikshāh until 1092, when the Assassins stabbed him to death. He was one of the greatest Persians of his day. He wrote the *Siyāsatnāmè* ('The Book of the Art of Politics') which, besides being what its title says, is also a valuable, though biased, source for studying the history and doctrines of the Ismailis, and of Islamic heresies in general. One dramatic episode will give an idea of the courage and audacity of the devout Ismaili *fidā'ī*. On an expedition which Malikshāh (or, according to some sources, his son Sanjar) was leading against Alamūt, a message was found one night in his well-guarded tent, pierced by a dagger thrust into the ground. It read: 'The dagger that has opened the hard earth might well have penetrated thy softer breast. Beware!'. The expedition ended in retreat. A common practice of the *fidā'ī* who were arrested and subjected to terrible tortures, was to confess, at the point of death, the names of their secret friends. But such was their diabolical ingenuity that the names that they gave were in fact those of their bitterest enemies. A witchhunt would follow, and thus the heroic *fidā'ī* would succeed in dragging their opponents into the grave with them!

On the death of Malikshāh, a struggle for the succession arose between his sons Barkiyāruq, Muhammad, and Sanjar, and the omnipresent Ismailis played their part in these intrigues. Barkiyāruq died in 1104, Muhammad perished in an assault on the fortress of Alamūt in 1118, while the third, Sanjar, despite the misfortunes which marked his reign (he was attacked and even taken prisoner by his own kith and kin, the still uncivilized Ghuzz from Central Asia), became famous as the patron of a number of great Persian poets. He died without leaving an heir in 1157, and thereafter the empire split into various districts governed by the *atābeg* (masters or teachers of servile origin) of the princes of the ruling house, who gradually made themselves independent.

A basic characteristic of the political system of the Seljuk period is its lack of centralized organization, despite the efforts of officials such as Nizamu'l-Mulk, who, in his *Siyāsatnāmè*, put forward a plan for harnessing the strength of the Turks to the administrative methods of the Abbasid caliphs inherited from the Sassanids. In the Seljuk period we witness the full development of a flourishing feudalism, different as this is in many ways from its European counterpart. But at the same time the invasion of the Seljuk Turks created, or rather enlarged, the class of Persian officials who proved indispensable, at least in the initial stages, to the less experienced invaders from Central Asia. This official class often found an ally in the old aristocracy, though their aims were not always identical. The ruling class, which we misleadingly term the 'aristocracy', was far from being united. A document dating from the turn of the ninth century provides the information, most interesting on account of its detail and of the area concerned, that of the forty-one 'noble' families in the district of Baihaq in Khorāsān, twenty-four were of Arab extraction (though by now Iranized), three were descended from pre-Islamic *dihqān*, nine belonged to the Samanid official class, and one to the merchant class, making in all twenty-four families of Arab stock against thirteen of Persian origin. These lived in the city of Sabzavār but held lands in the surrounding area. The proportion of merchants and officials (both secular and religious) increased progressively during the time of the Ghaznavids and particularly during the Seljuk rule. Though one cannot speak at first of the existence of an actual middle class, there developed a 'serving aristocracy' which, in the

Islamic world unconcerned with differences of race, succeeded in asserting itself even more firmly than in Europe.

The institution of the *iqtā'* continued to evolve, becoming hereditary. It is interesting to note on this point the contrast between the theoretical opinion of Nizāmu'l-Mulk—who tended to oppose feudal decentralization—that the *iqtā'dār* or *muqta'* (the beneficiary of the *iqtā'*) had no rights of ownership to the land or to the peasants settled on it, and the actual situation as expressed a little later in the words of a wealthy Syrian *iqtā'dār* of the twelfth century, reported by the Arab historian Maqrīzī: 'The *iqtā'* is our property: our descendants will inherit it from father to son, and we are ready to fight for it'. With the increasing decentralization, certain central offices began to lose their importance, such as, for example, the *dīvān al-kharāj* (the central tax office), and the collection of the *kharāj* fell into the hands of the *atābeg* and other local officials, while various local 'offices' sprang up. On the one hand, this decentralization produced positive effects. For example, in the past the *iqtā'dār* had been interested merely in getting as much as they could out of the land in the form of taxes and other contributions from the peasant farmers. Now they were concerned in maintaining the land in a good state of productivity, since it was substantially their own property, and in making the conditions of the peasants who worked it bearable. On the other hand, it made it even more difficult for a determined peasant revolt (if such a thing could ever have occurred at this time in the East) to break out. It has, in fact, been noted that the endemic revolts of the over-exploited peasants which characterized the eighth to tenth centuries seem to die down in this period.

The processes at work in the cities, outlined in the previous chapter, were consolidated, while there was a considerable development in the arts and crafts. Trade expanded particularly with Europe, due to contacts with the Crusaders, but above all with the Mediterranean area, and especially Italy. (With reference to the Crusaders, one must bear in mind that for a long time Syria formed part of the Seljuk empire, and that it is impossible to write a history of Iran as a distinct ethnic unit within the medieval Muslim world.) The craftsmen in the cities continued to be completely dependent on the feudal lords allied with the merchants, but with the remarkable development during this period of mysticism and Sufi fraternities, the very interesting craft guilds grew stronger, taking on mystical elements which, however, were not generally pantheistic, though pietistic, and which were not always heterodox. One of the most important of these fraternities was that of the *akhī* ('brothers'), also known as the *futūwa* ('chivalry' or 'knights'), which sometimes presented a noble and fairly organized opposition, based on Islamic precepts, to tyrants and social injustice.

Culturally, the Seljuk period is one of the most outstanding in the whole of Persian history. At certain moments, orthodoxy and mysticism, Ismaili innovations and a sincere *pietas*, art and life, appear to achieve a state of balance, though, alas, it was ever short-lived. This is the period, from the death of al-Ashʿarī (935) to that of al-Ghazzālī (1111), during which the whole of the present form of orthodox Muslim theology was moulded, while al-Ghazzālī himself invested it with mystical elements. It was also during this period that treatises on Ismaili gnosticism flourished. In the rich atmosphere of Iran, all those features which form an essential part of Islamic culture through the succeeding centuries down to our own times, were now gathered together and interwoven, forming a clearer pattern as the period drew to an end. Hellenistic gnosticism was Islamized. Religious fraternities sprang up. (The most ancient fraternity of the Dervishes, the *qādiriyya*, dates from the twelfth century.) Theology and mysticism flourished. During this period, nearly all the forms of Persian literature evolved. It is true that some, especially a particular type of erotico-mystical lyric, perhaps reached their highest peak at a later date, but it was during the Seljuk period that they were shaped. This was the age of perhaps the most poised and thoughtful of the Persian poets, Nizāmi (1141–1209/13), who appears to have belonged to the fraternity of the *akhī* or at least to have been influenced by it. Nizāmu 'l-Mulk founded some of the first and greatest universities in the Islamic world, or in the entire civilized world, for that matter. That which he built in Baghdād, to which Malikshāh's capital was transferred from Isfahān in 1091, was named Nizāmiyya after him, and he set up others in

Nīshāpūr, Balkh, Mosul, Herāt, and Merv. Among those who received his protection were al-Ghazzālī, one of the greatest thinkers in the history of Islam (although he wrote nearly all his works in Arabic, he was Persian), and Omar Khayyām, so famous in Europe that he cannot be ignored. For long more renowned in the East as a mathematician and a man of science than as a poet, Omar Khayyām presided over a commission of astronomers and mathematicians set up in 1074 by Nizāmu 'l-Mulk to reform the calendar. In architecture certain important features developed. From the eleventh century onwards, the classical type of mosque, of Arabo-Byzantine origin, began to be replaced by that in the form of a smallish square or octagonal building with a cupola, thought by some to have originated in Iran in ancient times. (Examples are to be found in the Friday mosques of Gulpāyagān, Qazvīn, Ardistān, Isfahān, and elsewhere.) Later, square courts were to be added to these mosques, with cloisters and with four large arched portals. The typical Muslim pointed arch predominated in the eleventh and twelfth centuries. Persian pottery reached its zenith, the finest ceramics being produced in Rayy and Kāshān, which gives its name to *kāshī*, the Persian word for ceramic ornaments. Particularly famous was the glazed pottery decorated with ornamental designs. The Persians appear to have held turquoise glazes in particularly high esteem, but they also employed cobalt blue and a tin oxide white glaze. From the twelfth century the highly prized lustre-ware came into use, produced by employing a mixture of silver and copper salts, arsenical sand, etc, and giving a second firing in a reducing kiln. A formula for this is given in 'The Treatise on Precious Stones' by Abu 'l-Qāsim 'Abdullāh ibn Abī Tāhir of Kāshān (twelfth century).

From the world of science the greatest names in Iran and indeed in all of medieval Islam really belong to the preceding Ghaznavid period, though it is often difficult to make a cultural distinction between that and the period of the Seljuks. Avicenna died in 1037, and al-Bīrūnī, perhaps the greatest man of science of Islam, in 1048. Rāzī, a Persian and the greatest experimental scientist in the history of Islam, had already died in 923. The Seljuk period, in fact, was one in which the discoveries of the scientists of the preceding age were applied and developed.

It is difficult to analyze the varied causes of this upsurge of intellectual activity. It is true to say, however, that, with the Turkish invasions which created the Seljuk power, a new social class was born, a bureaucracy of intellectuals recruited by the new invaders from among the Persian population, a bureaucracy quite different from the *dihqān* class of the preceding period which was partly a continuation of the small landed nobility of the Sassanids. An excellent example of this difference is to be found in the literary field. Firdausī is a typical representative of the *diqhān* whereas Nizāmī is an equally typical representative of the new ruling class of intellectuals. Furthermore, the very fact of an invasion by a foreign people, unless it is thoroughly destructive like the Mongol invasion, may contribute to a healthy mixing of the social classes and at the same time may serve to sharpen a people's creativity. Some scholars, such as Barthold, have tried to interpret the Ismaili opposition as an attempt to return to an Iranian form of feudalism, an attempt to re-establish the patriarchal attitude of the country *dihqān* in opposition to the new people of the cities. But this interpretation is too simple and fails to take into account the fact that there was no single fixed type of Ismailism but many different forms, and that Ismailism itself had adherents among the artisans and other inhabitants of the cities. Moreover, the Ismailis also dreamed of a unified Islamic world, though on another plane and in another way, just as the early Seljuks, whose ambitious intentions were expressed by Nizāmu 'l-Mulk, aimed at unification. The Ismaili intellectuals came in the main from the same new class of citizens and officials, and Ismaili gnosticism gave much of the tone to the culture of the era, which analyzed man rather than nature, and added considerable psychological depth to the more elementary literary and cultural outlook of the preceding period. Persian culture, which at this time offered infinite possibilities of further development, might well have moved on in unexpected directions and would probably have made considerable advances if at this moment the third, and certainly the most devastating, of the invasions Iran had to suffer in her long history, had not broken upon her. The Mongol invasion was once again to alter the line of development of Persian culture and the whole of eastern Islam.

CHAPTER VI

The Mongol period

Slowly the Seljuk empire broke up. New tribes were appearing in Central Asia, and one of the first regions of Iran to come under their sway was the outlying state of Khārizm, south-east of the Aral Sea. Qutbu'd-Dīn Muhammad, son of a Turkish slave from Malikshāh, had been appointed governor of the region in 1097 with the title of *Khārizm-shāh* (King of Khārizm). His successors remained unreliable vassals of the Seljuks until 1172, when the kings of Khārizm began to overrun Seljuk territory. They had a hard struggle with the Ghurids, another dynasty in the extreme east of Iran. Ghūr is the name of the mountainous region situated between the valley of the Helmand and Herāt (modern Afghanistan). The local princes had been subdued and converted to Islam by Mahmūd of Ghazna. A certain Fakhru'd-Dīn made himself leader of the Ghurid princes and extended his rule as far as Balkh and Badakhshān. Another branch of the Ghurids had succeeded in occupying Ghazna, whence they were dislodged by the Seljuk Sanjar. Ghazna was then reoccupied by the brothers Ghiyāsu'd-Dīn and Mu'izzu'd-Dīn. In 1186 the latter conquered Lahore and thus brought an end to Ghaznavid rule in India. Meanwhile, Ghiyāsu'd-Dīn was defending himself against the Khārizm-shāh, who finally destroyed the Ghurids in 1215.

Having driven the Ghurids out of Khorāsān after a fierce struggle, the Khārizm-shāh, 'Alā'u'd-Dīn Muhammad (1199–1220) extended his conquests in Persia and seized Bukhārā and Samarkand. For a time he paid tribute to the fickle Qarakhitai barbarians, who came from Manchuria, but in 1210 he overthrew them and after taking Otrār became complete master of the whole of Transoxiana. A few years later he entered Ghazna and so brought Ghurid rule to an end in this area.

At this time Khārizm was one of the richest and most powerful states in Islam, for amongst other things it was a commercial centre of the utmost importance for trade between the Far East and the Islamic and Western world. But this period of greatness marked the final stage in the history of Khārizm. Emboldened by his success, 'Alā'u'd-Dīn Muhammad decided to conquer Iraq and overthrow the Abbasid caliphate. He assembled a large army and set out for Baghdād in 1217, but was forced to turn back on account of the rigorous winter weather. At the same time, there occurred a fatal incident with the Mongols. It was probably occasioned by the capture of a caravan from Mongolia, and the murder of all those accompanying it. When Chingīz Khān, the Great Khān and lord of the nomadic Mongol 'hordes' (*ordu, orda* is the Turko-Mongol word for 'encampment') was moving across Central Asia, learned that one of his ambassadors, who had been on a mission to demand certain reparations, had been killed, he sent his troops against 'Alā'u'd-Dīn, and the new tactics which they employed and the fear that they inspired quickly led to the annihilation of the Khārizm-shāh's army. 'Alā'u'd-Dīn fled, hard pressed by troops who harried him from Balkh to Merv, from Merv to Nīshāpūr and Rayy, until he finally died in 1220 on a small island in the Caspian Sea. His son Jalāl ad-Dīn, the last of the Khārizm-shāhs led a fantastic expedition which reached Ghazna. In vain he tried to win back the lost kingdom, fighting many a brave battle not only with the Mongols but also with the Georgians, local Indian princelings, and other enemies. In 1231 he was assassinated by a Kurd.

The Mongol state had only recently been unified and moulded into a powerful force by Chingīz Khān himself (the name appears to mean 'lord of the world'). Its organiza-tion was that of a pastoral, nomadic feudalism, with at its head the *khān* or *qāān* (Turk. *qāghān*). Leading each *ulus* (tribal unit, nation) was a vassal prince, and under him came the *noyon* who moved about the grazing grounds within a particular area, with their *nüker* (which gives rise to *noukar*, 'servant' in modern Persian) and *arat*. This social structure at the same time provided a powerful military force sub-divided into groups of *tümen* comprising 10,000, a thousand, a hundred, and ten, which also conformed with the old tribal division. The ties uniting the ordinary soldiers to their military commander, who was also the head of the tribe or sub-tribe, were therefore extremely strong. The Great Khān had a personal guard of 10,000 (*keshik*), made up of the young men from the families of the aristocracy. They provided the senior officers of the army and the governors of conquered provinces. Traditional law was based on the Great *Yasa* (law). The Great Khāns were elected at a *kurultay* (an assembly which also decided other important matters) of the princes and lesser *khān*. The Mongol strength lay in the rigid discipline which ran through the entire fighting nation, and the comparatively democratic form of military government of the state which, being of nomadic and pastoral origin, had no agricultural tradition. This was the secret of the Mongol expansion, which led to the invasion of China, Tibet, Eastern Turkestan, Central Asia, Iran, Transcaucasia, and Nearer Asia as far as Dasht-i Qipchaq and Russia, and the countries of Eastern Europe. When the Mongols entered in strength into countries with a highly developed culture such as Iran, this barbarian simplicity led to terrible destruction and a radical disorganization. The ruin which they brought upon in the cities which they successively conquered with astonishing ease, was appalling: only a few hundred people would succeed in saving themselves from the ensuing massacre. It has been said that some of the cities of Persia and Central Asia still show the consequences of this devastation to this day. Once flourishing cities were reduced for all time to small villages of few inhabitants and no importance, while new commercial and cultural centres arose elsewhere. The Mongol invasion, like an earthquake, affected the very geography of the country.

Chingīz Khān died in 1227, but his work was continued by his successors. At the *kuraltay* of 1229, Ugädäi (1229–41) was proclaimed Great Khān, and his armies were active from Korea in the east to Russia in the west. In 1246, the *kurultay* of the Mongol princes placed Güyük (1246–8) on the throne. Despite the terrible ravages which the Mongols caused (and at first the conquering hordes had to be lodged and fed by the local population), the unification of such enormous stretches of territory, and the fact that the khāns were Shamanists and later Buddhists and in general tolerant in religious matters, brought certain advantages, such as a great easing of trade over wide areas. (A safe conduct from the *khān* was enough to terrorize any robber or other person with ill intentions.) Commerce was largely in the hands of the big Muslim traders of Iran and Central Asia, who at this time were called *urtāq* (ancient Turk. 'travelling companion'). Even the Mongol khāns themselves invested large sums in trade.

At the death of Güyük there was disagreement over the choice of his successor, and it was not till the *kurultay* of 1251 that Möngke (1251–9) was elected. This *kurultay* is particularly important for the history of Iran, for besides electing the Great Khān it also decided to subdue those states which were still active after the first waves of invasion. In the west, Hūlāgū Khān was entrusted with putting down the Assassins of Alamūt and the Abbasid caliphate in Baghdād, while in the east Qubilay Khān (like Hūlāgū, a brother of Möngke) was given the task of finally subjecting China to Mongol rule.

The situation in Iran prior to Hūlāgū's campaign was complex. In 1237, Isfahān had been conquered, together with Jazīra or Upper Mesopotamia. By about 1250, the Mongols held Khorāsān, Sīstān, Māzandarān, Persian Iraq, and Azerbaijān. Relations with the Mongols in southern and south-western Iran were somewhat different. At Kirmān there was a Qarakhitai *khān* (see p. 106) who had received recognition from the Mongols. In Fārs Seljuk *atābeg* (masters or teachers) of the Salgharid dynasty still reigned. Luristān was divided between two small dynasties of Seljuk *atābeg*. In the western part of Luristān the lands of the *atābeg* bordered on the remaining lands of the Abbasid caliphate, still untouched by the Mongols as was also as the fortress of Alamūt. In Mongol-held Khorāsān the Mongol governor Chintīmūr and his successor Kurkuz tried to repair the initial destruction by rebuilding some of the cities and, since they were especially responsible for sending taxes to the central coffers of the Mongols, re-establishing at least rudimentary forms of agriculture on which these taxes could be based. In order to achieve this it was essential for there to be some collaboration between the Mongol leaders and the Iranian ruling classes who had fled before the storm. This policy, which was typical of the governors of Khorāsān during this period, was however strongly opposed by other Mongol khāns, who preferred not to fraternize in any way, and restricted themselves to the ruthless exploitation of the people, without attempting to enlist the co-operation of the former local aristocracy.

Hūlāgū's campaign was a complete success. News of his entry into Khorāsān no sooner spread than all the small rulers of Persia, including the Grand Master of the Assassins, were terrified into offering their submission. Hūlāgū accepted in every case, with the one exception of Ruknu'd-Dīn, Grand Master of Alamūt, to which fortress he proceeded to lay siege. On the advice of his crafty astrologer Nasīrū'd-Dīn Tūsī, a famous Persian man of science and the author of various treatises on ethics, Ruknu'd-Dīn surrendered on the assurance that his life would be spared, but subsequently he was assassinated with all his followers. Soon afterwards all the other fortified stongholds of the Ismailis fell. Nasīrū'd-Dīn entered into the service of the pagan Hūlāgū, advised him on the conquest of Baghdād, obtained his agreement (as a good Shi'ite) that the Shi'ite holy places in Iraq should be respected, then took charge of the building of the observatory at Marāgha in Azerbaijān which Hūlāgū had commissioned, and carried out other work at Hūlāgū's court. He is a typical example of that large group of Persian intellectuals who, *faute de mieux*, hastened to come to the assistance of the Mongols, acting as annalists and secretaries and thus providing the administrative and bureaucratic services necessary to successful government. During this period in Persian literature, prose histories flourished.) Being a Shi'ite, Nasīrū'd-Dīn must have hated the Abbasid Sunnite caliphate in Baghdād: at least, his advice was taken and proved successful. The ancient capital of the Abbasid empire, where there still existed a phantom caliph, al-Musta'sim, fell easily into the hands of the Mongols, who, it is said, massacred hundreds of thousands of people, though the figures are probably exaggerated, while the caliph, in accordance with Mongol tradition which forbade spilling the blood of princes, was put in a sack and beaten to death (1258). The universal Islamic caliphate was brought to an end for ever.

After the successful outcome of his campaigns, Hūlāgū remained in Iran, and in 1261 his brother Qubilay Khān, who had meantime become Great Khān, officially invested him as sovereign of all the territories he held and granted him the title of *il-khān* (lit. 'tribal *khān*' or 'local *khān*'), which was handed down to his descendants, who, under the nominal sovereignty of the Great Khān, continued to govern a vast area. In the north the Caucasus formed the frontier with the land of the Golden Horde, which was another state of Mongol origin. In Transcaucasia, Georgia and the state of Shīrvān (the area around modern Baku), where the court language was Persian, were Hūlāgū's vassals. On the Black Sea the empire of Trebizond (formed in 1204) paid Hūlāgū tribute. In Asia Minor the Seljuk sultanate of Rūm was a vassal state (though not occupied by the Mongols), as was the Armeno-Cilician kingdom (1080–1375) to the south-east. The Euphrates formed the frontier with the territories of the Mamlūks, who succeeded in resisting the Mongol hordes and even inflicted their first defeat on them in 1260. In the south, Hūlāgū's kingdom stretched to the Persian Gulf, while in the east the border with the lands of the Indian princes ran through the desert from the Indian Ocean as far as the Amu Darya, passing slightly east of Tirmiz. Herāt, now in Afghanistan, was the centre of the Kart state, which was also a vassal of Hūlāgū. In the north-east the Amu Darya formed the frontier with another Mongol state, belonging to the descendants of Chagatai. In the north, the border with the Golden Horde ran south of Urgench to the eastern shore of the Caspian Sea.

On Hūlāgū's death a local *kurultay* (at first the descendants of Hūlāgū copied the model of the central Asian Mongols), elected his son Abāqā (1265–82) to the throne, and he maintained his father's policies. After his death, disagreement arose over the two candidates for the succession, his brother Taqūdār and his son Arghūn. Taqūdār was eventually successful, and he became the first of Hūlāgū's descendants to accept Islam. He adopted the name of Ahmad, and tried to carry out a policy similar to that of Chintīmūr in Khorāsān, which displeased a large section of the conservative and anti-Islamic Mongol aristocracy. Ahmad tried to flee, but was executed by being beaten to death in order to avoid spilling his blood. He was followed by Arghūn (1284–91) who, with the support of the feudal aristocracy of the nomadic Mongols, brought about the downfall of the extremely wealthy Juvainī family, Muslim Persians who had acted as secretaries to the Mongols and had accumulated an immense fortune in the service of Hūlāgū Khān and his successors. A very great part was played at court by the Mongol prince Buqāy, a member of the Jalā'īr tribe, whose excessive power, however, led to his own execution. Arghūn did not trust the Persian Muslim administrators, and decided to replace some of them with Christians and Jews. His vizier was the famous Jew Sa'du'd-Daula, who succeeded to a certain extent in restoring the state finances, which had been appallingly administered. Through his struggle to end corruption in the administration, however, he attracted the hatred of both the Mongol nomad aristocracy and the Muslim bureaucracy, who brought about his downfall. He was executed during the period of Arghūn's last illness in 1291, his property was confiscated and his relatives were sold as slaves. Given Arghūn's political outlook, it was natural that European Christian rulers should continue their attempts to ally themselves with the Mongols against the common enemy, Islam. The exchange of embassies, though it did not achieve any important political results, contributed considerably in increasing the East and West's knowledge of each other.

After a struggle for power between the khāns, in 1291 another son of Abāqā, Gaikhātū (1291–5), was elected *il-khān* of Persia. He attempted to pacify the various religious groups, for hatred of the overbearing Sa'du'd-Daula had resulted in the Muslims carrying out pogroms against the Jews. Gaikhātū's minister, the Muslim Sadru'd-Dīn Ahmad Khālidī, faced with an almost empty treasury, suggested introducing paper money, as had already been tried out in China, which was to serve for internal trade, while all coin was to be kept in the treasury. These banknotes, known by the Chinese name of *chao*, the first of their kind in the world, were issued from Tabrīz, which for all practical purposes had become the capital of the *il-khān* in 1294, and the people were forced to accept them under pain of death. The consequences were disastrous: the bazaars closed down and every form of merchandize disappeared. The *chao* had to be abolished, and the treasury coffers remained empty. Sadru'd-Dīn, whose name signifies 'support of religion', came to be called 'paper support'. Gaikhātū's reign was brought to an end by an uprising led by his brother Bāidū, which was in part backed by the Mongol aristocracy. He seized power in 1295 by killing his brother, but he himself ruled for only a few months.

During the period of the Il-Khānids, the ruling class consisted of four social groups: the pastoral and warrior aristocracy, made up of Mongols, Turks and Kurds; the urban bureaucracy, consisting mainly of Persians, some of whom, such as the house of Juvainī, were extraordinarily wealthy (the income of Shamsu'd-Din Muhammad Juvainī, brother of the well-known historian of the Mongols, 'Atā Malik, was equivalent to 20% of the annual revenue of the whole of Hūlāgū's state); the senior members of the Muslim religious hierarchy; and the remnants of the local provincial Iranian aristocracy who were not part of the central government. The first group held most of the political power. Much of the last group had ceased to exist and the lands of the Persian provincial aristocrats had passed into the hands of the state or of the *khān*. The administration concentrated on extorting the maximum sums in the form of taxes, from the inhabitants. The head of the civil service was the *sāhib-dīvān* or 'vizier of the great divan', who was mostly occupied by finance. He also controlled the *kārkhānè* (a term nowadays used in the sense of 'factory' or 'workshop'), where those artisans who had been reduced to slavery as a result of the conquest or their descendants, worked for the Mongol state. The office of tax-gatherer was contracted out, and the actual collection of taxes was planned in advance with all the care of a military campaign. At first this resulted in vast sums of money entering the treasury's coffers, but such an absurd system quickly threw the peasant farmers into a state of terror and they fled from whole areas, leaving them completely deserted. The Mongol pastoral soldiers who had come to Iran with their families and slaves, continued to lead a nomadic life, spending the summer months in the pasturelands of Azerbaijān, Transcaucasia and Khorāsān. These feudal nomads remained faithful to their traditions and were little inclined to mix with the native population. This attitude led to a certain amount of decentralization, while on the other hand the policy of the Iranian bureaucracy and of those Mongol *khāns* willing to fraternize with the inhabitants tended to create a unified state modelled on that of the Ghaznavids.

During the early period of the *il-khān* the land was divided up into various categories. There were the *dīvānī* or state lands; *injū* or *khāss injū* lands belonging to the *khān* and his relatives; *mulk* or private land belonging to Mongol or indigenous feudal vassals; and *vaqf* or pious foundations. The revenue from the *dīvānī* lands covered state expenses, while the income from the *injū* lands went to support the *khān* and his relatives, and, when possible, to maintain the army. The revenue from the *vaqf* supported the Muslim priesthood. The taxes paid by the peasant farmers who lived on *dīvānī* and *injū* land were collected either directly by the supreme *dīvān* or *dīvān injū*, or by contractors who were either feudal vassals or big merchants. A large proportion of the *dīvānī* lands were held by the Mongol aristocracy in the form of *iqtā'*.

The condition of the peasants at this time was appalling, for they were subject to anything from fifteen to thirty different kinds of tax or tribute. One of the basic taxes was the *māl* or *kharāj*, a land tax paid either in kind or, particularly in the neighbourhood of the cities, in cash. The rate varied from region to region, and often an additional sum (*far'*) was imposed which consisted of ten per cent of the tax itself. The invaders also introduced a tax known as *qupchur* which at first applied only to the pastoral population and consisted of one per cent of the head of cattle owned, but was later also imposed on the farmers and townspeople in the form of a per capita payment in cash which varied over the years. This head-tax was not limited to Jews, Zoroastrians and Christians, as laid down by Islamic law, but also applied to Muslims, who regarded it as particularly offensive. The peasant farmers also had to pay various other forms of tribute in cash or kind, known as *ikhrājāt*, which went to support the emirs, soldiers, officials, treasury messengers (*īlchī*), etc. The farmers also had to supply forage and provisions to the army (services known as *'alāfè* and *ulūfè* respectively), and had to make special contributions of grain and beverages (known as *tagar*). Furthermore, the officials employed as tax-gatherers were subject to no control, and on occasions, after collecting the sums due to the treasury, they made a second and even a third collection which went into their own pockets. The number of insolvent peasants increased, and from 1250 to 1270 they and their families could even be reduced to slavery.

It was a common practice to grant princes, emirs and officials a *barāt*, that is to say, letters patent which allowed a pension to be drawn from the taxes of a particular region or village. Rashīdu'd-Dīn, the famous historian of the Mongols, recounts how someone going to collect his *barāt* from a village found it deserted. All the inhabitants had fled, except for three peasants who had been caught by a group of Mongol soldiers. The latter had hung these up by their feet and were beating them savagely in order to make them confess where their fellow-villagers had fled, so that they could collect payment of their *barāt*. Equally burdensome for the peasants were the numerous services they were called on to provide. These included the *ulāgh*, upkeep of the horses and asses used by the postal service; and *bīgār*, forced labour employed on cleaning and repairing the canals and building forts, palaces and roads, work that often remained unfinished or completely ineffective. Really burdensome for the peasant was the duty to provide (*nuzūl*) for a visiting Mongol emir or official and his retinue, who might requisition as many as a hundred houses. The *nüker* of these state officials plundered voraciously and often violated the women. In order to avoid them, the peasants were forced to keep their houses in a deliberately semi-ruined condition. It was during the Mongol period that the peasants became in fact slaves of the soil, a position previously unheard of in the Islamic world and under Islamic law, which regards workers on the land as freemen. In Mongolia in the time of Chīngīz Khān the pastoral soldier (though not an actual slave) was considered to be everlastingly bound to his hereditary lord, to the pastoral noble, to his nomad camp, and to his military unit of a hundred or of ten men. This traditional law, enshrined in the *Yasa*, the Mongol code, had perhaps made sense in the pasture-lands of Mongolia, but the Mongol invaders also applied it to the peasant farmers of Iran.

The lot of the peasants varied, however, according to the type of land they lived on. For example, on private land (*mulk*) it was not too bad, in so far as the proprietor was concerned in keeping the land productive, unlike the officials and tax-gatherers whose interests were entirely predatory. It is a fact, however, that towards the end of the thirteenth century these various systems of taxation had turned whole regions into desert. The peasants had fled, and in many areas, according to Rashīdu'd-Dīn, only a tenth part of the land was cultivated.

The towns destroyed by the invasion were slow to revive. The attempts of the Mongol governors, and later of the first *il-khān*, to rebuild these towns or create new ones were largely unsuccessful. Furthermore, the fact that the markets were no longer being supplied with farm produce from the neighbourhood meant that they dwindled in size, while the townspeople themselves were burdened with taxes and other obligations. One of the main taxes they had to pay was the *tamgha*, first introduced by the Mongols, which was levied on workshops, on trade—both wholesale and retail—and even on goods which the peasants brought to sell at the town markets, and on every product of the cottage industries. Also a source of hardship was the *tarh*, a system by means of which both the peasants and craftsmen were forced to sell goods and farm produce to the treasury at below market prices. The same term was applied to the system whereby merchants and craftsmen were forced to buy, at four to five times the market price, goods and other products which the treasury had received from the peasants and others as payment in kind of their taxes. Special tolls (*bāj*) were also levied on the transport of goods. The greater part of these town taxes eventually fell on the shoulders of the craftsmen, since the big merchants (*urtāq*) traded under the protection of the *khān* and thereby benefited from special exemptions. And like the peasants, the artisans were also subject to the imposition of forced labour for building works, road repairs, etc. Worse still, of course, was the position of those craftsmen who had sunk to the rank of slaves and were employed in the state workshops (*kārkhānè*), the first of which made their appearance in Iran in 1230–40.

The Mongol conquest, therefore, reduced the feudal economy to the even worse form of a slave economy. We know, for example, that the two market gardens of Rashīdu'd-Dīn near Tabrīz employed 1,200 slaves of both sexes, amongst whom were Greeks, Georgians, Abyssinians, and Negroes. The supply of slaves was mainly provided by prisoners of war, but they could also be bought from merchants who obtained them from the Crimea, Russia, the steppes of the Qipchaq, India, Africa, Egypt, and Asia Minor. Moreover, the defaulting debtor or taxpayer could be reduced to slavery. Usury, strongly prohibited under Islamic law, was rife, and served to worsen the situation. All this led to a decline in the country's productivity and a weakening of the economy. As we have seen, by the end of the thirteenth century the treasury was almost empty.

One important aspect of the Mongol conquest is that for the first time Persia and other large areas of the Muslim world found themselves governed, at least from 1221 to 1295, that is to say for three generations, by non-Muslim rulers, pagan shamanists or Buddhists who ignored differences of religious belief among their subjects, who used Christian auxiliaries, and who employed Jewish ministers alongside administrators from the Far East. This humiliation for the Muslim world is paralleled only by the colonial system of government of modern times. However, it has been remarked by some scholars that, despite the terrible devastation that it brought with it, Mongol rule did provide certain virtues, such as the reunification of large areas, safety of travel, the establishment of new trade routes, etc. The fact that the *il-khān* had made their capital in the extreme west of the Iranian plateau, at Tabrīz in Azerbaijān (already Turkicized by the Seljuks, and to-day a Turkish-speaking region), and that the lines of communication which the empire straddled were now open because they were practically all controlled by the Mongols, greatly increased exchanges between the West and the Far East. Persian miniature painting came under the influence of Chinese painting. Persian literature flourished in the hands of such a great writer as Saʿdī (1184–1291), who nevertheless lived in the tiny semi-independent state of the *atabeg* of Fārs, and of the mystic Jalu'd-Dīn Rūmī (1207–73), who likewise lived in vassal state of the Mongols which was not directly governed by them, the Seljuk sultanate of Konya in Asia Minor.

For the Sunnites the annihilation of the Assassins was an act of liberation. At the same time, the destruction of Alamūt itself had important consequences, for, as recent studies have shown, it resulted in Ismaili ideas in a disguised form entering various streams of Islamic thought, particularly Sufi mysticism, and enriching them with gnostic features. Indeed, is appears that many Ismailis, though outwardly defeated, continued to spread a modified form of their propaganda under the cloak of the mystics. Mysticism, which had already made a promising start under the Seljuks, continued to develop at an attitude to life, perhaps even as some kind of consolation for the hard lot to be endured in the tangible world. The accounts by some of the astounded and terrified historians of the Mongol invasion convey a certain sense of the imminent end of the world. In Persia, poetry became inextricably involved with mysticism, and though this gave rise to some of the masterpieces of the literature of the world (such as the *Masnavi-i Ma'navi*, the 'Spiritual Poem' of Jalu'd-Dīn Rūmī), to some extent it contributed to the weakening of the robust human and civil virtues and the vigour of Islam in its early days.

When Hūlāgū reached Persia (after 1251), the number of Mongols of pure blood under his command was about 100,000, but these were soon decimated, especially as a result of his campaigns against Egypt, whose rulers, the Mamlūks (from *mamlūk*, 'slave', for they were former court slaves who had come to power), were the first to withstand the deluge of the Mongol advance. It soon became impossible to maintain control over vast territories and a large population by means of a few foreign troops (either Mongols or Christians from the Caucasus), whose origins and religions were so different from those of the local inhabitants. This was one of the reasons—besides perhaps an actual act of faith—why in 1295 the Buddhist Ghāzān Khān (1295–1304), a descendant of Hūlāgū and son of Arghūn Khān, became a Muslim and took the name of Muhammad, thereby associating himself with the majority of his subjects and at the same time converting his entire army. This was a triumph for the policy of assimilation favoured by part of the Mongol aristocracy. The *il-khān* of Persia also broke the tenuous connection that nominally still attached them to the Great Khān of all the Mongols, now residing in distant China. The contemporary sources reveal Ghāzān Khān as a man of considerable personality. Having mounted the throne at the early age of twenty-four, he showed a knowledge and appreciation of Iranian culture, and a particular interest in medicine and the natural sciences (he even gathered herbs and strange plants when out on his hunting parties). Besides Mongolian, he spoke fairly good Persian and Turkish, and had some knowledge, it appears, of Arabic, Hindi, Kashmiri, Chinese and 'Frankish' (perhaps Latin or French). His basic policy consisted in struggling against the decentralizing tendencies of the traditionally minded Mongol vassals and in reforming the disastrous financial system. This naturally led him to seek the support of the local Muslim officials. One of the most important of his counsellors, who was the inspiration behind a number of his policies, was the famous historian, physician, and encyclopaedist, Rashīdu'd-Dīn Fazlullāh of Hamadān. On gaining the sovereign's favour he brought about the downfall of Sadu'd-Dīn, 'paper support', and for all practical purposes the most important person after the Khān. Through him Persian officials acquired a new authority, while Ghāzān Khān seemed to place less faith in the aristocracy, Persian or Mongol.

The first and most important of Ghāzān's reforms consisted in fixing the *kharāj* (land tax) and *qupchur* (head tax) at definite and unalterable rates. These rates, which varied in the different provinces, were inscribed on iron and stone tablets, which were displayed publicly in every area. Officials or feudal lords who arbitrarily increased the taxes were severely punished. The institution of the *barāt*, the ruinous billeting system, and the head tax on Muslims, were all abolished. Treasury funds were carefully recorded and checked, and no sum could be withdrawn without the khān's written authority. In order to provide for the army, many state lands were granted as *iqtā'* to the soldiers by means of a system of drawing lots, especially in Azerbaijān, not far from the summer and winter pastures of the pastoral warriors. These *iqtā'* could not be sold, and though they were handed down from father to son, in the case of poor service they could be withdrawn, in which case they returned to the state. As well as improving the organization for collecting taxes, Ghāzān Khān strengthened the peasant farmers' attachment to the land. Peasants were strictly forbidden to abandon the lands assigned to them, while at the same time the use of slaves for agricultural work was retained. In order to repopulate and reclaim land that had been abandoned and had become desert, Ghāzān granted special tax concessions to whoever worked it and restored it to productivity. This, together with the numerous grants of *iqtāʿ* to the soldiers, led to an increase in the amount of land in private ownership, which in the long run helped to raise the level of agricultural production. As a zealous Muslim, Ghāzān increased the *vaqf* holdings.

Ghāzān Khān was also determined to put down usury, which had been poisoning the life in the towns and even in the courts of the khāns. He therefore took the radical step of discharging insolvent debtors not only from their liability to pay interest to the usurers, but even from their liability to pay back the original sums borrowed. This measure caused considerable discontent and certain concessions had to be made to the usurers. In many towns the *tamgha* was abolished, while in others it was cut by half. At the same time, a monetary reform abolished the various currencies previously in circulation and established a new system of silver coinage, based on the silver *dirham* weighing 2.15 grams. Six *dirham* made a silver *dīnār*. Ten thousand *dīnār* made a *tūmān* (a Mongolian term for 10,000 which is still used in Iran for 10 reals). A unified system of weights and measures was also introduced. Furthermore, Ghāzān Khān improved the conditions of the slave craftsmen who were employed in the state *kārkhānè* to make arms, saddles, clothes, etc. He embellished his capital of Tabrīz by building, during his lifetime, his own magnificent mausoleum, together with a madrasa and mosque, an observatory, a hospital and other buildings. It is said that Rashīduʾd-Dīn, who as a minister became extraordinarily wealthy, owned an entire quarter of Tabrīz containing 30,000 houses (perhaps an exaggerated figure, or it may just represent the number of rooms or apartments), 24 caravanserais, 1,500 shops, paperworks, dyeworks, and so on. Many of the craftsmen had been brought from other parts of the country. Within ʿRashīdʾs quarter' (*rubʿ-i rashīdī*) there was also a hospital, which employed fifty physicians from India, China, Egypt and Syria, a library containing 60,000 volumes, and a theological school with 6,000–7,000 students. The whole of this wealthy quarter was confiscated after Rashīduʾd-Dīn's downfall and execution (1318) under Abū Saʿīd. Ghāzān Khān's wise reforms helped to replenish the treasury, increasing its funds by about twenty-five per cent from 1,700 *tūmān* to 2,100 *tūmān*. Despite everything, however, agricultural production and living standards failed to reach the levels achieved before the Mongol invasion.

In the middle of the fourteenth century, the Mongol empire broke up, and its Persian territories, partly populated by the remnants of a succession of invasions, had no time in which to achieve political unity, with the result that a number of principalities arose in different parts of the Iranian plateau.

Ghāzān Khān was succeeded by his brother Oljaytu Khudābanda (1304–16), who had been baptized as a child by his Christian mother, and who in general maintained the policies of his predecessor. He was followed by his son Abū Saʿīd (1316–35), who gave a freer reign to the traditionally minded Mongol aristocracy, inimical to the reforms of Ghāzān Khān and particularly to his source of inspiration, Rashīdu'd-Dīn. The feudal lords succeeded in bringing about the latter's downfall, and he was condemned to death and his vast possessions were confiscated. Abū Saʿīd died without issue, and thereafter none of his successors as *il-khān* managed to maintain their rule over Hūlāgū's former empire in its entirety, or even the whole of Persia. Thus, while the Jalā'ir Mongol princes held sway in Iraq (1336–1411), in Persia the areas of Isfahān and Shīrāz, the heart of Persis or Fārs, were governed by the Muzaffarids (1313–93), officials in Mongol service who boasted of their Arab origin. They were continually involved in internal wars, but they were patrons, particularly Shāh Shujāʿ (1358–84), of the great poet Hāfiz. The interesting Shi'ite republic of Sabzavār was ruled for a hundred years by its vigorous rebel chiefs (twelve of them between 1337 and 1381), who were known as *sar-be-dār*, 'with the head in a noose', meaning that they were prepared to go to extremes and risk all. Herāt was governed by the Karts (1245–1384), who were of Ghurid descent and former vassals of the Mongols. These and other principalities were eventually engulfed by the next wave of invaders led by Tamerlane, which brought about a new unification but also once again caused terrible devastation.

Some scholars have laid particular stress on features to be found in the formation of certain of these states which reveal a national revolt or popular liberation movement. Certainly, there were elements of a people's revolt, especially in the case of the republic ruled by the *sarbedārī*, who combined forces with a brotherhood of mystics and Shi'ites founded by *shaikh* Khalīfa (d. 1335) and continued by Hasan Jūrī. Contemporary sources mention the egalitarian and anti-aristocratic tendencies of some of their leaders. But at the same time there were internal struggles between the moderates and the extremists, the latter taking a more religious line and being more closely linked with Khalīfa and Hasan Jūrī's 'order' Indeed, the religious side of the *sarbedārī* movement is particularly interesting, for it offers an example of the ancient connection between certain forms of Shi'ism and Sufism, although the two movements were in theory substantially different (the Sufis believe that anyone can become united in the godhead, while for the Shi'ites only the legitimate *imām* is in a sense a manifestation of the divine). Yet this connection is also to be found in the early development of the much more important Safavid movement, which was later to mark a turning-point that was to have incalculable repercussions on the history of Iran. It is doubtful, however, whether there was any conscious awakening of the mass of the people (one can really only speak of this in the nineteenth century), for the social structure of medieval Persia was such that the genuinely popular features that developed in Western European society at a fairly early stage were unable to make their appearance.

Instead of continuing the logical development of Ghaznavid and Seljuk feudalism, the Mongol invasion shattered this very development by reintroducing and actually reinforcing a pastoral feudalism and slave economy, which had fast been disappearing. It created or strengthened institutions which were foreign to the more ancient Muslim Middle Ages and to Islamic law, such as usury and tying the peasants to the land. This further retarded the emergence of a new social order in Islamic Iran. Though it would be an exaggeration and over-simplification to attribute to the Mongol catastrophe and to the Turco-Mongol invasions in general, Islam's decadence and inability to evolve after its initial auspicious leap forward, there is no doubt that the earlier collaboration and fusion that obtained in Iran after the Arab conquest was culturally much more productive than that in Iran under the Mongols.

CHAPTER VII

Tamerlane and the Timurids

Ghāzān Khān's wise reforms and the improvements in agriculture in Iran once again came to nothing, because of the arrival of new waves of invaders from Central Asia, who also brought with them a feudal social structure based on nomad pastoralism. Tamerlane's rule was reactionary in the etymological sense of the word, for it restored the Mongol type of pastoral nomad aristocracy which had suffered a set-back as a result of Ghāzān Khān's reforms. One of the reasons for the backwardness of Persian agriculture to-day is to be found in this succession of invasions—at fairly short intervals of time—by nomads ignorant of farming methods, who regarded the possession of land as a quick source of plunder, and had no understanding of the technical exploitation of agricultural resources. If these invasions by pastoral tribes had not occurred, Persian agriculture, which was quite flourishing before the arrival of the Mongols, would probably have developed along quite different lines. (Compare the pattern in Western Europe, for example, which never suffered invasions from Central Asia: the barbarian invasions were of a different type, and occurred at a much earlier period in history.) In a general sense, one can say that even in modern Persia there still remains evidence of the apparently illogical and arbitrary effects that are the typical outcome of a pastoral nomad society and culture, to which, moreover, the country is subject on account of its climate and geographical position.

Tīmūr (Turk. 'iron') was the name given to one of the sons of the Turkish governor of Kish (modern Shahr-i Sabz, 'Green City'), south of Samarkand, situated in one of the small states, theoretically dependencies of the Mongol *khān*, which arose when the empire of Chīngīz Khān broke up. Later, on account of a wound about which the chroniclers disagree (those hostile to the conqueror claim that he received it while sheep-stealing), he was called *lang*, meaning 'lame'. This gave rise to Tīmūr-lang, from which we derive the name Tamerlane. After various romantic exploits which reveal him as a born warrior and adventurer, he became lord of the city of Balkh at the age of thirty-four (1369). The next ten years he spent in extending and strengthening his authority over Transoxiana and Khārizm, until in 1380 he set out on his campaign against Persia. Though the Timurid conquest led to the restoration of traditional nomal feudalism, nevertheless Tamerlane's policies also included certain new features which had been unknown to the *il-khān*. Most important, for example, was his policy of enriching Transoxiana, his country of origin. His depredations of the countries he conquered served to construct irrigation works, to embellish cities and built new ones—but all in Transoxiana. His determined decision to conquer Iran, Arab Iraq, Transcaucasia, and Asia Minor was largely based on his plan to control the caravan routes linking Asia and Europe. The more northerly ones running across the steppes near the Black Sea and the Caspian which he was unable to control, he tried in every way to close. This explains his destruction of cities such as Urgench, Saray, Berke, Astrakhan, Azov, and others which lay along the northern route.

In the spring of 1381, Tīmūr entered Khorāsān and subdued the Karts of Herāt. Due to their continuing state of civil war, the *sarbedārī* also in the end became his vassals. When they rose in revolt at Sabzavār at the end of October 1383, the city, together with its well-fortified castle, was destroyed; two thousand men were buried alive in the walls of the new fortresses that Tamerlane built, and many others perished under appalling torture. In the same year Sīstān and Qandahār were conquered; even to-day the ruins of the cities of Sīstān, which lie in land that was once fertile but that is now uninhabited because the canals from the river Helmand were destroyed, bear eloquent witness to the passage of Tamerlane. Everywhere pyramids of corpses and human heads were raised, visible signs of the conqueror's anger. In 1384, Tīmūr overran Gurgān, and in the following year he subdued northern Iran from Dāmghān to Sultāniyè. The Jalā'ir state, torn by internal struggles, was unable to resist Tīmūr, particularly as Tokhtamish, the *khān* of the Golden Horde, fearing Tamerlane's advance into Iran, had laid it waste in 1385, ravaging Tabrīz and carrying off to his own country rich booty and 90,000 prisoners, including the famous poet Kamāl from Khujand. In 1386, Tīmūr reoccupied the devastated city of Tabrīz, put an end to the Jalā'ir state, and despatched the finest craftsmen to Samarkand. By 1387 he was already in Georgia, and wherever he went he destroyed and massacred on a scale that can only be compared with that of the Mongols of Chīngiz Khān.

A rebellion by Shāh Mansūr, the last of the Muzaffarids of Fārs, quickly brought Tamerlane to central and southern Persia. Isfahān surrendered, but the garrison of 3,000 men which Tamerlane left there was shortly afterwards massacred by the inhabitants. In his rage Tīmūr spared only the Muslim *ulema* and the men of learning: 70,000 human heads were piled up to form 120 tall pyramids outside the city walls. Shāh Mansūr himself was finally defeated and killed near Shīrāz in 1393, following a second revolt. According to Persian literary tradition, it was at about this time that Tamerlane met Hāfiz, the great poet of Shīrāz, and one of the greatest in the whole of Persia, but the story is almost certainly apocryphal. In the first verse of one of his famous odes (*ghazal*), Hāfiz had said: 'If that beautiful Turk of Shīrāz were to take my heart in his hand, I would give Samarkand and Bukhārā for his black beauty-spot.' During his tempestuous stay in Shīrāz, Tamerlane, therefore, is supposed to have desired to meet the poet who had so despised his two principal cities. On seeing Hāfiz standing before him, somewhat shabbily dressed, he exclaimed: 'I have conquered half the world with my illustrious sword in order to embellish my native cities and the seats of my government, Samarkand and Bukhārā, and yet thou, craven wretch, would give them away for the beauty-spot of a Shīrāz Turk.' 'Sire,' replied the poet, 'it is on account of my excessive generosity that I find myself reduced to my present state.' And besides being pardoned, it is said that he even received a gift.

After shattering the power of the Mongol Golden Horde in the West (he even reached Moscow, which he devastated), Tamerlane turned his eyes on India, and in 1398, when he was over sixty years old, he entered Delhi. Then he returned like lightning to his western territories in order to put down a revolt of the Jalā'irs and to punish his own faithless son Mīrān Shāh, who had sought refuge with the Ottoman ruler, Bāyazīd. In 1401, he reconquered Baghdād (making pyramids of 90,000 heads), seized Syria, marched against the Ottomans, laying waste their capital city of Brusa, and taking the sultan prisoner (1402), and then returned to Samarkand. When he died in 1405 at the age of seventy, he was still full of youthful vigour and was making plans for the conquest of China.

Tamerlane's death was followed by four years of chaos, with wars of succession between sons and nephews. Eventually one of the sons, Shāh-rukh (the name means 'to castle', because Tamerlane, a keen chess-player, received the news of his birth as he was about to make this move), gained the upper hand, and his reign brought some peace. He is described by the historians as being a man of peace, a generous prince, a poet, artist, and scholar. On his death (1447) a rapid decline set in. Ulugh Beg, the son called on to succeed him, was fifty-four, and had devoted his entire life to study. He was a man of letters, an artist, and above all an astronomer of note, who in 1421 had built a celebrated observatory at Samarkand, where he and other Persian, Turkish and Arab scholars had compiled a famous set of astronomical tables. He was less successful in the civil wars which ensued on his succession. the state broke up into various small princedoms which, in Persia, were able to offer only the meagrest resistance to the forces of the Safavids, while in Transoxiana the Timurids were reduced to controlling the country surrounding Bukhārā and Samarkand. By the end of the fifteenth century they had been supplanted in Persia by the Safavids, and in Transoxiana by the Shaibanid Uzbeks.

A number of the Timurid princes of the period of decadence are important in the cultural history of Persia. Bāisunqur, one of Shāh-rukh's sons who was governor of Astarābād and died in 1433, is regarded by some as one of the world's greatest bibliophiles. He also initiated one of the most elegant styles of Persian calligraphy and miniature painting. Abū Sa'īd (not to be confused with the Mongol Abū Sa'īd mentioned earlier), who was a grandson of Tamerlane's rebellious son Mīrān Shāh, ruled in Central Asia and eastern Persia, and was killed in 1468 by the Turkomans of Uzun Hasan's 'White Sheep' Turkomans, was a patron of scholars, theologians, and men of letters. He is the 'Busech' referred to in the interesting accounts of the Venetian ambassadors who visited Uzun Hasan's court. Even more important from the literary point of view is Sultān Husain Bāiqarā (1469–1506), who held a brilliant court at Herāt and was the patron of the Persian poet Jāmī. His minister was the famous Mīr 'Alī Shīr Navā'ī (d. 1501), who was a patron of poets and himself a poet and man of letters, especially in Chaghatai or Uzbek, the Turkish language of central Asia which he tried to raise to the same literary level as Persian. The Turks of Uzbekistan to-day regard him as the great founder of their national literature, but to us his *Muhākamat al-lughatain*, 'Contest of the Two Languages', appears little more than an elegant literary diatribe, and his Turkish poetry a graceful stylistic experiment within the traditions of Islamic culture. One should not forget that Babur, who conquered India and founded the dynasty of the Great Moguls, was a Timurid, and also wrote excellently in both Turkish and Persian.

With regard to the Timurid dynasty, we cannot do better than quote what Minorsky has to say in his brief but perspicacious essay on Persian cultural history entitled 'Iran: Opposition, Martyrdom and Revolt' in *Unity and Variety in Muslim Civilization*, edited by Gustave E. von Grunebaum (Chicago, 1955, pp. 193–3):

'The conquest of Tīmūr swept away the principalities which had been formed on the debris of the Mongol empire. The conqueror himself was a follower of the Sunna, but to the rigor of his doctrines he added an extreme veneration for the saints and shaikhs supposed to possess supernatural powers. Even more curious among his beliefs were survivals of certain superstitions which he had inherited from his pagan Turkish ancestors. Tīmūr left Persia disorganized and stripped of its artisans, scholars, and artists, whom he had carried off to Central Asia . . .

'In spite of the triumph of the Sunna, even in the time of Tīmūr, Fadl Allāh Astarābādī (1339–93) founded the new secret sect of the Ḥurūfīs. The outward characteristic of his doctrines was the use of the numerical values of words, but

apart from this cabalism the Ḥurūfī books which have survived reveal little about their actual mysteries. Tīmūr's son,
Mīrān Shāh, executed Faḍl Allāh in 1393, and his lieutenants
emigrated to Turkey, where they grafted their doctrines
upon those of the Bektāshī order. Even in the east the clandes-
tine propaganda continued. The instigators of the attempt
on the life of Shāh-rukh in 1427 were accused of Ḥurūfism. If
it was not merely a pretext for the accusation, one might
conclude from it that behind the abstruse theories there was
hidden some political idea which took no account of the pre-
rogatives of the very pious Sunnite king.' Despite the very great
importance of the Timurid period in the history of the figurative
arts in Persia (the name of the miniature painter Bihzād,
who was born sometime after 1455 and died in 1533, is known
throughout the world), in the field of literature it was an age
of refined weariness, a silver age *par excellence*. The principal
cultural centres were Herāt and Tabrīz.

The various periods of Persian history, especially from the
Mongol invasion onwards, appear to follow the same cyclic
course: the conquest of all or at least a large part of the country
by someone of exceptional personality; a period of apparent
prosperity after the initial terror; a flourishing regeneration of
the decorative arts and handicrafts; and the final break-up
of the state once more, with a number of areas producing their
own magnificent styles of decorative art. Despite the attempts
of many scholars, particularly those subscribing to a Marxist
interpretation of history, to discover a group of events which
would demonstrate the existence of a continuous line of
development, from the Mongol conquest up to the middle of
the nineteenth century, the state of the forces of production
and the condition of Persian society remained almost unchanged, and at the stage of the early Middle Ages. The
historian is therefore obliged to discuss, and even perhaps
overrate, situations which are no more than simple variations
on a theme.

During the second half of the fifteenth century, Persia was
once again subject to Turkish rulers, though this time they
came from the west. (Apart from a few brief intervals, throughout the period from AD 1000 to 1925 it was Persia's fate to be
ruled by successive Turkish dynasties.) From this time onwards,

Khorāsān plays an ever less important part in Persian history, which is now more and more affected by events in Azerbaijān. The Safavids themselves had their spiritual roots firmly fixed in the west. The Mongols had driven some of the Ghuzz tribes out of the Seljuk empire towards Armenia, Syria and Asia Minor, and now these Turkomans (a word whose etymology is still uncertain) tried to fill the vacuum produced by the debility of Tamerlane's descendants and their continual civil wars. The two Turkoman dynasties were known as the Qara-qoyunlu, 'those of the Black Sheep', and the Aq-qoyunlu, 'those of the White Sheep', the names being taken from their tribal insignia. The Qara-qoyunlu, who had seized Tabrīz from the Timurids in 1406 and made it their headquarters in Persia, had in some mysterious way become indoctrinated with Shi'ite beliefs, some of them in an extreme form.

Though initially a vassal of Shāh-rukh, the Qara-qoyunlu Jahān-shāh (1434–67) set out on a campaign of conquest which soon made him master of Persia from Herāt in the east to beyond Baghdād in the west, as well as of the whole of Iraq. He built the *Gök Masjid*, the Blue Mosque, whose remains are still one of the most beautiful monuments in Tabrīz. The Qara-qoyunlu dynasty was brought to an end by the Aq-qoyunlu Uzun Hasan, 'Hasan the Long', who killed Jahān-shāh in battle, and defeated his son, together with his ally Abū Sa'īd. Uzun Hasan, who now ruled Persia, Iraq, Azerbaijān, and Armenia from his capital of Tabrīz, was happy to receive embassies from all those who opposed his western neighbours and natural enemies, the Ottomans. The Venetians in particular have left us colourful accounts of their travels in Persia at this time. They called Uzun Hasan Ussun Cassano or Assambei (Hasan Bey), and, forgetting, understandably, his Turkish origins, compared the splendour of his court with that of the empire of Darius and Xerxes. From this period dates the traditional enmity between the Ottoman Turks and the Persian upper classes (themselves of Turkish origin), due not so much to racial as to the general political, social, and geographical differences, while under the Safavids religious differences also intervened.

With the death of Uzun Hasan (1478), the Aq-qoyunlu dynasty began to decline. During the reign of Uzun Hasan's son

Ya'qūb, the Safavid family of Ardabīl, in modern Azerbaijān extended their political power, and one of them, Ismā'īl, was to bring Aq-qoyunlu rule to an end and found the Safavid dynasty in Persia. In Minorsky's opinion, it was now that there arose the sect or religion of the *Ahl-i Haqq*, 'People of the Truth', also known as 'Alī-allāhī, who are still to be found scattered in small groups throughout Persia. They had some connection, though what it was is not clear, with the Safavid dynasty-cum-sect-cum-brotherhood. Their members, who are nowadays drawn from the lower strata of the community—nomads, petty traders, goatherds, and servants—should not be confused with other extremist Shi'ite communities, with their exaggerated adoration of the fourth caliph, 'Alī, and his descendants. The *Ahl-i Haqq* believe in seven cycles of divine manifestation, of which 'Alī presides over the second, while the truth was completely revealed only in the fourth cycle, that of Sultān Ishāq, who laid down both rites and dogma. In any case, the origins of this sect are to be sought in the west, among the Druses, Nusayris, and popular anti-Ottoman movements in Turkey.

Under the Timurids the feudal economy attained its maximum development. Of particular interest is the evolution of the *iqtā'* system, which becomes transformed into the *soyurgal* (Mongolian 'bestowal', 'donation'), first recorded in the mid-fourteenth century. *Soyurgal* lands were to be found both in the Jalā'īr, Qara-qoyunlu, and Aq-qoyunlu states in the west of Iran, and in the Timurid principalities in the east. The *soyurgal* was a hereditary concession of land granted by the sultan or ruler to one of his vassals, and could vary in extent from a single village to an entire province. The recipient of the *soyurgal* (*sāhib-i soyurgal*) was obliged to serve his lord in a military capacity and to provide a certain number of armed horsemen from among his dependants. The essential difference between the *soyurgal* and *iqtā'* was that, besides the tax exemptions enjoyed by the holders of *iqtā'*, the hereditary owners of *soyurgal* were also immune from legal proceedings and independent of the central government. For all the officials within the territory of the *soyurgal* were appointed by the beneficiary himself and were entirely dependent on him, while government officials were expressly forbidden to enter *soyurgal* lands. This is clearly stated in the formal letters granting the concession with the Persian phrase *qalam va qadam kūtāh va kashīdè dārand va pīrāmūn na-gardand*, 'that they may restrain and withdraw their foot and quill and not rove around', that is to say, they are not to have any business communication with the holder of the *soyurgal*, nor are they to set foot in his territory. This immunity from government officials made the proprietor of the *soyurgal* absolute master in judicial and military matters, while his exemption from the payment of taxes meant that he collected for his own benefit all the tribute of his subjects (*ra'īyat*) that had previously gone into the coffers of the central treasury. When the *soyurgal* consisted of an entire province, the feudatory also had the right to distribute part of his lands in the form of *soyurgal* to his own vassals. The owners of large *soyurgal* had their own private armies and bodies of officials. *Soyurgal* were granted to the warrior aristocracy and the ecclesiastical hierarchy. (In theory, Islam has no clergy, since there are no mysteries nor sacraments, but only a body of doctors of the law, who in practice, however, as this example goes to show, held a position in society very similar to that of our own medieval clergy.)

The other forms of feudal landownership remained more or less the same as in the preceding period. But the amount of land held by the state continued to decrease, while the *mulk* (hereditary freehold land) and the *vaqf* (pious foundations) underwent an important change in that many *mulk* enjoyed tax exemption (*mulk-i hurr*, 'free possession'), and this was subsequently granted to the *vaqf* as well. Ownership of the land continued to be concentrated in the hands of those who possessed huge estates. The amir Bābā Hājjī Qavardī, for example, received in *soyurgal* from the Qara-qoyunlu Qara Yūsuf six hundred villages, large and small. The same ruler granted another amir, Shamsu'd-Dīn, chief of the nomadic Rūzaki, a Kurd tribe, four vast districts in southern Armenia in *soyurgal*. The *iqtā'* lands (by now the term is synonymous with *soyurgal*) held by the Timurid prince Bāisunqur in various parts of Gurgān, Khorāsān, Persian Iraq, and Fārs, were valued at 600 *tūmān*, or six million silver *dīnār*, each *dīnar* containing two *misqāl*, or 9 grams, of silver. The *vaqf* possessions of the Mansūriyyè madrasa in Shīrāz, which was exempted from the payment of taxes, consisted of 50 villages in Fārs with an annual income of 242,000 *dīnār*. The famous Persian poet 'Abdur-rahmān Jāmī, who was under the protection of the Timurid Sultan Husain of Herāt, owned such large estates in the Herāt area that he was able to disburse 100,000 *dīnār* a year for his 'ordinary expenses'. The political influence of the great feudal lords was measured not only by the extent of their lands and the size of their income, but also by the number of their *noukar* (at this period the term means 'vassals' rather than servants), for the most part small landholders who could be called on to render military service. By the end of the fifteenth century, the most powerful vassal of the Timurid Sultān Husain Bāiqarā of Herāt was the Amir Khusrau, who held in *soyurgal* the territory stretching from the Amu Darya to the Hindu Kush.

The widespread bestowal of administrative immunity and tax exemption throughout the Timurid and Aq-qoyunlu states during the fifteenth century considerably weakened the central government, which thereby lost a large part of its income to the great feudal lords, along with judicial and military authority. Moreover, the distribution of these concessions was only theoretically in the keeping of the sultans themselves: in reality they were forced to satisfy the claims and demands of the feudal lords. During this period there arose the *tarkhān*, vassals both large and small who enjoyed not only immunity but also various personal privileges, such as a preferential share of the spoils of war, and dispensation from legal responsibility for a certain number of future crimes (usually up to nine). At the beginning of the sixteenth century, the Timurid prince Babur, who conquered India, decided to dismiss from his service a *tarkhān* with whom he was displeased, but he was met with the response, 'Until such time as I have committed nine misdemeanours, no one can punish me!'. Thereupon Babur enumerated, one by one, not nine but eleven offences which he had committed, but allowed him to emigrate to India with his family and possessions.

As before, the community was divided into four basic groups: the aristocracy of the pastoral nomads, Mongols, Turks and Kurds, who were referred to in general as *ahl-i shamshīr*, 'people of the sword'; the sedentary provincial aristocracy, which was not involved in government service; the senior members of the Muslim hierarchy; and the civil servants, *ahl-i qalam*, 'people of the pen'. The majority of the members of the last three groups were of Iranian stock. As before, everything was paid for by the peasants. Letters patent granting feudal concessions list in one case twenty-seven, in another thirty-one, and in a third sixteen different forms of tax and service which the peasants were bound to pay to their feudal lord.

CHAPTER VIII

The Safavids

At the turn of the sixteenth century, Iran was in part governed by various Aq-qoyunlu rulers. Prince Alvand held sway in Azerbaijān and Armenia, while Sultān Murād ruled over Persian Iraq. In Fārs, Yazd, Kirmān, Arabian Iraq, and Diyarbekir, there were other Aq-qoyunlu princes, who were independent of Sultān Murād. Khūzistān was governed by the Shi'ite Arab dynasty of the Musha'sha'. Abarkūh, Kāshān, Semnān and Sīstān all had local rulers, while Māzandarān was divided up between nearly a dozen princelings. In Gīlān there were two amirates or khānates, Lāhijān and Rasht, and Talish also formed an independent khānate. In the east, Khorāsān, including roughly present-day Afghanistan and southern Turkestan, was governed by the Timurid Sultān Husain Bāiqarā (1469–1506) from Herāt, while Balkh and Qandahār were ruled by local prices independent of Herāt. Nearly all of these 'states' then had their vassals who were governors of whole provinces. The main enemies of the Aq-qoyunlu and Timurids were respectively the Ottoman Turks in the west and the nomadic Uzbeks in the east, whose leader Muhammad Khān Shaibānī relieved the Timurids of their Central Asian possessions in 1499–1500.

The Safavids were a Turkish-speaking dynasty-cum-mystical brotherhood, whose doctrines were in many ways similar to those of the *ahl-i haqq* and the Shi'ite extremists of some of the Turkoman tribes of Asia Minor. They succeeded in imposing on the Persians by force a moderate form of Shi'ism, known as the Twelver, whose texts were mainly written in Arabic. In order to disseminate their beliefs throughout Persia, the Safavid rulers imported preachers from northern Arabia and Syria. Nevertheless, even to-day many modern Persians and European scholars seem to regard this period—one of the most arid from the point of view of Persian literature—as one in which there was a revival of feelings of nationhood and of the existence of an Iranian race. This is a paradox which can only be understood after a study of Persia's foreign relations during the period.

According to tradition, Ismāʻīl, the Safavid conqueror of Persia, was a sixth-generation descendant of Shaikh Ishāq Safīuddīn, who was believed by his followers to be descended from the seventh Shiʻite *imām* Mūsā al-Kāzim. Recent studies, however, have shown that the Safavids' claim to Arab descent was false: it appears, from what little can be discovered, that they were of Kurdish stock, and therefore in a sense Iranian. There is no doubt, however, that they spoke a Turkish dialect of Azerbaijān. Safīuddīn, who had an extraordinary reputation for piety and sanctity, and who died in his native city of Ardabīl in 1334, was head of a *tarīqa* or mystical brotherhood, which was named Safavid (Pers. *safavī*) after him, and whose leadership was handed down to his descendants. Shaikh Safī was a Sunnite: the legend about descent from the Caliph ʻAlī was used by his successors to attract the support of the Shiʻites. Shiʻism was particularly widespread among the peasants and the artisans in the towns, and Khwāja ʻAlī, who was head of the brotherhood from 1392 to 1427, had Shiʻite leanings. In due course, the Safavids became feudal lords of the city of Ardabīl and its surrounding province. Khwāja ʻAlī, however, was still regarded as a holy man in such fiercely anti-Safavid and anti-Shiʻite works as the *Taʼrīkh-i ʻālam-ārāy-i amīnī* of Fazlullāh ibn Rūzbihān Khunjī (see Bibliography), which maintains that the person who 'changed the way of life of his ancestors' was in fact Shaikh Junaid, who ruled over the brotherhood from 1447 to 1456. He organized the community on a military basis, and in addition he made his 'followers in Rūm' (Anatolia) refer to him as 'god'. This is a particularly interesting statement, for it confirms the popular origins in Anatolia of the Safavid religion, and at the same time it refers the source of Shāh Ismāʻīl's singular ideas to the period that preceded him. Shāh Ismāʻīl has left an important collection of poems in Turkish, in some of which he clearly refers to himself as 'god'. These highflown, semi-mystical, semi-martial verses were intended to be sung as hymns by his followers. Members of the brotherhood were known as 'red heads' (Turkish *qizil-bāsh*) on account of a red twelve-pointed cap, representing the twelve Shi'ite *imāms*, which they had begun to wear in the time of Shaikh Haidar (1456–88), son of Junaid and father of Shāh Ismā'īl.

In the fifteenth century, the brotherhood received its main military support from the tribes of Turkish nomads in Azerbaijān. (Traditionally, there were seven of these tribes, Shamlu, Rumlu, Ustajlu, Tekelü, Afshar, Qājār, and Zulqadar, but in fact there were many more.) The *qizilbāsh* shaved their beards but let their moustaches grow to a great length (this can be seen in some of the portraits of Shāh 'Abbās the Great, who still followed this custom), and shaved their heads, leaving only a single tuft of hair. It was during this period, and particularly in the reign of Shaikh Junaid, that the peaceful *tarīqa* of the Safavid dervishes developed into a sort of religious military order, which some scholars have compared with the Order of the Templars. There are a number of differences, however, one of the most important of which is the pastoral and nomadic origin of the *qizilbāsh* aristocracy.

Shāh Ismā'īl was only fourteen years old when, in 1499, he took over the leadership of the *qizilbāsh* order. In 1500–1, he defeated the *shīrvānshāh* Farrukh Yasār and ravaged Shīrvān, near the modern Baku, routed the Aq-qoyunlu Alvand, seized southern Azerbaijān, and occupied Tabrīz, which he made his capital and where he took the significant title of *shāhinshāh-i Īrān* (1501). Having defeated the army of Sultān Murād, the other Aq-qoyunlu ruler, near Hamadān, and put him to flight, he conquered the whole of Persian Iraq. In 1503, the *qizilbāsh* overran Semnān and Fārs, with its capital of Shīrāz, and in 1504 Yazd fell to them. Between 1502 and 1509, the rulers of Khūzistān, Kurdistān, Gīlān, Māzandarān, and practically the whole of western Iran, surrendered. The Timurid Sultan Husain of Herāt attempted to come to terms with Shāh Ismā'īl, but without success, and after his death a large part of his kingdom was conquered by the Uzbek Muhammad Khān Shaibānī (1507). The *qizilbāsh* therefore inherited from the Timurids a new enemy—the Uzbek Shaibanids. It was Muhammad Khān's intention to conquer the whole of Iran, and this naturally led to a struggle between the two opposing powers. The decisive battle took place in

1510 near Merv, and resulted in the defeat of the Shaibanids and the death of Muhammad Khān himself. Khorāsān, apart from the area round Balkh, fell into the hands of the *qizilbāsh*. But their attempts to conquer the whole of Central Asia, however, failed before Uzbek resistance.

Religion played an important part in this struggle. The Uzbek Shaibanids, like the Safavids' enemies in the west, the Ottomans, were Sunnites, though all three groups were of Turkish origin. The Ottomans were particularly concerned at the rise of the Shi'ite Shāh Ismā'īl, because they feared that it could, under cover of religion, lead to the outbreak of revolts among the Shi'ite subjects of the Ottoman empire. (According to the estimate, which is certainly exaggerated, contained in a Venetian document, four-fifths of the population of Asia Minor at this time were Shi'ites and held strong pro-Safavid sympathies.) The Ottoman sultan Selim the Grim (1512–20), reversed the weak policy of his predecessor Bayazid II, and had some 40,000 Shi'ites who lived within his frontiers, massacred on the grounds that they were Safavid spies. On 23 August 1514, the Ottoman army inflicted a severe defeat on Shāh Ismā'īl at the celebrated battle of Chaldiran in southern Azerbaijān, after which it is said that Ismā'īl never again smiled for the rest of his life. (The Ottomans had the advantage of excellent artillery: firearms had first appeared in Iran around 1387 where they were known as *radd-andaz*, 'give-a-push', and at the end of the fifteenth century a few very primitive cannon were being produced at Herāt.) Because of affairs at home, Selim was unable to take full advantage of his victory, and returned to Turkey, leaving the Safavids still masters of southern Azerbaijān and Arabian Iraq. Safavid rule was also retained over the territories of Transcaucasia, and in 1517 Shāh Ismā'īl subdued eastern Georgia. His death in 1524 was followed by a long period of turmoil. His ten-year-old son Tahmāsp I succeeded him, and ruled for fifty-two years but lost territory on his eastern and western frontiers, and when he died, civil war broke out. The succession was practically decided by the *qizilbāsh*, that is to say, Turkish troops faithful to the brotherhood, who sided now with one Safavid prince now with another.

With the arrival of the Safavids, Iran began to become a

Shi'ite state, and thus to distinguish herself from the surrounding countries which are all to-day officially Sunnite, even though they include—particularly Iraq—Shi'ite minorities. Recent studies, however, have shown that it is unreasonable to make too strict a division between the beliefs of the Sunnites, the moderate Twelver Shi'ites, and the Sufis. As Molé has shown, the documents relating to the early period during which Iran began to adopt Shi'ite beliefs, are difficult to define in a precise way. Nevertheless, there is no doubt that the peasant movements, which regularly erupted during the long period of Iran's history before the Safavids, were to some extent coloured by Shi'ite thought, while it is well known that craft guilds in the towns had Shi'ite leanings. However, it is a fact that when the Safavids arrived the majority of the Persian population was Sunnite, and the change to Shi'ism was a conscious and deliberate policy carried out by the Safavids themselves. As soon as Shāh Ismā 'īl had conquered Tabrīz in 1501, he issued a decree that, 'in the public places the people should loosen their tongues in order to curse and execrate Abū Bakr, Omar, and 'Uthmān: whoever should dare to oppose this shall have his head cut off'. It is very probable that these orders were only servilely respected, and that in the early days the Shi'ite following was fairly superficial. The effective conversion of the mass of the Persian people to Shi'ism must have taken place much later than is suggested by some of the sources, which are generally concerned only with the outward and visible signs, and probably occurred in the eighteenth century. Religious unity—even if imposed under duress—turned the Persian population into an actual 'people' in the only way possible at the time, by uniting them under common religious laws and dogmas which effectively isolated them from their neighbours. It was through the acquisition of this unity provided by the Shi'ite religion, and not due to any ancient racial characteristics, that there arose that extraordinary sense of self-sufficiency, of nationalistic aloofness, which distinguishes the Persians even to-day in their relations with their neighbours, and which has also led to their regarding themselves as Aryan, as more 'European' than the surrounding Arabs, Turks and Indians. With the creation of a compact body of Shi'ites in Persia, for the first time in the history of Islam, Shi'ism, previously merely an ever-present source of fairly extremist and heretical religious ideas which had seldom, and then only briefly, been accepted as a basis of government, found itself organized as a political entity. In a way that had never happened before (for the *shī'a/sunna* division had not been a geographical one, but was founded on groups, centres, classes), the unity of the political world of Islam had been shattered. Before the Safavid period, Shi'ism had verges towards extremism on the one hand, and Sufism on the other, or simply towards a form of pro-'Alī Sunnism, which is traditionally the most orthodox.

From the point of view of the Persian nation, in which the Aryan element is only one of many, it can be said that the resulting isolation was what really saved the Persians. The state founded by Ismā'īl was a theocracy, which Minorsky has exaggeratedly compared with the Tibetan government of the Dalai Lhama. It was held together by a religion and by a single party—that of the *qizilbāsh*. The sources speak of disputes among the followers of the Shāh, who was also the superior of the brotherhood, and these were resolved on appeal to the sovereign's infallible authority. Some of the documents, however, and this is a point of great interest, remark on the ignorance of theology—even of the theology of the Shi'ite Twelvers which was to become official—of the early Safavid shaikhs and kings. The *qizilbāsh* Hasan Rūmlū confesses that the only guide on questions of the Shi'ite religion available to the followers of Shāh Ismā'īl in 1501 was an incomplete copy of a work by al-Hillī (d. 1326), which a cadi of Tabrīz happened to possess! In the initial stages, therefore, there was simply a desire for Shi'ism, and an enthusiastic faith, half religious, half militant, in a semi-divine leader. Theology, drawn from ancient treatises and taught by Arab theologians, came later. However, though these teachers reintroduced the less exuberant orthodoxy of Twelvist Shi'ism and proclamations of divinity such as that made by the founder were no longer possible, the fact remains that the people became accustomed to regarding the *shāh* as a holy person, the descendant of the venerated *imāms* to whom religious obedience was due. From this time, too, dates that particular regard for monarchy which is so much stronger in Iran to-day than in the other

Islamic countries. Without all this, Persia would perhaps have been once more invaded, and submerged beneath the ever-stronger waves of Ottoman Turks from the west, Uzbeks in the east, and probably reduced to the condition of the former Iranian lands in Central Asia, where Turkish languages predominate. The new doctrine, which had no philosophical connection whatever with the Persians as a people or a nation, nevertheless provided a platform from which they were able to defend themselves from losing their identity in an all-absorbing Islam, and in particular, since the nearest representatives of Muslim Sunnism were the Turks, from being engulfed in the Turkish ocean. But the Persians became aware of all this only much later, probably in the Qājār period. The claim that contemporary Iranian nationalism goes back to the ancient pre-Islamic past must be rejected. What we have in fact is a Persian variation—though with many highly typical Persian features—of Islamic culture whose origins date from the Safavid period, which is therefore of fundamental importance in the history of Iran. Moreover, it is well known that the Safavids encouraged their poets to write above all on religious subjects, to weep over the tragic fate of the ancient martyrs of the Prophet's family, particularly revered by the Shi'ites, or to study the new Shi'ite theology from Arabic treatises, and in this way made only the slightest contribution to one of the most important aspects of any genuine national renaissance—literature. Indeed, as Edward G. Browne discovered to his unjustified amazement, from a literary point of view the Safavid period is very poor. The true renaissance, within certain limits, occurs later, under the Qājār dynasty. Yet besides these theological treatises, the Safavid period saw the flowering of a new popular and semi-popular religious poetry, which is unfairly despised by the Europeanized Persian nationalists of to-day. This consists of poems written in stanzas, often vigorously expressed in honour of the Shi'ite martyrs, sacred plays similar to our medieval mystery-plays, and written by people who had a rudimentary learning only and used a form of language that was more crude but often more original and immediate than the classical style, together with poems in praise of the saints. This lesser stream of semi-popular literature, drawing perhaps unconsciously on the secret traditions of the people, flourished under the Safavid sovereigns.

Up to the time of Shāh 'Abbās the Great, however, the Safavids failed to introduce any innovations in the economy or the agricultural condition of the country. The four groups of the aristocracy remained, the first, that of the pastoral nomads, strengthened by the *qizilbāsh*, and the last, that of the government officials, enlarged to meet the needs of the increased centralization of the government. At the same time there arose a new Shi'ite rank among the clergy, that of the *ahl al-'amā'im* or 'turbaned ones'. The chiefs of the nomad tribes (*mīr-i īl*) were often also the hereditary feudal lords of the lands (and of the peasants working them) around their tribal grazing grounds. The lands which the king had granted to the tribal chiefs were known sometimes as *yurt* (a Mongol word meaning 'tent'), sometimes as *ojaqlïq* (a Turkish term, from *ojaq*, 'hearth'), and sometimes as *jā-u-maqām* (Arabo-Persian 'place'). In 1553, Shāh Tahmāsp I granted Khalīl Khān, chief of the Kurdish tribe of the Siyāh Mansūr, the district of Abhar, Zanjān and Sultāniyyè, on the understanding that three thousand of his warriors would enter the royal army. Besides the cultivated land and its peasants, the *yurt* included the usual summer pastures (*yailāq*) in the mountains, and the winter pastures (*qishlāq*) in the valleys, and were granted in theory to the tribe as a whole (*īl*, plur. *īlāt*), but in practice to the chief himself. Other lands consisted of *dīvānī* (state lands), *khāssè* (lands belonging to the royal family), *mulk* (private property), *vaqf* (pious foundations), and *soyurgal* (hereditary feudal land). Naturally, as always happens after a country has been overrun, there were many changes among the landowners and their assignees (in this case, the *qizilbāsh*), and in the distribution of the land between the different forms of ownership. Due to the tendency to centralization of the Safavid monarchy, the state lands (*dīvānī*), the royal lands (*khāssè*), and the *yurt* of the *qizilbāsh* were extended at the expense of the *mulk* and *soyurgal*. Indeed, the Safavid sovereigns avoided granting further *soyurgal*, though they continued to recognize many of those already in existence. Instead, they began to distribute among the aristocracy and government officials a new kind of feudal benefit, the *tuyūl*, admittedly first mentioned by Abd ar-Razzāq Samarqandī, a fifteenth-century writer, but particularly widespread in the sixteenth century. The *tuyūl* consisted in the grant of an interest (which could be 100%) in the revenue of certain feudal lands. Some *tuyūl* were attached to a particular position or office, and were enjoyed by the assignee during the entire period in which he held such office. Others were granted as a reward for personal services rendered, and were enjoyed by the holder for life, but were not hereditary. In no case was there any question of administrative exemptions or concessions. In other words, institution of the *tuyūl* was an attempt on the part of the central government to restore the system of the *iqtā'* to its original form as a temporal benefit. The *tuyūl* were granted on the *dīvānī* or state lands.

All local rulers, including the chiefs of the nomad tribes as well as the old Iranian rulers, were considered to be *hākim* (governors), that is, officers of the state appointed and dismissed at the will of the *shāh*. The chiefs of the nomad tribes bore the title *khān* or *sultān* (during the Safavid period the title of *khān* was regarded as higher than that of *sultān*), and both were also referred to as amir. The local sovereigns on settled land had the title of *malik* (king). Some of the *malik* came under the authority of royal governors, the *beglerbeg*, while others, such as the rulers of Luristān, Kurdistān, and Arabistān, were directly responsible to the *shāh* and were known as *valī*. The condition of the nomads (*īlāt*), who formed the backbone of the feudal army, was considerably better than that of the peasants (*ra'iyat*), who suffered from the usual impositions of a feudal economy. Once again, Iran was being governed along the lines of pastoral nomadic feudalism.

Discontent among the *qizilbāsh* and particularly the *lālā* (tutors) of the various princes led to disorder and civil war. There was a serious revolt of dissatisfied peasants in Gīlān (1568–70) and of town artisans in Tabrīz (1571–3). The disturbances continued after the death of Tahmāsp I (1576), who had removed the capital from Tabrīz to Qazvīn, west of Teheran. A new era opened in 1587, when 'Abbās, a grandson of Tahmāsp I, received the recognition of the *qizilbāsh* troops as successor to the throne. He promptly had his two brothers blinded, and imprisoned at Alamūt.

The reign of Shah 'Abbās, known as 'the Great' (1587–1628),

is universally regarded as the most glorious in the annals of modern Persia. Using alternately force and subtle diplomacy, he succeeded in securing the state frontiers, and even in incorporating within them Iraq and Mesopotamia. The latter he seized from the Ottoman Turks, but ever since pre-Islamic times it had always been considered a natural part of the Persian empire. His possessions in the east included towns such as Qandahār and Herāt, which to-day belong to Afghanistan. Fully realizing the weakness inherent in the praetorian nature of the *qizilbāsh* troops, 'Abbās determined to form a strong military force which would make him independent of their every caprice and their constant abuse of power. Besides creating bodies of sharpshooters, recruited after the model of the Ottoman Janissaries (from *yeni cheri*, 'new troops') from among Georgian and Armenian Christians converted to Islam, he is supposed to have formed a personal bodyguard of *shāh-seven*, 'those who love the king', recruited from various Turkish tribes. Recent studies, however, have shown this to be a myth: Iskander Beg Munshī, our main and most reliable source for the period of Shāh 'Abbās, makes no mention of the *shāh-seven*, who probably date from the middle of the seventeenth century. However, Shah 'Abbās certainly broke the power of the *qizilbāsh* (he even destroyed one of their tribes, the Tekelü, in 1596), and strengthened the position of the town bureaucracy, which was largely of Persian origin. The presence at his court of the brothers Sir Anthony and Sir Robert Sherley gave Shāh 'Abbās the opportunity of learning to make good artillery and of exercising his troops in the European manner.

By historical coincidence, the period of Shāh 'Abbās's reign is one in which great rulers are to be found throughout the world: Philip II of Spain, Queen Elizabeth I of England, Sulaiman the Magnificent in Turkey, and Akbar the Great in India. The splendour of the court of the Grand Sophy, as the Safavids were called in Europe, became proverbial even in the West. As Fabian says in *Twelfth Night* (II.v.168), 'I will not give my part of this sport for a pension of thousands to be paid from the Sophy'. Shāh 'Abbās moved the Safavid capital once again, this time from Qazvīn to Isfahān. A number of magnificent buildings were put up, such as the great Masjid-i-

Shāh ('The King's Mosque'), the Chihil Sutūn ('The Hall of Forty Columns'), the great Allahvardi Khān bridge over the Zāyandeh Rud, and the Chahār Bāgh ('The Four Gardens'). Thanks to Shāh 'Abbās and his early conception of town planning, Isfahān still remains one of the few cities worthy of the name in modern Iran. The prosperity of the capital, the welcome with which foreigners were received, and the tolerance with which Christians were treated, attracted many European merchants and missionaries to 'Abbās's court. Europe's principal enemy at the time was the Ottoman Turks, and the enemy's enemy is a friend.

The sovereign showed as favourable an attitude to artists, scholars, men of letters, and especially to Shi'ite theologians, but he did not reveal great piety and forbearance. Our horror at some of his acts may be lessened when we consider the standards of behaviour that obtained even in Europe during these times, but we certainly cannot admire him for having put out the eyes of his brothers; or for killing in cold blood his eldest son Safī, who had gained too great an ascendancy over the people; or, frightened by the report of his astrologer that in the year 1000 of the Hegira (=1591–2) the king of Persia would be killed, for having abdicated for three days, placed on the throne a certain innocent Yūsuf, and had him assassinated, in order to be able to re-ascend the throne himself in safety!

With Shāh 'Abbās's death in 1628, the days of glory of the dynasty came to an end. Attacks from east and west alike placed the frontiers in danger. The names of his descendants mean little to the European reader, and we shall mention merely Shāh 'Abbās II (1642–66), during whose reign Persia seems to have recovered some of its past greatness, and whose sumptuous court was described with admiration by European travellers. In the reign of the incapable Husain (1694–1722), Afghan hordes occupied Isfahān and dethroned the Safavids. Once again the usual cycle is repeated: invasion by pastoral nomad people, the creation of a new short-lived state, followed by decadence. Certain features of this immensely important period, however, stand out, religious reform, and the considerable political and social changes, which derived from the restoration of an efficient central government, based on an urban bureaucracy as well as on unstable and unreliable nomad tribes. The fulcrum of the state was moved from Turkish Azerbaijān to Isfahān in the heart of Persia. the Persian language, already the language of official and diplomatic correspondence (the often ferocious exchanges of letters between Ottomans and Safavids was generally carried on in Persian, though in the early Safavid period there are examples of the Ottoman sovereign writing in Persian, and the king of Persia writing in Turkish), continued to gain in importance in official circles, though military terms, and also some of the technical terms of government, were still largely Turkish, and it appears that Turkish was spoken at the court. In fact, the structure of modern Persia had now been laid down.

A particularly important feature of Shāh 'Abbās's internal policy—apart from the centralization of the government—was the tendency to strengthen the Persian economy at the expense of conquered territories: the complete opposite, in fact, of the policy of Tamerlane and other rulers whose centres of empire lay outside the traditional Iranian frontiers. For example, after the occupation of Shīrvān (1607), 'Abbās demanded from the Turkish subjects the enormous sum of 50,000 tūmān (500 million dīnār), though he was able to collect only 30,000. In Luristān he obtained 10,000 tūmān, and similar sums elsewhere. On his return to Isfahān after making peace with Turkey in 1612, he exempted the inhabitants of the capital from the payment of taxes for three years. In Persian Iraq, the central region of Iran, he abolished the tax on sheep and cattle (chobān-begī). Taxes which had been increased in the years 1570–90, were reduced to the earlier rates. 'Abbās's famous action of transporting a large part of the Armenian population from the city of Julfa on the Araxes to Isfahān was also carried out for the purpose of enriching the Isfahān area. The intention was to transfer the international centre of the silk trade —which was in the hands of the Armenians of Julfa—to Iran, and to divert the Silk Route through Isfahān and Bandar 'Abbās. (The latter was a port on the Persian Gulf, the former Gumrān or Gombrun near Hormuz, which had been renamed after the shāh when it was seized from the Portuguese.) For these Armenians 'Abbās built 'New Julfa', a suburb of Isfahān itself, and made the new 'city' self-governing, while at the same time exempting it from taxes. Unfortunately due to lack of hygiene and the hazards of travelling, only 3,000 of the original 13,000 Armenian families who had set out on the journey, actually reached New Julfa. But silk became the main Persian export at this time. On other occasions 'Abbās ordered large-scale deportations of people, always in order to promote the interests of Iran itself, which had lost so much of its population in earlier periods. In 1605, for example, some 70,000 Armenians and Azerbaijānis were removed from Nakhchavān to Iran, but many who took part in this great *surgun* (in Turkish *surgun* means 'emigration') died on the way. As a result of the expedition into Georgia, some 100,000 Georgians were resettled in Iran, and so on.

In order to improve trade, Shāh 'Abbās strove to introduce a unified monetary system. The new monetary unit was the *'abbāsī*, named after the sovereign himself, equal to 200 *dīnār* or one *mithqāl* (4.6 gr.) of silver. A *tūmān* was therefore worth 10,000 *dīnār*, or 50 *'abbāsī*. When we recall that in the time of Ghāzān Khān at the beginning of the fourteenth century one *dīnār* contained nearly three *mithqāl* of silver (see p. 120), while in the seventeenth century it took three *'abbāsī* or 600 *dīnār* to make up three *mithqāl* of silver, we realize how greatly the *dīnār* had fallen in value over 300 years. But the attempt to establish a unified monetary system failed, and in seventeenth-century Iran besides the *'abbāsī*, there were in circulation a number of different currencies of varying values, including Turkish and European coins, and the exchange rates varied in the different regions.

As far as society was concerned, 'Abbās's policy of centralization resulted in considerable variations in the relative sizes of the classic four groups of the feudal aristocracy. In particular, the introduction of a new type of aristocracy of serving soldiers, drawn from the *ghulām* or royal slaves (often Georgians or Armenians), for the express purpose of weakening the power of the pastoral nomad aristocracy of the *qizilbāsh*, brought about many changes. A comparison of two lists of amirs (*khān* and *sultān*, i.e. high-ranking members of the warrior aristocracy), one dating from 1576, before 'Abbās's reforms, and the other from 1628, reveals the importance of these developments. The first list contains the names of

114 amirs, all belonging to the pastoral nomad group, and nearly all *qizilbāsh*. The second list contains the names of 90 amirs, made up of 35 *qizilbāsh*, 34 non-*qizilbāsh* members of pastoral nomad tribes (mostly 'Iranian Kurds and Luri), and 21 royal *ghulām* who, like the other amirs, had their own grants of land (*ölke* in Azeri, Pers. *ulka*), and kept up their own feudal armies (*qushūn*, a Mongol word still in use in modern Iran). At the same time, there was a considerable increase in the amount of land held by the state (*dīvānī*), which was administered by the ever more powerful civil service, and in that owned by the royal family (*khāssè, khāssè-sharīfè-i pādshāhī, khālisè*).

Not only the Isfahān area and the hereditary Safavid domain of Ardabīl, but even entire regions such as Gīlān, were now *khāssè* lands. Included among the state lands (*dīvānī*), however, were those granted as *tuyūl* (see p. 142). There were also very extensive *vaqf* belongings to Shi'ite religious institutions. At the beginning of the seventeenth century the *vaqf* of the great Safavid mosque at Ardabīl included 650 parcels of arable land (*juft-i 'avāmil*) worked by tenant farmers, making over 10,000 acres of irrigated and cultivated land in all. In 1671, the *vaqf* possessions of the same mosque included 40 villages in southern Azerbaijān alone, and, in the city of Ardabīl, 200 houses, 9 public baths, 8 caravanserais, the entire main square of the market (*maidān*), the large covered market for the wholesale trade (*qaisariyyè*), 100 stalls, and the right to collect excize duty (*bāj*) from all the merchants. To this should be added 100 houses and 100 shops in Tabrīz, several caravanserais and baths at Qazvīn, and lands and other sources of income in Mughān, Gīlān, and Gurgān.

For obvious reasons the central government, particularly during the reign of Shāh 'Abbās, preferred to grant *tuyūl* rather than *soyurgal*. According to contemporary sources there were ten times as many *tuyūl* as *soyurgal* during this period. The post of *qurchī-bāshī* (commander of the guard of mounted archers or *qurchī*, an extremely important position), carried with it the *tuyūl* of the district of Kāzerūn, with an annual return of 13,917,200 *dīnār*. The post of *tufangchī-bāshī* (commander of the fusiliers), carried with it the *tuyūl* of the district of Abarqūh, with an annual return of 7,115,300 *dīnār*, and so on. Lesser officials naturally received less lucrative *tuyūl*, known as *hamè-sālè*. This was the term applied to the concession, granted in return for services rendered, of a fixed sum (paid in cash or in kind) obtained from the taxes of a particular territory, but with no right to administer the territory itself. The sums were paid in the form of cheques (*havālè, barāt*) drawn on the treasury of a given district, on presentation of a certificate to show that the assignee had been in active employment for *hamè-sālè*, 'for the whole year'. Taxes, which had been reduced under Shāh 'Abbās, were again increased by his descendants for various reasons, including the cost of disastrous wars. The main source of revenue was, as usual, the land tax or *kharāj* (now more often called *māl-u-jihat* or *māliyāt*), generally paid in kind on the basis of fifteen to twenty per cent of the harvest. Sheep-farmers, on the other hand, paid a tax called *chobān-begī*, which consisted of one seventh of the wool sheared, one in seven of newborn lambs, and one-third of the value of colts and asses. The system of special taxes continued during this period: the *ikhrājāt* to pay the expenses of high officials, the *'avāriz* (supplementary taxes), the *alāfè* and *ulūfè* to provide forage for armies on the move, as well as the peasants' gifts to their feudal lords on festive occasions (*'īdī*). Depending on the type of land, these taxes went either in their entirety to the state (in the case of *dīvānī* lands), or in their entirety to the feudal landlord (in the case of *soyurgal, vaqf*, or *yurt*), or were divided between the landlord and the state in a fixed proportion (as in the case of *mulk* lands). If the landowner had received tax exemption (*mu'āfī*), than all the taxes collected went into his own pocket: in other words, exemption rarely benefited the peasants, who were nearly all tenant farmers. In order to retain a plot of land, generally on a hereditary basis, the peasant farmer paid the landlord the *bahrè-yi mālikānè*, 'the landlord's share'. In the case of *dīvānī, khāssè, soyurgal*, and *vaqf*, this *bahrè* included the ordinary taxes. The *bahrè-yi mālikānè*, which gave the peasant the right to enjoy the land and the irrigation system, often reached a figure of one-fifth to one-third of the harvest, or a half to two-thirds of the fruit from orchards. The rate increased if the farmer had received from the landlord seed or the use of draught-animals, when it could reach eighty to ninety per cent of the harvest, but included all taxes. The traveller Jean Chardin reported that in the flourishing oasis of Isfahān the peasants were better off than their contemporaries in France, but if this were true in the neighbourhood of the cities, it did not apply to the whole of Iran. Chardin also says that, nevertheless, the peasants were subject to the absolute will of the shāh and his officials, and they had no possibility of legal redress.

The pastoral nomads remained of fundamental importance in the Persian economy. We have no figures for their numbers during this period, but since at the end of the nineteenth century thirty per cent of the entire population was nomadic, we can assume that the proportion was even higher in the seventeenth century. Few nomads, and then only the most wretched, ever settled on the land, and the condition of the settled peasant farmer was definitely worse than that of the nomad. The latter was to some extent protected by his tribal organization, he had a right to a portion of the booty when serving in the army, and, above all, he was armed, while the peasant was unarmed, and subject to every form of oppression and imposition without any means of defending himself. Slaves existed, but during this period they were employed solely as men-servants and as guardians of the harem. They were of different types, and included prisoners of war (asīr), those 'bought for money' (zarkharīd), and those 'born in the house' (khānè-zādè), that is to say, slaves of the second or third generation. These last were the best treated, since it was customary not to sell slaves born in the house, though there was no law prohibiting this. Hardly any slaves were employed on the land or in the workshops and, although they still worked in the royal silk factories in the years 1530–40, by the seventeenth century the silk-workers were all freemen. In fact, one can say that by this time virtually all traces of a slave society had disappeared. The reports of contemporary travellers reveal that the domestic slaves were treated much like the old family retainers in the noble households of Europe, and infinitely better than the slaves on the American plantations in the nineteenth century.

There was an improvement in agriculture for a number of reasons. The landowners had gained more authority, 'Abbās had reduced the taxes, there was a long period of peace from 1640 to 1722, and marketing had developed. Though the high level of pre-Mongol days was not reached, the quantity of farm produce was much greater than it had been in the thirteenth to sixteenth centuries. This is also partly accounted for by the high standards of the irrigation system, which led Chardin to remark that there was no people in the world who knew how to construct such perfect subterranean canals as the Persians. These were the famous kārīz, an ancient feature of Iranian irrigation, which, as Chardin adds, could stretch for 20 to 25 miles, and reach a depth of 30 to 50 feet below the ground.

This improvement in the economy was reflected in the cities. Contemporary documents often mention the craft guilds (sinf, plur. asnāf), with their three grades of shāgird (apprentice), khalīfè (pre-master), and ustād (master), and their special initiation rites to the grade of master. The Tazkirat al-mulūk, an anonymous source which describes the administration of the Safavid period though it is dated 1725, states that 'the inhabitants of every ward, of every village, and of every guild nominate one of themselves whom they consider trustworthy, write out a certificate for him, and fix his honorarium. This document, to which is affixed the seal of the naqīb (a sort of assistant mayor), is presented to the kalāntar (the town mayor), from whom they then receive the necessary authorization (ta'liqè) and a ceremonial dress for their elected candidate, who thereupon can begin to carry out his work.' Without the authorization of the head of the guild, no one was able to open a new workshop. The masters of the guilds held their own meetings, and in the first three months of each year the kalāntar of the city called them all to his house to discuss with them the taxes (bunīchè) that each guild was to pay. This shows the considerable influence that the guilds had achieved in the running of the city, much greater indeed than they had enjoyed in the times of the Seljuks and Ilkhanids. The taxes were paid in produce or in coin: according to Chardin each workshop paid between 10 and 20 sous annually, that is to say, about one 'abbāsī.

The masters of the court workshops (now generally known by the Arabic word buyūtāt, 'houses') were in a privileged position, and were no longer slaves but freemen under the supervision of the *nāzir-i buyūtāt* (controller of the workshops). The *nāzir* fixed the price of articles in agreement with the masters. Nevertheless the cities were not genuinely self-governing. At the head of the administration was the *kalāntar*, a kind of mayor chosen by the royal governor from among the local aristocracy (the local landlords who had interests in the wholesale trade), and occasionally from among the big merchants. Only the Armenians in the New Julfa quarter of Isfahān had the right to elect one of their own number (always a wealthy merchant) as their own *kalāntar*. The individual wards and guilds enjoyed a restricted independence.

The most important of the local industries was weaving, and very fine and costly textiles were produced, while the manufacture of carpets reached a very high standard during the seventeenth century. The carpets were mainly exported to Europe via Baghdād and Turkey, and for this reason came to be known as 'Turkish carpets'. Contemporary travellers particularly admired the carpets of Kirmān. Persian porcelain and maiolica also enjoyed a great reputation and after a long period of decadence the art of pottery began to again flourish. Articles in leather and morocco were highly esteemed, and Persian bows and sabres were considered the finest in the world. According to Olearius, the best steel came from the shores of Lake Neirīz, and the best sword-blades from the city of Qum, where they cost from 16 to 80 *'abbāsī*. Travellers and contemporary documents also refer to jewellery, dyes, glassware and articles in crystal, paper-making factories (though the paper produced was inferior in quality not only to European paper but also to that of Central Asia), and soap factories. Cheap soap was made from mutton fat scented with herbs. The upper classes imported a better quality soap from Aleppo.

The wholesale trade no longer accepted credit-notes, as in earlier times, but insisted on cash payment. On the other hand, according to Chardin there were many merchants who had agents as far afield as China and Sweden. Thanks to the fact that the feudal aristocracy was often closely involved in business on a large scale, and thanks also to the attitude of Islam, the position of the merchant was a highly honoured one, whereas this cannot be said of Europe until the Renaissance. The Muslim countries do not hold with our old-fashioned and snobbish attitude towards the 'common shopkeeper'. On the whole, foreign trade was in the hands of non-Persians, mainly Armenians, but also the Dutch, French, and English, who traded with Russia and Western Europe, and Hindus, who controlled the trade with India and the Far East. Internal trade, however, was largely handled by Muslims. The Armenians of New Julfa, who virtually had the monopoly of the silk trade, paid in taxes the enormous sum of 580 *tūmān* per year. But besides the Armenians, the Dutch and English also had the right to export silk, they had their own factories, and there was continual rivalry between them. In the years 1770–9, the Dutch exported silk to Europe to the value of 500,000 to 600,000 gold 'livres', or 11 to 13,000 *tūmān*.

The breakdown in the economy which occurred at the end of the seventeenth century, and the renewed exploitation of the peasants, combined with the impoverishment of the land and the decline of internal trade had an extremely bad effect on trade and industry. The increase in taxes and excessive excise duties, the oppressive government, which was particularly pernicious as far as the craftsmen and smaller merchants were concerned, and the feudal rulers' arbitrary control of the cities, eventually overcame the progressive tendencies of the beginning of the seventeenth century. For this reason it was impossible for a unified market to be formed in the cities, and the capitalist economy which was developing was unable to become the predominant form of production. During this period a healthy economy was to be found only in the cities of Iran proper (Isfahān, Shīrāz, Qazvīn, Hamadān, Kirmān, Rasht, etc.), and southern Azerbaijān (Tabrīz and Ardabīl). Apart from Qandahār and the Shi'ite holy city of Mashhad, the cities of Khorāsān, once the cultural and economic centre of Iran, underwent an economic decline, partly because of the falling off of their trade with Central Asia, which was now in the hands of a hostile power.

One of the characteristics of the Safavid period, which is partly due to Iran's acceptance of Shi'ite Islam, is this closing of the frontiers, this defining of the limits of what was to become modern Iran.

CHAPTER IX

The Afghans, Nādir Shāh, and Zands

The period between the Safavids and the Constitution of 1906 can be regarded, at best, as one of incubation, at worst, as one of complete decadence. In Europe, and to some extent in India and elsewhere, the eighteenth century was immensely creative; in Persia it was one of the darkest and dullest periods for literature and the arts.

The century opens with the downfall of the Safavids and the short-lived Afghan invasion. The decline in the economy at the end of the seventeenth century had considerably impoverished the peasants, with a consequent diminution of the revenue of the state and landowners, while at the same time the demands of the civil service and the feudal aristocracy actually increased as a result of the financial and commercial development of the preceding era. There was only one way in which to satisfy such demands, and that was by increasing taxes. This produced a vicious circle which became especially serious under the last of the Safavids, Sultān Husain (1694–1722), during whose reign taxes were doubled and trebled, while three new forms of taxation were introduced. A much-hated census was maintained, and those who attempted to avoid the vigilant eye of the government had their property confiscated or were otherwise punished. As in the Mongol period, this resulted in many peasant farmers taking flight, and also in further attempts to tie them to the land by means of royal firmans, such as that of Sultān Husain in 1710. In his autobiography the Persian poet Muhammad ʿAlī Hazīn (d. 1766) notes that in the case of his family's hereditary lands in various parts of Gīlān, 'as a result of the devastation of the region and of the fact that there was no one capable of looking after the land, after my father's death the income decreased, until the entire annual return was insufficient to pay the essential expenses for more than a few months'. This situation caused discontent not only among the peasants but also among the feudal landlords, of whom Hazīn was one, and loosened the bonds of loyalty to the central government. It was therefore not so much the weakness and personal errors of the last Safavid *shāh* that brought about the downfall of the dynasty, as the general economic position of the country.

Chardin states that in the first six or seven years of Shāh Sulaimān's reign (1669–94) the customs' duty collected in the ports of Bandar 'Abbās and Kong, near Hormuz, varied between 400,000 and 500,000 *livres* (910–1,100 *tūmān*), compared with 1,100,000 *livres* (2,444 *tūmān*) in the time of Shāh 'Abbās II (1642–66). The main reason for the decline in foreign trade was the fact that the quantity of goods crossing Iran along the caravan routes had decreased, and trade with countries on the shores of the Indian Ocean had fallen into the hands of Dutch and Indian merchants. Throughout the seventeenth century European merchants tended to make full use of the sea route to India round the Cape of Good Hope, which had been discovered by Vasco da Gama in the fifteenth century, and this resulted in a decrease of traffic along the great Asiatic caravan routes in general, and the Iranian ones in particular. In order to increase the revenue from foreign trade and to strike at the Dutch merchants' monopoly, Sultān Husain concluded two commerial treaties with France, in 1708 and 1715, which were important not only because they granted the usual customs exemptions and other privileges, but because they conceded to the French merchants extra-territorial rights. The Persian government renounced its right to judicate in the case of disputes between the French themselves, and a form of mixed tribunal had to be set up to try cases involving both French and Persian subjects. This is the first instance of a thorough-going capitulation agreement being conceded to by Persia.

Last but not least, Sultān Husain earned the resentment of many of his subjects on religious grounds. He was a fanatical Shi'ite who, under the influence of the famous theologian M. Bāqir Majlisī persecuted the numerous Sunnites who still lived within his domains, particularly in the Causasus, Kurdistān, Afghanistan, and Azerbaijān. This indicates that even at the end of the Safavid period, Shi'ism was far from being the undisputed national religion. In the early decades of the eighteenth century, large numbers of the population in Fārs, in the very heart of Persia, were Sunnites, and in the region of Lār in 1722 their hatred of the Shi'ite government led to their giving aid to the Afghan invaders. But by far the most serious revolt was that of the Ghilzāī, an Afghan tribe who lived in the Qandahār area. An Afghan prince, Mīr Veis, declared himself independent, and his example was followed by other Afghan chieftains, such as the *abdālī* of Herāt. The rebels even had the support of a *fatvā* (a ruling on a point of Islamic law) from Mecca, stating that it was legitimate for Sunnites to rise in revolt against a heretical overlord. Mīr Mahmūd, son of Mīr Veis, occupied Kirmān in 1720, and in 1722, after the battle of Golnābād, he entered the Safavid capital and deposed Sultān Husain. Again, despite the appalling conditions that existed at the end of the Safavid period, the Afghan invasion did not prove to be a liberation but was merely a further example of a feudal conquest by nomadic and semi-nomadic tribes. At first there was some amelioration in the condition of the most oppressed classes, and yet in many cases the *'avāmm*, the common people, rebelled against the Afghan invaders. Indeed, Afghan rule lasted only a short time: in 1725, Mīr Mahmūd was assassinated by one of his cousins, and there followed a period of anarchy, which was only brought to an end under the leadership of the General Tahmāsp-qulī Khān, later to be known as Nādir Shāh. In fact, while Tahmāsp II, Husain's successor, fled before the victorious Afghans, an amir of the Afshār (a Turkish tribe), who, to show his devotion to Tahmāsp, had taken the name of Tahmāsp-qulī (in Turkish, 'Tahmāsp's slave'), placed himself at the head of the Persian forces and fought on all sides to expel the enemy from Safavid territory. The Afghans were defeated, and so were the Ottomans, who, taking advantage of Persia's weakness, had attacked from the west. But Tahmāsp II decided to maintain hostilities against the Ottomans on his own account, was himself defeated, and had to accept humiliating conditions. Infuriated by this, the general deposed him, put Tahmāsp's infant son 'Abbās III on the throne, and concluded the war victoriously by conquering Azerbaijān and Georgia, partly with the assistance of Russian advisors.

Complete political reunification had been achieved, but the state of the country was deplorable. As usual, it was the peasants in the countryside who had suffered most. In the oasis of Isfahān alone, a thousand villages—that is to say, two-thirds of the area—had been ravaged and were virtually in ruins. Particularly serious was the fact that the dykes, *kārīz* and canals, which were essential for irrigating the land, had been either destroyed or allowed to fall into disrepair. An inscription on the doorway of the mosque of Vanand (Nakh-chavān), dated 1732/3, states 'Because of the famine and distress of this unhappy time, the people were in hell, for in the course of a single year the village of Vanand and others in the neighbourhood were three times invaded and laid waste, and many believers, both men and women, were either killed or led into captivity, while the other servants of God were dispersed, crossed over the river Araxes, and settled on lands on the other side. In those days of an unfortunate conjunction of the planets, even trade came to a standstill'. Cities such as Isfahān, Shīrāz, Qazvīn, Yazd, and Tabrīz lost over two-thirds of their inhabitants. Worse still was the fact that neither the Turks, nor the Afghan invaders, nor the local landlords, nor even in due course Nādir, considered reducing the burden of taxation. Truly does the poet Hazīn write in his memoirs that the expulsion of the Afghans in no way brought relief to the population. The real value of the currency eventually fell to a tenth and a twelfth of what it had been at the end of the seventeenth century, and prices rose accordingly. According to Muhammad Kāzim, who wrote an important history of the period of Nādir Shāh, the *'Ālam-ārāy-i Nādirī*, in the Merv district at the beginning of Nādir's reign, a *mann* of grain cost 200 *dīnār*, while at Tabrīz, according to another source, it was 900 *dīnār*!

After 'Abbās III's death, on New Year's Day (Pers. *Naurūz*, 21 March, the spring equinox), 1736, Tahmāsp-qulī gathered in the plain of Mughān (in Azerbaijan, north-west of Ardabīl) the governors, amirs, and dignitaries of Persia to the number of some 30,000, together with almost 100,000 of their servants and attendants. He told them that, having completed his task, he now desired to retire to his estates in Khorāsān, and leave them free to elect a *shāh*. On being urged himself to become their king, he at first insistently refused (we do not know how sincerely), and eventually accepted only on the condition of a compromise between the Shi'ite Persians and himself, a Sunnite. Tahmāsp-qulī (who now took the name of Nādir Shāh) was not particularly concerned with religious questions, but in order to achieve peace with the Ottomans, he proposed resolving the *shī'a-sunna* problem by creating, alongside the four orthodox Sunnite schools, a further school known as the *ja 'fariyya* (after Ja'far, one of the most important and highly venerated of the twelve *imāms* of the Shi'ites), to which the Twelver Shi'ites should belong. It was a short-lived expedient which was to satisfy neither side. This attempt to lead the country out of Shi'ite isolation formed part of a deliberate plan by Nādir to return Persia once again— though this time by means of military conquest—to the fold of universal Islam.

In 1738 after taking Qandahār, where the Afghan revolt had originated, Nādir Shāh decided to attack the ill-protected provinces of the Great Moghul, which, since the death of Aurangzeb in 1707, had fallen into a state of decadence. On the pretext that Afghan fugitives were being harboured by the Moghul court, he carried out a swift campaign which resulted in the conquest of Ghazna, Kābul, Peshawar, and, in January 1739, Lahore. He then defeated the troops of the Moghul emperor, Muhammad Shāh, near Delhi, and entered, at first 'as a friend', the fabulous capital of India. A popular uprising against the invaders led to a terrible massacre, but Nādir, who did not wish to dethrone the Moghul sovereign, contented himself with seizing an enormous quantity of booty together with the territories to the north-west of the river Indus. On his return to Persia he hastened to confirm the loyalty of the north-eastern regions. He was amicably received by the amir of Bukhārā, and fixed the Oxus as his north-eastern frontier.

There were further wars with the Ottomans, who did not wish to accept his plan for the creation of a new legitimate Shi'ite school. These were brought to an end in 1747 with a peace treaty which left the religious question unresolved for all practical purposes.

An attempt on Nādir's life had been made in 1741/2, for his supposed complicity in which Nādir Shāh had his son blinded, and thereafter he developed a morose character which drove him to bouts of senseless cruelty. His campaigns had devastated the lands on his frontiers, but they had failed to enrich Iran. After he had seized the immense booty of the Moghul empire, Nādir proclaimed a three-year exemption of taxes. But due to the lack of even the most elementary form of industry and the primitive agricultural conditions under feudalism, these immense riches were either futilely hoarded or foolishly expended to no purpose, with the disastrous result that in 1743 Nādir decided to collect the taxes not only for that year but also for the three previous years which he had declared exempt! Demands for payment were accompanied by unheard-of cruelty. Against all the tenets of Islamic law— the study of which in individual Islamic countries very often shows it to be a form of human idealism although rarely applied—defaulters were barbarously mutilated or sold into slavery. According to Muħammad Kāzim during these two to three years, between 200,000 and 300,000 peasants unable to pay their taxes were maimed and imprisoned. Worse still, in 1744 there was a further large increase in the rates of taxation. For example, the district of Khoy in Azerbaijān, which formerly paid 3,000 *tumān* annually, was expected to find the absurd sum of 100,000 *tumān*: the only result was a general uprising of the inhabitants. Numerous revolts broke out, which were harshly and cruelly put down. Nādir tried hard to impose a policy of centralization, but though in the time of 'Abbās the Great, when the economic conditions of the country were fairly good, this could succeed, it now proved a utopian dream. In order to increase the area of state lands, Nādir Shāh confiscated many of the *vaqf* to the value of about one million *tumān*, and reduced the *yurt* estates of the *qizilbāsh*, and particularly of the *Qājār*. His intention was clearly to weaken the economic position of the Shi'ite religious author-ities and the *qizilbāsh* landlords, but he succeeded in alienating many other secular and religious leaders. He tried to find support from the feudal landowners in the eastern parts of his empire (mostly Turcoman, Uzbek and Afghan pastoral nomads), who had grown wealthy during the campaign of plunder in India. It was not by chance that Nādir had transferred his capital from the devastated city of Isfahān to Mashhad in the then comparatively prosperous region of Khorāsān and near to his favourite place of refuge—the fortress of Kalāt.

As was to be expected, the king, who at the outset of his career had raised the hopes of the oppressed Persian people, met his death in 1747 at the hands of a group of chiefs from his own tribe of the Afshār, who conspired together with some of the Qājār chiefs. In order to avoid the possibility of their producing any pretenders to the throne, his own family was almost entirely exterminated.

In general, Nādir's policy proved to be a futile outburst of undirected energy without any plan for the future, which succeeded solely in maintaining Persia's frontiers during a critical period. Nādir was, however, the first Persian sovereign to realize the usefulness of a navy. In 1743 John Elton, an English adventurer who took the name of Jamāl Beg, built ships on the Caspian, while in the Persian Gulf a flotilla of twenty vessels was formed. Yet even this turned out to be no more than a historical curiosity. The Persian navy has never played an important part in the history of the nation, even in the twentieth century.

Nādir Shāh's death was followed by a period of chaos and civil war in which relatives of the dead king, Afshār, Qājār, and Afghan chieftains, and the last of the Safavids took part. There were three main groups of feudal lords struggling for power: one in Fārs, led by Karīm Khān Zand; one in Astarābād, led by Muhammad Hasan Khān Qājār; and the third in southern Azerbaijān, led by Āzād Khān. Kārim Khān Zand was victorious, and in 1750 he founded the short-lived but beneficent Zand dynasty, which provided a lull in the internecine wars and a period of comparative peace and piety, fondly recalled to this day. The Zands were the first dynasty of Iranian stock after an interval of nearly a thousand years of Turkish rulers. From the very first, Karīm Khān Zand proclaimed himself regent on behalf of a hypothetical grandchild of the Safavid Shāh Sultān Husain, and never evinced any desire to assume the royal title of *shāh*. After defeating his Afghan and Qājār rivals and gaining control over a large part of Persia (excluding, however, Khorāsān), he took the title of *vakīl* (deputy) and ruled as such for some thirty years (1750–79) from his capital of Shīrāz. His main concern was to bring back order and prosperity to the impoverished provinces. He also attempted to revive the arts and crafts by setting up workshops for producing pottery and glass, and reduced the tax burden on the peasants by limiting the arbitrary powers of the landowners. He succeeded in partially restoring the irrigation system, especially in Fārs and southern Iran. In Shīrāz itself he put up a number of beautiful buildings which can still be admired to-day, such as the Vakīl Mosque, the Caravanserai, and the Mausoleums, since restored, of the two great Shīrāz poets, Sa'dī and Hāfiz. The only important military event in Karīm's reign was the seizure of Bassora (Basra) from the Ottomans in 1775, though it was lost to Persia again after his death.

On Karīm's death, civil war broke out again once more. The strongest opponent of the Zands soon proved to be the eunuch Āghā Muhammad Khān, son of Muhammad Hasan Khān and head of the Astarābād branch of the Qājār tribe. His father had been killed in the struggles with Karīm Khān Zand, and thereafter he had lived as a hostage at Kārim Khān's court. When the latter died, Āghā Muhammad fled to his native Māzandarān and placed himself at the head of his people. He showed himself to be an energetic politician and an able leader, but at the same time he revealed extremely cruel and sadistic tendencies which some attribute to the fact that he was a eunuch. (He had been castrated as an infant on the orders of Ādil Shāh, one of the short-lived successors of Nādir Shāh, and for this reason he was given the title of *āghā*, usually applied to the palace eunuchs.) Āghā Muhammad defeated one of the Zands, Ja'far Khān, in battle, and seized Isfahān. Thereafter, by means of careful negotiation, he was able to win the support of the *khān* and nomad aristocracy of northern Iran. He made Teheran his capital, partly because it was near the pasture-lands of his own tribe, but also because it lay on an important caravan route. Until this time Teheran had been a town of only secondary importance without any real historical tradition behind it (the first European to mention it was the Spaniard Clavijo, who visited Tamerlaine's court in the fifteenth century), although it is situated close to the ruins of the ancient Rhages, the Rayy of the Middle Ages. Even these arbitrary changes of capital and the mushroom growth of

new cities (Teheran to-day has a population of over two
million) are a typical outcome of the pastoral nomad society
to be found in Iran and other Islamic countries.

After his defeat, Ja'far Khān fled to Shīrāz, where he was
killed as the result of a conspiracy. In these struggles of the Zand
dynasty, which often changed its leader, an important part
was played by the 'king-maker' Hājjī Ibrāhīm, *kalāntar* of
Shīrāz and a member of the local Iranian aristocracy, who now
put on the throne Lutf 'Alī Khān Zand (1789). The struggle
between the feudal lords of the north with the Qājār at their
head and those of the south led by the Zands ended with
complete victory for the former. Hājjī Ibrāhīm deserted Lutf
'Alī Khān and handed Shīrāz over to Āghā Muhammad
Qājār, receiving in return the position of grand vizier. Lutf
'Alī Khān held out for a time in Kirmān in south-east Iran,
until he was betrayed and made prisoner by Āghā Muhammad,
who determined to put his eyes out personally (1794). Āghā
Muhammad Khān meted out terrible punishment to the
people of Kirmān for having given their support to Lutf 'Alī.
The young women were distributed as slaves among his soldiers,
while the men were blinded. Twenty thousand pairs of eyes
were presented to the tyrant, who had threatened to blind
those who were detailed to carry out the task if they missed a
single one.

The victory of the northern group of feudal lords, led by the
Qājār, was not fortuitous. Throughout the eighteenth century
the economic superiority of the northern areas of Iran had
become more and more evident. From these regions were
exported silk and cotton, while through them passed the
caravan routes which connected Russia and Turkey with
central and southern Iran and Central Asia, and they included
the ports and harbours of the Caspian which served the
increasing trade with Russia. The southern regions, however,
despite the efforts of Kārim Khān Zand, failed to regain the
privileged position they had held prior to the Afghan invasion.
During this period the trade passing through the ports on the
Persian Gulf was less than that with Russia. Consequently,
the northern lords were richer and more powerful than those
in the south.

Āghā Muhammad Khān (once again the dynasty was

Turkish, after the brief interlude of the Zands) strengthened the authority of the central government by removing the restless *khāns* of Kurdistan, Fārs, Arabistān, and elsewhere, and revived commercial exchanges between the various parts of the country which had been disrupted by the long period of civil war. The peasant farmers were treated harshly, but the new *shāh* did not dare to increase the taxes. He attached great importance to the reconquest of the Caucasian lands, which had, to all intents and purposes, remained independent since the death of Nādir Shāh. (They provided excellent sources of raw materials and a ready market for Persian handycrafts.) In 1795, he mounted a campaign against Azerbaijān and Armenia, which resulted in the destruction of Tiflis and the carrying off of 22,000 peaceful Georgians as slaves. In 1796, Āghā Muhammad Khān had himself crowned in Teheran and assumed the traditional title of *shāhinshāh*. Immediately afterwards he invaded Khorāsān. The blind Shāhrukh Afshār was taken prisoner, and forced under torture to reveal where he had hidden his treasure. Doubts as to Russian intentions in the Caucasus gave the *shāhinshāh* the opportunity of again invading Transcaucasia in 1797, when he seized the city of Shusha and forced the inhabitants to submit to appalling torture. During this blood-bath, he himself was assassinated by two of his servants whom he had condemned to death sometime previously, but whom, in some extraordinarily casual way, he still continued to keep around him. The army withdrew to Iran, where Āghā Muhammad Khān's nephew, Bābā Khān, was proclaimed *shāh* and took the name Fath 'Alī Shāh (1797–1834). The Qājār dynasty was destined to be a lengthy one, for it was to rule over Iran until 1925.

CHAPTER X

The Qājār dynasty to modern times

Under the Qājārs, Persia found herself for the first time seriously involved, though powerless to do anything about it, in the European colonization of Asia. (Under the Safavids, European contacts had been fairly superficial, and almost non-existent during the reign of Nādir Shāh.) Within Persia, the Shi'ite religious authorities quickly recovered from the partial eclipse from which they had suffered under the Sunnite Nādir, and began to play an extremely important part in public life, retaining the privileges they had won under the Safavids and completely paralyzing the country's progress. Politically, this is a period of defeat and humiliation; socially, it is one of conservatism; while culturally it reveals the first seeds of a further renaissance.

Āghā Muhammad's successor, Fath 'Alī Shāh was a vain ruler, famous for his long beard and his vast harem. It was his desire to be portrayed beside the Sassanid bas-reliefs of Tāq-i Bustān, for we now enter the period of ever-increasing nationalism and glorification of the pre-Islamic past. During his long reign, Persia came under repeated pressure from the English, the Russians, and the French under Napoleon, who wanted a base from which to invade India. In 1807, Fath 'Alī sent Mīrzā Muhammad Rizā Qazvīnī as Persian ambassador to France, and thus he became one of the first of a series of inquiring, sometimes intelligent, often ingenuous Persians immortalized in James Morier's *The Adventures of Hajji Baba of Ispahan*, first published in 1824. (Some of these travellers wrote lively and often hilarious accounts of their experiences in Europe.) A few months later, General Gardanne, with a large French mission seventy strong, including technical advisers and instructors, arrived in Persia, and permanent diplomatic relations with France were established. The success of Gardanne's mission—it resulted amongst other things in the signing of a defence treaty, in French engineers bulding fortifications, and French instructors being attached to the Persian army—put England on her guard. In 1808 Sir John Malcolm was sent by the Government of India to counteract the French influence at the court of Fath 'Alī Shāh. A treaty was signed and the French alliance repudiated. In the following year, the *shāh* appointed an ambassador to England, who set out in the company of James Morier.

In court circles, one of the leading advocates of cautious reforms was the enlightened prince 'Abbās Mīrzā, heir presumptive to the throne and at the same time, as was the custom during the Qājār period, governor of Azerbaijān. Amongst other things, 'Abbās Mīrzā encouraged the translation of French and Russian works on military fortifications and the art of war.

Between 1800 and 1828, a number of disastrous campaigns against Russia took place. In 1813, following a heavy defeat, Persia was forced to renounce for ever her claims to Georgia and the other Caucasian provinces by the Treaty of Gulistān, while by the Treaty of Turkmānchāy in 1828 she ceded Armenia to Russia, promised to maintain no ships on the Caspian (the only comment of Fath 'Alī Shāh's incompetent minister was: 'We are not ducks that we need the waters of the Caspian.'), and for the second but not the last time in her history conceded extra-territorial rights. The death of the heir to the throne, 'Abbās Mīrzā, in 1833, the only person who might perhaps have saved Persia, was a great blow to his country and his father, who survived him by only a year.

Fath 'Alī Shāh's son and successor, Muhammad Shāh (1834–48), had during his father's lifetime attempted to carry out a diversion in the east against Afghanistan, or rather against the prince of Herāt, with the aid of Russian officers. He now suffered a defeat at the hands of the English, who forced the Persians to raise the siege of Herāt by threatening the Persian Gulf. Although the embassy, under the 'chief adjutant' Husain Khān, which Muhammad Shāh sent in 1838–9 to defend the Persian position at the court of Louis Philippe, and before Metternich and Lord Palmerston, was a political failure, we owe to it a delightful unpublished diary written in beautifully simple Persian prose by Husain Khān's secretary.

During Muhammad Shāh's reign there occurred in 1840 a revolt of the Ismailite followers of the Āghā Khān (descended from the ancient 'old man of the mountain'), and in 1844 the much more important advent of the Bābī religious movement. A young man called 'Alī Muhammad, from a family of Shīrāz merchants, suddenly proclaimed himself the *Bāb* (Arab. 'Gate') and the hidden *imām* who, according to Shi'ite tradition, was due to arrive at the end of the world. The Bāb interpreted Shi'ite eschatology in a symbolic sense, and declared that the 'end of the world' signified the end of an era, of a cycle of prophets. He then revealed himself as the initiator of a new cycle and forerunner of one even greater, 'He whom God will make manifest', who would announce a new era in the social and religious life not only of Persia but of the entire world. If this movement had taken hold, it would have destroyed the privileges of the Shi'ite clergy and would have had a definitely beneficial influence on the life of the country, but it was bitterly opposed by both the religious and political authorities. Thousands were martyred for supporting the new faith, and Renan later compared its beginnings with those of the early Christians. The Bāb himself, after a long period of imprisonment, was eventually shot in Tabrīz in 1850, during the reign of Muhammad Shāh's successor, Nāsiru'd-Dīn Shāh (1848–96). The latter quickly dismissed the old minister and tutor Hājjī Mīrzā Āghāsī, an incompetent conservative, and put in his place the much more zealous Mīrzā Taqī Khān. At first, Nāsiruddīn was faced with the problem of putting down the heroic uprisings of the Bābīs (1849–52). The Bāb's followers were drawn not only from the lower classes and the growing middle class of traders, but even from among the aristocracy. Although initially the movement was extremely successful—some Europeans in Persia believed that the country might have become completely Bābī—it was apparently broken by the bitterly cruel persecutions of 1852, followed by an unsuccessful attempt made on the *shāh's* life by two Bābīs seeking vengeance for their leader's death. Among the victims of the persecutions was the learned and beautiful Bābī poetess Qurratu'l-'Ain, known as Tāhirè ('the Pure'), who may be regarded as one of the world's earliest feminists (the Bābīs were opposed to the segregation of women which is so typical of Muslim society). The Bābīs who had sought refuge abroad, however, reorganized themselves in Baghdād under the leadership of Bahā'u'llāh, whom the majority of Bābīs regarded as the future and greater prophet proclaimed by the Bāb. At the same time, the movement declared that it was a new universal religion and adopted a more pacifist and humanitarian attitude. To-day there are 30,000 Bāha'ī in Teheran alone, and followers are to be found in more than 300 countries throughout the world. The Bahā'ī have now achieved considerable success in the ex-colonial territories of Africa and Asia and in Latin America.

After the political failure of the Bābī movement, the new Persian middle classes, consisting largely of traders, found in the liberal ideas which percolated through Europe a further way of freeing themselves from the autocracy of the *shāh*. On his own travels in Europe the sovereign himself was greatly impressed by European progress (he wrote a simple, colourful, and sometimes rather ingenuous account of these), and as a result he welcomed foreign missions indiscrimately and granted them concessions that were often unwarranted. The first printing-press had been set up in Tabrīz in 1816–7, and in about 1850 the first Persian newspaper (*Rūznāmè-yi vaqāyi '-i ittifāqiyè*, 'The journal of events that occur') was produced at the instigation of the minister Mīrzā Taqī Khān. However, it appears that a certain Mīrzā Sālik had already started a printed weekly paper covering events in Teheran in 1841. In 1852, the first university was founded, the *Dāru'l-Funūn* ('House of the arts'), again on the initiative of Mīrzā Taqī Khān, who fell into disgrace shortly before its inauguration. Its first director was the critic and man of letters Rizā Qulī Khān Hedāyat (1800–72), who recruited mainly Austrian teachers. On first opening it had 100 students, and instruction was given not only in military affairs but also in geometry, medicine, surgery, pharmacy, and mineralogy, as well as European languages, particularly French. (As in Europe, France dominated the culture, though not the politics, of Persia.) The *Dāru'l-Funūn* also concerned itself with the translation of books from European languages. Among the first to be translated (and the list shows the indiscriminating taste of the day) were a *History of Napoleon*, Fénélon's *Télémaque*, *The Count of Monte Cristo*, *The Three*

Musketeers, Stanley's *Travels*, George Rawlinson's work on the Sassanids, *The Seventh Great Monarchy* (a further example which shows how the modern interest in the pre-Islamic past dates from the Qājār period), as well as books on mathematics, anatomy, physics, geometry, etc.

Increasing trade with the West further strengthened the European influence. James Baillie Fraser, who travelled through Persia in 1821, wrote: 'Persia, it is true, is a poor country and only a small part of its population can indulge in superfluous luxuries; but its increasing contacts with Europe and European comfort have created a desire to possess the luxuries and commodities brought from Europe, so that its consumption of these is extensive and constantly growing'. Direct commercial exchanges between Great Britain and Persia were renewed in 1830 (previously English goods had in general been imported from India). A trade route through Trebizond in Turkey was opened, and within a few years it was carrying goods to the value of a million pounds sterling and the amount was increasing continuously. Between the years 1845 and 1865, the maritime trade through the Persian Gulf increased fivefold. In the financial year 1868–9 the value of the import and export trade (excluding that carried by small coastal boats) across the Persian Gulf and through Oman was estimated at £6,000,000. Trade with Russia became very active, particularly after the Treaty of Turkmānchāy. Russian exports to Persia, consisting mainly of manufactured goods handled by Georgian merchants from Tiflis, were estimated at approximately one million ducats annually. In 1904, Russian exports to Persia were valued at £2,000,000, and imports at £1,750,000. Shipping routes were developed on the Caspian, chiefly with Russian capital. In 1867, fourteen steamships as well as a large number of small sailing ships of 40 to 100 tons were trading between Astrakhan and Anzalī. In the Persian Gulf, a line of steamers sailed regularly every fourteen days between Bombay and Basra, calling at the Persian port of Bandar 'Abbās.

In 1858–9, the Persian Government began the construction of the country's first telegraph line, linking Sultāniyyè with Teheran. Then in 1860, this was extended to Tabrīz, and to Julfa in 1863. Other lines followed, most of them constructed by the British. Particularly important was the telegraph line from London through Russia to Teheran which the Indo-European Company built in 1870.

Because of Persia's feudal conditions and the absence of any Tariff controls, this sudden opening up of trade with European nations resulted in a huge increase in the import of goods, and reduced almost to nil the production of those articles which she needed and which she could have manufactured herself. Thus, local industry eventually degenerated, despite the attempts of 'Abbās Mīrzā to build factories along European lines, to be run by Europeans, and despite the existence of various ordinance factories in Tabrīz (mentioned by George Fowler in 1841), set up by a Persian who had been sent to Europe to study the subject. In 1872, Nāsiru'd-Dīn granted a disastrous seventy-year concession, against insufficient guarantees, to Baron Julius de Reuter to construct railways, irrigation works, etc., throughout the entire country, but popular opinion forced him to withdraw it. In 1890, the *shāh* made a further mistake when he granted the famous tobacco concession to a certain Major Talbot, who was to have a fifty-year monopoly of all buying, selling and manufacture of tobacco within the country and abroad in exchange for an annual sum of £15,000 and a quarter of the profits. The Persian tobacco-growers and producers, as well as the tobacco-smokers, were so indignant that once again the concession had to be withdrawn.

During this period (1886–90) there appeared at the Persian court a number of odd figures, such as the Muslim agitator Jamālu'd-Din al-Afghāni (1838–97), who supported a somewhat liberal and modern form of Islam, and was fiercely opposed to the tobacco concession. Another was Malkom Khān, an extraordinary Armenian adventurer who had been converted to Islam (his father had named him Malkom in admiration of Sir John Malcolm!), and who began his career at court as conjuror, no less. He was the founder of Persian freemasonry (*farāmūsh-khāně*, 'the house of oblivion'), became Persian minister in London, called himself 'prince', inaugurated a lottery, and edited an independent liberal newspaper, *Qānūn*, 'The Law'. The personality of Malkom Khān, a highly intelligent man but lacking any moral sense or serious ability, demonstrates the limitations of the so-called political liberalism in Persia, which gained the unjustified enthusiasm of certain Europeans who, having no historical understanding, placed it on the same plane as the liberal movements which had been current in Europe a few decades earlier. In fact, liberal and modern ideas, which had not sprung from the Persian society of the times but had been directly imported from abroad, were being simply imposed on an economic structure that was still basically feudal. Persian society could have achieved a truly modern development only as the result of an internal revolution, such as that intended by the Bābīs, for example.

In 1896, Nāsiru'd-Dīn Shāh was assassinated by a follower of Jamālu'd-Dīn al-Afghāni, while preparations were being made to celebrate the fiftieth anniversary (in lunar years) of his reign. The liberal and revolutionary tendencies which had gathered strength during his lifetime, exploded during the reign of his successor, Muzaffaru'd-Dīn Shāh (1896–1906). The new *shāh* was an invalid who spent much of his time on trips to Europe. In order to fill the empty coffers of the treasury and to pay for his travels, he borrowed money from foreign countries in exchange for concessions which were economically harmful to the country. For example, in 1900 the Banque d'Escompte de Perse, which was Russian-owned, granted a loan of £2,400,000 in exchange for all the customs revenue of the entire country with the exception of Fārs and the Persian Gulf. In 1902, the Russians granted a loan of 10,000,000 roubles, in exchange for the concession to build a road from Julfa to Teheran via Tabrīz and Qazvīn. When some merchants of Teheran were given a sentence of corporal punishment in 1905, the people's resentment of the corrupt minister 'Ainu 'd-Daulè exploded. (The merchants, who formed the kernel of the new and somewhat liberal middle classes, were, and to some extent still are, the most reliable and honest group of people in Persia.) A large proportion of the Shi'ite Muslim clergy also added their powerful support to the 'constitutional' movement. Despite the reactionary influence of many *'ulamā*, during this period it was certain factions of the clergy, rather than the Europhile bourgeosie with their liberal theories which provided the people with their last hope, for the people themselves were powerless against an oppression that contradicted the tenets of Islamic law. Eventually, the *shāh* was forced to concede the election of a Constitutional Assembly or Parliament (*majlis-i shūrā-yi millī*, 'national consultative assembly', known in short as the *Majlis*). Obviously, in view of the social organization, the electorate was very limited, but the Assembly met in October 1906 and drew up a constitution, which was signed by the *shāh* a few days before his death.

During the reign of Muhammad 'Alī (1907–9), Persia reached the nadir of decadence. In 1907, an Anglo-Russian agreement divided the country into two spheres of influence, English in the south, Russian in the north, and Persian sovereignty became almost nominal. In 1908, intolerant of the constitution and other restrictions, the *shāh* ordered the bombardment of the Parliament building, and this led to an actual revolution, which was supported by many influential *mujtahids* (Shi'ite clergy) and the powerful nomadic tribe of the Bakhtiārī. The revolutionaries (*mujāhidīn*, 'fighters of the holy war') were victorious, deposed the *shāh*, and placed on the throne his infant son Ahmad Shāh (1909–25).

The constitutionalists, however, did not provide the country with a much better government. It was only a Europeanized elite who held liberal, constitutional views, and it was not supported by the traditional classes as a whole. It is even said that, in order to persuade the Bakhtiārī to fight for the constitution (*Mashrūtè*), they were told that this mysterious *Mashrūtè* was a venerable old man, who was a saint and a close friend of the *shāh*. The situation became even more chaotic in the years immediately preceding and following the First World War. There were revolts in Mashhad, the shrine city of the Shi'ites in Khorāsān, which the Russians committed the sacrilege of bombarding in 1912. (The memory of this incident is still so alive in the people's minds to-day, that the anti-Communists use it for the purposes of anti-Soviet propaganda, though of course it was the Tsarist regime that was involved.) Muhammad 'Alī Shāh attempted an uprising, and the British and Russians invaded. There followed the convention of 1919—quickly denounced—by which Persia became little more than a British protectorate.

During the Qājār period the ever-increasing pressure of Europe transformed the feudal economy into a money economy, and the economic and social condition of the country took on a complete new shape. The various forms of fiefdom were changed irreparably, to the advantage of the new middle classes created by commerce and the change of circumstances. An urban middle class developed, though lacking the historial experience of its European counterparts, which in the Middle Ages had passed through a phase of living in free cities. In Iran, therefore, the middle classes were born in a 'colonial' manner, since the special circumstances in which the economy had developed and in particular the pastoral nomad type of feudalism had impeded them from appearing of their own accord. Iran thus had all the disadvantages of being a colony without any of the few advantages, such as the creation of industries either to the direct benefit of the colonizers or for their military purposes, improvements in the juridical system, and so forth. One could even claim, paradoxically enough, that the present situation in Iran would perhaps have been better if the country had for a time become a British or Russian colony: but this was not possible, due to the proximity of the two giants, the need to maintain a balance of power, and the complex political situation in Europe at the time.

The early years of Qājār rule did not bring any major changes in the Persian economy or social life. On the one hand, the Qājārs had inherited from the Safavids the idea of a sacred and absolute monarchy, and therefore strove to strengthen the central authority; on the other, as good Turkish *khāns* they partly revived the ancient but dangerous practice of distributing land as *tuyūl*. The army was composed of a small force of regulars—that is to say, the royal bodyguard—and a number of provincial, mainly tribal contingents. For example, in 1808–9 the governor of Shīrāz had in his service 1,000 horseman, 200 of whom (the number provided by the nomadic tribe of the Bakhtiārī) formed his bodyguard. In an emergency he was able to put 20,000 horsemen into the field. The troops provided their own arms and clothes, and received an annual sum of 40 piastres, and a daily allowance of one *mann* ($7\frac{1}{4}$ lbs) of barley, 2 *mann* of straw, and $\frac{1}{4}$ *mann* of wheat, except in spring when their horses were free to graze in the pasture-lands. Furthermore, they each had a plot of land whose produce supported their families. When a new levy was required, each tribal chieftain produced the number of men requested of him. Such an army did not stand a chance against the regular soldiers of the Russians and the Indian sepoys of the British. 'Abbās Mīrzā attempted on several occasions to improve the system of recruitment, but with little success, and it was not until 1879, when the famous Cossack Division was founded, with its Russian officers and instructors, that Persia first began to have a fairly efficient military force. But wherever they were sent, whether it was to put down a local insurrection or to fight the enemy on the frontiers, the troops generally brought devastation to the lands through which they passed.

The *tuyūldār* (beneficiaries of *tuyūl*) tended to become the hereditary proprietors of the land, though in theory their rights were limited to the collection of taxes. Government taxes, therefore, came to be identified with the *bahrè-yi mālikānè*, the 'proprietor's share' of the produce of the land which he had come to own. The powerful nomadic tribes (now to some extent semi-nomadic) were completely submissive to their chiefs, who were therefore made personally responsible for the collection of taxes, often in their case paid in kind. Customary law (*'urf*) prevailed in many districts, and this was often less humane than Islamic law. In this the nomadic tribes, who also had their special rights, their council of elders, and so on, differed from the rest of the population and formed a kind of state within the state. Requisitions, false demands for the payment of tax arrears, out-of-date land registers (which could lead to a once wealthy but now impoverished village being exorbitantly taxed, and vice versa), and other injustices of all kinds were everyday affairs.

While on the one hand there was a slight decrease in the extent of *vaqf* lands, the *khālisè* increased as a result of confiscation, or 'annexation' in times of famine in order to supply the state with seed, and so on. According to J. Scott-Waring, an eighth of Fārs and Persian Iraq was the property of the *shāh*. The transition from feudalism to the modern world was not a sudden one: it proceeded slowly, and indeed there is much that is feudal in the social and agricultural systems in Iran to-day. Even in the days of Nāsiru'd-Dīn Shāh it was clear that the only way to improve the country's condition was to reform the taxation system, and at the same time to sell off the excessive *khālisè*, and thus transform them into private property, rather than giving individuals the right to a share of the *khālisè* revenue (i.e. *tuyūl*). Amīn us-Sultān, Nāsiru'd-Dīn Shāh's minister at the end of his reign, initiated many decrees concerning the transfer of land. Newly acquired private property which had formerly been *khālisè* (*khālisejāt-i intiqāli*) was, however, made subject to a particularly high tax, estimated in terms of produce, which was then converted into its money value at a fixed rate known as *tas'īr*. Such private property still had certain restrictions on it, for though it could be inherited, it could not be sold to a third party. A large amount of crown land was sold in this way towards the end of Nāsiru'd-Dīn Shāh's reign. There was a special form of ownership in the case of lands held by nomadic tribes as winter and summer grazing-grounds (*qishlāq* and *yailāq*, or, in Persian, *sardsīr* and *garmsīr*), and these were subject to special taxes.

The taxation system was administered by various local *mustaufi* (fiscal accountants), at the head of whom was the *mustaufi al-mamālik*. A sum was fixed for each village, and then the local authorities or village elders decided how much was due from each peasant. Towards the end of Nāsiru'd-Dīn Shāh's reign, unsuccessful attempts were made to standardize the absurdly complicated system of taxes. Various edicts and decrees were issued, which merely served to confuse the situation even more. The relationship between the various types of landowner and the peasant farmers differed in the different regions. In certain cases—as in the earliest and most recent times—the individual plots of land were assigned to this or that peasant on a permanent basis, while in others, the plots of farm land were redistributed annually or at other fixed intervals. However, according to James Baillie Fraser, in the early years of the nineteenth century one could still find villages in Azerbaijān where the peasants' rights were safeguarded by a rudimentary form of democracy, subject nevertheless, to the whims of the central government or government officials.

It is interesting to glance at the annual balance-sheet of a peasant farmer at the turn of the century, just prior to the constitutional reform, which was published by the Russian scholar Tigranov in 1905. While the farmer in this example exploited the landless farm-labourers, he was not himself a true landlord in the capitalist sense of the term but rather the tenant of a powerful landowner, by whom he in turn was exploited to the full.

Taxes and expenses	Corn (in Russian poods: 1 pood = 16.38 kg. or about 36 lbs)	Value (in 1900 roubles)
Tithe (*ushr*) to the treasury	59	20.50
Tithe to the landlord	50	17.50
Tax on head of cattle	18	6.00
Straw and hay	11	4.00
Dast-andāz and *barkardè* (gifts to landlord and cartage *corvée*)	17	6.00
To the *mubāshir* (landlord's factor) and state official	14	5.00
To the factor (*brevi manu*)	10	3.50
Donations, tolls, fines, etc.	14	5.00
To watchman and herdsman	12	4.00
Obligatory free work and hire of day-labourers (60 working days)	35	12.00
Loan of half the seed-corn	45	16.00
Interest on borrowed corn	11	4.00
Ecclesiastical dues	10	3.50
Total	306	107.00

Besides the recognition of private property and the assurance that no one could be deprived of his land except in cases approved by the *sharī'a* (Islamic law, which freed believers from tyrannical and inimical usages), the constitution of 1907 introduced the following important reforms: 1) The many pensions and special concessions granted to a large number of princes and dignitaries were abolished or reduced. 2) The extraordinary and arbitrary taxes which governors were in the habit of exacting to provide for their expenses and those of their dependants were incorporated into the regular taxes, and the central government was made responsible for the proper payment of its officials' expenses. (An idea of how high these supplementary taxes could be is seen in an example from Kirmān, where the regular tax payable was 44,000 *tūmān*, while with the supplementary taxes the total came to 170,000 *tūmān*!). 3) The *tūyūl* system was abolished. 4) The *tas 'īr* system was abolished. In many cases, for example, the price of grain increased but the beneficiaries still paid their taxes at the old rate, since price variations were not taken into account.

Though these reforms remained largely theoretical on account of the increasing powerlessness of the central authorities in the years leading up to the First World War, the abolition of the *tūyūl* had great symbolic meaning, for it represented the official end of the feudal period. The American Morgan Shuster, who was appointed treasurer general in 1911 in order to reform and reorganize the country's finances, retained a very unfavourable opinion of the social and economic situation in the new 'liberal' Persia. (In due course he was forced to leave the country as a result of Russian diplomatic pressure.) As the central government collapsed, local chieftains, large landowners, and tribal *khāns* became virtually independent rulers in their own areas, and the situation became even worse that it had been in the preceding feudal era.

Emulating the earlier example of Nādir Shāh (though the comparison must not be pressed too closely), Rizā Khān, an officer in the Persian Cossack Division from Māzandarān, carried out a *coup d'état* in 1921. He marched on Teheran and then served as minister of war in the new cabinet and its short-lived successors, eventually founding the present *Pahlavī* dynasty. He was mainly concerned with the reorganization of the armed forces and the subjugation of the nomadic tribes, which had become semi-independent and were in a continual state of rebellion. The successes of Rizā Khān, combined with the absence of Ahmad Shāh (who as usual was undergoing so-called medical treatment in Europe), and the example of Mustafa Kemal in Turkey, led to the development of strong Republican feelings which were quickly suppressed by the reactionary Shi'ite *mujtahid*. When a ministerial crisis arose early in 1925, the *Majlis* gave Rizā Khān full military powers. A law passed in June of that year abolished the pompous medieval titles and instituted the use of the family name. Rizā Khān adopted the name of Pahlavī, by which he wished to recall the glorious past of pre-Islamic Persia, and this became symbolic of his reign, as it is to a large extent of the present one. Etymologically, *Pahlavī* means 'Parthian', while linguistically it is applied to Middle Persian. In modern Persian it is often used to signify 'ancient Iranian'. In October, Parliament declared Ahmad Shāh deposed (he died in exile in Europe), and in December the new Constituent Assembly pronounced Rizā Khān (now Rizā Shāh) the new *shāhinshāh-i Īrān*.

It is not easy to pass judgment on the work of Rizā Shāh, who died in exile in 1944, but is now known as *Rizā Shāh-i Kabīr* (Riza Shah the Great). To a great extent he tried to imitate the nationalism of Mustafa Kemal, but he was less radical. He strove to his utmost to limit the Shi'ite clergy's intervention in political and cultural affairs, prohibited the use of the veil by women, fostered feminine emancipation, forbade the wearing of old-fashioned national dress such as the turban (except in the case of those who had a religious title to it), and abolished the traditional religious processions of the Shi'ites in the month of *muharram* in commemoration of the martyrdom of the Prophet's grandson Husain, together with the associated sacred performances (*ta'ziè*). He introduced a new law regarding marriage and divorce, reduced the number of official holidays from forty to twenty-three, prohibited the use of the religious lunar calendar in business affairs and replaced it with the Persian solar calendar (beginning on *Naurūz*, 21 March), and inaugurated a plan for settling the nomadic tribes. But he would not, and perhaps could not, understand that all these reforms, which were sometimes of little effect and which often had to be imposed with pointless violence, would have come about quite naturally if firm, radical steps had been taken to carry out a revolutionary land reform. But the *shāh* was involved with the elite of large landowners. (The fact that he had persecuted some of them and confiscated their lands means nothing, for even the earliest feudal sovereigns had done as much!). Instead, he tried to allay the people's discontent with nationalistic slogans which harked back to ancient pre-Islamic Persia rather than the Persia of Islamic tradition which was more historically and realistically related to the contemporary Persian scene. In some cases the reforms led to uprisings, which were firmly suppressed.

In the cultural field, the *shāh* founded the University of Teheran, established the Academy of the Persian Language (*Farhangistān-i Īran*), and celebrated with great splendour the millennium of the birth of Firdausī in 1933. He paid particular attention to education at all levels and the educational system was standardized to such an extent that foreign schools which did not conform to government requirements were closed. And yet, since this was not accompanied by concomitant social reforms, eighty per cent of the people of Persia are still illiterate to-day. The Academy of the Persian Language was given the task of purifying the language by removing foreign words. When one considers that almost fifty per cent of the Persian literary vocabulary is taken from Arabic, one can easily understand the difficulties of the task and the almost complete failure to be adopted of the list of new words which the Academy produced.

As far as the economy was concerned, there was a monetary crisis. The authority to produce banknotes was withdrawn from the Imperial Bank of Persia (an Anglo-Qājār concern in origin), and transferred to the new National Bank (*Bānk-i Millī*). Since he desired a more favourable contract, the *shāh*, despite British protests, repudiated the concession of the Anglo-Persian Oil Company, which had no alternative but to accept the new terms imposed, which were more favourable to the Persian economy. One of the most important achievements of Rizā Shāh's reign was the construction of the Trans-Iranian railway, begun in 1927, which connects the Persian Gulf with the Caspian Sea over 865 miles of difficult terrain. The determination with which all these innovations were pushed through, combined with the superficiality of the results, has given modern Persia the appearance, at first glance, of a highly Europeanized country (when one arrives at Teheran airport one has the impression one is in a European far more than an Asiatic capital), which still requires very substantial reforms.

At the outset of the Second World War, Persia declared herself neutral and went on with the work she had been carrying out in peacetime. This included the construction of further railway lines, so that to-day there exists an east-west line running from Tabrīz to Mashhad, which crosses the north-south line at Teheran. (The rolling stock is excellent.) When Germany invaded the Soviet Union in 1941, the *shāh* reiterated his somewhat insincere declarations of neutrality, but to little purpose, for in August that year Persia was simultaneously occupied by Russian and British forces. In September the *shāh* abdicated in favour of his son and heir, Muhammad Rizā, and was deported to Mauritius.

Muhammad Rizā had a much less powerful personality than his father. His reign, at least during the years 1941–53, followed a theoretically more democratic course. (One must apply the word 'theoretically' because, despite all pretences, it is unrealistic to speak of democracy where the great majority of the people are illiterate, and where in the country the elections are in practice run by the large landowners.) In fact, despite the nominal existence of free elections and a parliament, Rizā Shāh 'the Great' had practically governed the country as a dictator. As was to be expected in a state that was a democracy only in name, strength returned to the Shi'ite religious authorities and the large landowners, who together form a clan made up of a few families. They in fact rule over the ignorant masses, who are incapable of taking practical advantage of the means of government which the democracy in theory puts at their disposal.[1] Rizā Shāh's reforms could have had a positive value only if they had been rigorously carried out and their consequences pursued to their logical conclusions, as happened in the case of Ataturk's reforms in Turkey. Instead, they turned out to be half-measures, partly on account of the Persians' preference for moderation and good sense. Consequently, the most insipid achievements were a form of vacuous nationalism imitated from Europe but quite devoid of any sense of history and a terrible economic conservatism disguised under the European façade adopted by the dominating classes who, nevertheless, are more advanced than in other Islamic countries. Even Communism, which has a large following among students and intellectuals who look to Moscow rather than London, Paris, or Washington (or Bonn—the elite has shown considerable admiration for Germany since before the War), seems to be superficial and not to have taken deep root. Communism feeds not only on the vast economic variations between the classes but also on local nationalism—particularly that of the Kurds and Turks. For example, the Turks of Azerbaijān, who form a compact group numbering

1 On the manner in which elections are still held to-day, see G. R. Scarcia, 'Intorno alle elezioni persiane', *Oriente Moderno*, XL, 1960, pp. 537–52.

some millions, with their centre at Tabrīz, and who could boast of holding the most liberal views at the time of the constitutional struggles at the turn of the century, are forbidden in the name of 'Aryan' nationalism to have a newspaper in their own language. At the same time, all the Kurds' requests for national autonomy are suppressed. It is therefore not surprising that in 1946 Azerbaijān rose against the central government and set up a Communist-inspired autonomous republic. This was put down with severe reprisals at the end of the year, once the Soviets had withdrawn their aid. The events that brought Musaddiq to power in 1951, and those that swept him away again in 1953, are a serious reminder of the latent discontent of the people and of the contradictions of the complex and fluid social situation. They are, however, too recent to be dealt with at length in these pages.

Contemporary Persian society suffers above all from the fact that, in a comparatively brief period, it has passed from (or is still passing from) a feudal structure, largely based on pastoral nomadism, to a capitalist structure in decline, largely due to external pressures. Persian society has undergone neither a Reformation, nor a Renaissance, nor a French Revolution so far, but merely variations on a theme of feudalism. The immense task of the Persian ruling class appears to be to find their *own* way of achieving simultaneously a religious Reformation (though the majority prefer an outworn scepticism *à la* Voltaire, combined with a decrepit tradition), a Renaissance (but the spiritual break is too great for a 'return to the Achaemenids' to have the same effect as the European rediscovery of Greece in the fifteenth century), and a French Revolution (which, to be effective, must be integrated with a social revolution also). So far, however, and we say this with sincere regret, the Persian elite does not appear to have realized where its historical duty lies.

Bibliography

There is as yet no general history of Persia that is both scholarly and covers the whole period, though the Cambridge University Press is preparing a *Cambridge History of Persia* which is to appear in several volumes. To date (1970) the following two volumes of this have been published: Vol. I: *The Land of Iran*, ed. by W. B. Fisher (Cambridge 1968), Vol. V: *The Saljuq and Mongol Periods*, ed. by J. A. Boyle (Cambridge 1968). P. M. Sykes' *History of Persia* (3rd edn, 2 vols., London, 1930) is superficial and out of date, as is Sir John Malcolm's much earlier *History of Persia* (2 vols., London, 1815; 2nd edn, 1829). There are good general text-books in Russian, amongst which we may mention V. Bartol'd, *Iran: istoricheskii obzor* (Tashkent, 1926); M. S. Ivanov, *Ocherk istorii Irana* (Moscow, 1952), and the volume produced in collaboration by N. V. Pigulevskaya, A. Y. Yakubovskii, I. P. Petrushevskii, L. V. Stroevska, and A. M. Beleniskii, *Istoriya Irana a drevneishih vremen do konca XVIII veka* (Leningrad, 1958), which, however, does not include the Qasar and modern periods. There are two excellent summaries in Italian, A. Pagliaro, *Iran antico*, and V. Minorsky, *Iran Islamico*, to be found in vol. 1 of *Le Civiltà dell'Oriente* (Rome, 1956, pp. 383–513). All these works contain useful bibliographies. Also useful (though, unfortunately, it lacks a bibliography) is *La civilisation iranienne* (Paris, 1952), a collection of essays by leading French scholars in the field. See also: R. N. Frye, *The Heritage of Persia* (London, 1963). An important bibliography of Persian historians and European historians of Persia is found in *Historians of the Middle East*, ed. by B. Lewis and P. M. Holt (London, 1962).

Chapter 1: The Aryans on the Iranian Plateau

The main sources, besides the Assyro-Babylonian tablets, the Greek authors and the Bible, are the *Avesta* and the cuneiform inscriptions of the Achaemenids. The most important complete translations of the *Avesta* are:

J. Darmesteter, 'Le Zend-Avesta, traduction nouvelle avec commentaire', in *Annales du Musée Guimet*, vols. XXI, XXII, and XXIV, Paris, 1892–3; photo. repr., intro. E. Benviste, 3 vols., 1960.

F. Wolff, *Avesta, die Heiligen Bücher der Parsen*, Strasbourg, 1910; new edn, Berlin and Leipzig, 1934.

The Achaemenid inscriptions are reproduced, together with an English translation, in:

R. G. Kent, *Old Persian*, New Haven, 1950; repr. 1961.

The most important studies of the Medean and Achaemenid period are:

C. Huart and L. Delaporte, *L'Iran antique*, Paris, 1943.

I. M. D'yakonov, *Istoriya Midii*, Moscow, 1956.

R. Ghirshman, *Iran from the earliest times to the Islamic conquest*, Harmondsworth, 1954.

G. G. Cameron, *The History of Early Iran*, Chicago, 1936.

A. T. Olmstead, *History of the Persian Empire*, Chicago, 1948.
B. Bretjes, *Die Iranische Welt vor Mohammed*, Heidelberg, 1967.
W. Culican, *The Medes and Persians*, London, 1965.
H. Bengtson, *Griechen und Perser. Die Mittelmeerwelt im Altertum*, I vol. Frankfurt a.M., 1967. Eng. trans: London, 1969.
E. Herzfeld, *The Persian Empire*, ed. by G. Walzer, Wiesbaden, 1968.
On the revolt of Gaumāta-Bardiya:
M. A. Dandamaev, 'Sotsial'naya sushchnost' perevorota Gaumatyi' in *Vestnik Drevnei Istorii* 1958, vol. 4, pp. 36 et seq.
On Alexander's conquest:
A. Pagliaro, *Alessandro Magno*, Rome, 1960, which includes a bibliography.

Chapter 2: The period influenced by Hellenism

Primary sources. Besides the Greek, Syrian, Armenian and other sources, numismatics provide valuable information for the study of this difficult period:
Percy Gardner, *The Parthian Coinage*, 1877.
A. von Petrowicz, *Arsaciden Münzen Katalog*, Vienna, 1904.
W. Wroth, *Catalogue of the Coins of Parthia*, British Museum, 1903.
Allotte de la Fuye, 'Classement des monnaies arsacides' in *Revue numismatique*, 4th series, VIII, 1904.
There is no modern comprehensive work on the Hellenic and Parthian period, but see:
E. Bikerman, *Institutions des Seleucides*, Paris, 1938.
E. Wilhelm, 'Die Parther' in Sanjana, *Avesta, Pahlavi and Ancient Persian Studies*, 1st series, 1904.
George Rawlinson, *The Sixth Oriental Monarchy*, London, 1873.
A. von Gutschmid, *Geschichte Irans und seiner Nachbarländer*, Tübingen, 1888.
W. W. Tarn, *The Greeks in Bactria and India*, Cambridge, 1951.
F. Altheim, *Weltgeschichte Asiens in griechischen Zeitalter*, I–II. Halle, 1947-48.
Berthold Laufer, *Sino-Iranica*, Chicago, 1919.
G. Widengren, *Iranisch-semitische Kulturbegegnung in parthischer Zeit*, Cologne, 1960.
G. Widengren, *Der Feudalismus im alten Iran*, Cologne, 1969.
M. A. R. Colledge, *The Parthians*, London, 1967.
P. Daffina, *L'Immigrazione de Sakā nella Drangiana*, Roma, 1967.

Chapter 3: The Sassanid period

The sources, together with a full bibliography, are listed in an excellent work which has become a classic on the subject:
Arthur Christensen, *L'Iran sous les Sassanides*, 2nd edn, Copenhagen, 1944.
More Recently: A. D. H. Bivar, *The Sassanian Dynasty*, London, 1969.
On the heresies of Mani and Mazdak:
Henri-Charles Puech, *Le Manicheisme, son fondateur, sa doctrine*, Paris, 1949.
O. Klíma, *Mazdak. Geschichte einer sozialen Bewegung im sassanidischen Persien*, Prague, 1957.
On the relations between Iran and Byzantium:

N. V. Pigulevskaya, *Vizantiya i Iran*, Moscow, 1946.
On the cities:
N. V. Pigulevskaya, *Goroda Irana v rannem srednevekov'e*, Moscow, 1956.
On the Christians in mediaeval Iran:
J. Labourt, *Le Christianisme dans l'Empire Perse sous la dynastie sassanide*, Paris, 1904.
G. Messina, *Cristianesimo, Buddhismo, Manicheismo nell'Asia Antica*, Rome, 1947.

Chapter 4: The early centuries of Arab domination

Primary sources. First come the chroniclers and annalists who write in Arabic. Al-Wāqidī, d. 823 (*Kitāb al-Maghāzi*, ed. Kremer, Calcutta, 1855–56); al-Balādhurī, d. 892 (*Kitāb futūh al-buldān*, ed. De Goeje, Leiden, 1863); al-Dīnavarī, d. ca. 895 (*Kitāb akhbār at-tiwāl*, ed. Guirasse, Leiden, 1888); al-Ya'qūbī, d. 892 (*Ta'rīkh*, ed. Houtsma, Leiden, 1883); at-Tabarī, d. 923 (*Ta'rīkh*, ed. De Goeje, 15 vols., Leiden, 1879–1901); French trans. by H. Zotenberg of the Persian version of 'Alī Bal'amī, d. 974, 4 vols., Paris, 1867–74; al-Mas'ūdī, d. 956 (*Murūj adh-dhahab*, ed. and trans. Barbier de Meynard and Pavet de Courteille, 9 vols., Paris, 1861–77); Hamza Isfahāni, ca. 961 (*Ta'rīkh al-umam*, ed. Gottwald, Leipzig, 1844. Latin trans. by Gottwald, 1848).

Also very important are the 'Arab' geographers, nearly all of whom have been published in the *Bibliotheca Geographorum Arabicorum*, Leiden; and the anonymous tenth-century Persian geography, *Hudūd al-'Ālam* (ed. Bartol'd, Leningrad, 1930; Eng. trans. by Minorsky, Leiden, 1937). For the earliest form of taxation, see the famous *Kitāb al Kharāj* of Abū Yusūf (Būlāq ed., 1302 A.H., trans. Fagnan, Paris, 1921). The encyclopaedic *Fihrist* of an-Nadīm (ca. 988) gives bibliographical information of the first order on various aspects of the cultural history of the period (ed. Flügel, Leipzig, 1871). See also Ibn Miskawayh, d. 1030 (*Kitāb tajārib al-umam*, only partially edited and published); ath-Tha'ālibī, d. 1038 (*Kitāb al-ghurar*, ed. and trans. H. Zotenberg, Paris, 1900); al-'Utbi, d.1036 (*Kitāb al-Yamīnī*, important for the history of the Ghaznavids, Delhi, 1847; Lahore, 1883; ed. with commentary by Mānīnī, Cairo, 1869; Eng. trans. by Reynolds of a Persian version, London, 1958; al-Bīrūnī, d. 1048 (*Āthār al-Bāqiya*, ed. Sachau, Leipzig, 1878; trans. by Sachau, London, 1879).

The historians of this period writing in Persian (for a full bibliography see vol. I of Storey's *Persian Literature*, London, 1927–39) include the eleventh-century Gardīzī (*Zein al-Akhbār*, ed. S. Nafīsī, Teheran, 1954), and Beihaqi, also eleventh century (*Ta'rīkh-i Beihaqī*, ed. S. Nafīsī, 1947 and 1953).

An important local history is the *Ta'rīkh Bukhārā* of the tenth-century Narshakhī (ed. Shefer, Paris. Eng. trans. Frye, Cambridge, Mass., 1954).

Studies of the period by European orientalists include:
B. Spuler, *Iran in früh-islamischer Zeit*, Wiesbaden, 1952. A standard work containing a full bibliography and a selection of source material.
C. Huart, *Les Ziyarides*, Paris, 1922.

M. Nazim, *The Life and Times of Sultān Mahmūd of Ghazna*, Cambridge, 1931.

M. Habib, *Sultan Mahmud of Ghaznin*, Bombay, 1927.

A. Y. Yakubovskii, 'Mahmud Gaznevi. K voprosu o proishozhdenii i haraktere gaznevidskogo gosudarstva' in *Ferdovsi*, Leningrad, 1934.

C. E. Bosworth, *Sīstān under the Arabs, from the Islamic conquest to the rise of the Saffavids*, Rome, 1968.

C. E. Bosworth, *The Ghaznavids, their Empire in Afghanistan and Eastern Iran*, 994–1040, Edinburgh, 1963.

Chapter 5: The Seljuk period

Primary sources. Arabic: as-Sam'ānī, d. 1167 (*Kitāb al-ansāb*, a biographical dictionary, ed. Margoliouth, Leiden, 1912); al-Kātib al-Isfahānī, d. 1201 (best known from Bundārī's version at the beginning of the 13th century, *Zubdat an-nusra*, ed. Houtsma, Leiden, 1889); Ibn al-Athīr, d. 1234 (*al-Kāmil fī't-ta'rīkh*, ed. Tornberg, 14 vols., Leiden, 1851–76); Yāqūt, d. 1224 (*Mu'jam al-buldān*, geographical dictionary, ed. Wüstenfeld, Leipzig, 1866–70).

Persian: *Mujmal at-tavārīkh* (anonymous, ca. 1196, ed. Bahar, Teheran, 1939); Rāvandī, early 13th century (*Rāhat as-sudūr*, ed. M. Iqbal, *Gibb Memorial Series*, London, 1921); Nizāmu'-Mulk, d. 1092 (*Siyāsat-nāmè*, ed. and trans. Schefer, Paris, 1891–97; better edn by Khalkālī, Teheran, 1934; excellent Russian trans. by B. N. Zahoder, Moscow, 1949); Nizāmi 'Arūzī, mid-twelfth century (*Chahār Maqālè*, on the four court professions of secretary, poet, astrologer, and physician, with important material on the social and cultural life of the period, ed. Browne, Leiden, 1910; Eng. trans. by Browne, London, 1899; new and better edn by Mo'īn, Teheran, 1957); Muhammad Baghdādī, secretary to Kharizm-shāh Takash at the end of the 12th century (*Kitāb at-tavassul ila t-tarassul*, collection of state papers, letters, etc., ed. Bahmanyar, Teheran, 1936).

Important regional histories of Tabaristān (Ibn Isfandiyār, *Ta'rīkh-i Tabaristān*, ed. A. Iqbāl, 2 vols., Teheran, 1941–42; Eng. abridged trans. in *Gibb Memorial Series*); Sīstān (the anonymous eleventh-century *Ta'rīkh-i Sīstān*, ed. Bahār, Teheran, 1935); the region of Sabzavār (Ibn Funduq, Ta'rīkh-i Beihaq, written in 1168, ed. Bahmanyār, Teheran, 1938); Fārs (*Ibn al-Balkhī*, ca. 1125, *Fārsnāmè*, ed. Le Strange and Nicholson in *Gibb Memorial Series*, 1921).

Among the works of European Orientalists, besides that of Spuler listed for the previous chapter, see:

The Cambridge Medieval History, vol. IV, ch. X, 'Muslim civilisation during the Abbasid period. The Seljuqs'. Cambridge, 1923.

K. Süssheim, *Prolegomena zu einer Ausgabe der Chronik des Seldschuqischen Reiches*, Leipzig, 1912.

Mirkhond, *Geschichte der Seldschuken*, ed. J. A. Vullers, Giessen, 1838.

Sanaullah, *The Decline of the Seljukid Empire*, Calcutta, 1938.

M. T. Houtsma, 'Zur Geschichte der Seldschuqen von Kirman', in *Zeitschr. d. Deut. Morg. Gesell.*, 1885, pp. 362–441.

W. Barthold, *Turkestan down to the Mongol Invasion*, Eng. trans. of the Russian edn of 1898–1900, *Gibb Memorial Series*, N.S., V, London, 1928.

B. N. Zahoder, 'Horasan i obrazovanie gosudarstva Sel'dzhukov', in *Voprosui Istorii*, nos. 5–6, 1945.

I. A. Orbeli, 'Problema sel'dzhukidskogo isskustva', in *Tretii Mezhdunarodnuii Kong. po iranskomu isskustvu i arkheologi*, Moscow, 1939.

A. Y. Yakubovskii, *'Sel 'dzhukskoe dvizhenie i turkmeni v XI v.'*, in *Izv. Ak. Nauk SSSR*, Otd. Obshch. Nauk, n. 4, 1937.

H. Horst, *Die Staatsverwaltung der Grosselgüqen und Hōrazmsāhs* (1038–1231), Wiesbaden, 1964.

On the Ismailis:

M. G. S. Hodgson, *The order of Assassins*, The Hague, 1955. Contains a full bibliography.

A. E. Bertels, *Nazir-i Hosrov i izmailizm*, Moscow, 1959.

B. Lewis, *The Assassins. A radical sect in Islam*, London, 1967.

Also the numerous works of Ivanov, published in the *Ismaili Society Series*, Bombay.

Chapter 6: The Mongol period

Primary sources. Besides Ibn al-Athīr (listed in the bibliography for chapter V), who discusses the Mongol invasion in vol. XII, mention should be made of:

Nasavī, secretary to the last Khārizmshāh (*Sīrat as-Sultān Jalāl ad-Dīn Mankūbertī*, written in Arabic in 1241–42, ed. and trans. Houdas, 2 vols., Paris, 1891–95; *Nafthat al-masdūr*, his memoirs written in Persian in 1234–35, ed. Hidāyat, Teheran, 1930); Minhāj-i Sarāj, *ca.* 1260 (*Tabaqāt-i nasīrī*, ed. W. N. Lees, Calcutta, 1864; trans. Raverty, 2 vols., London, 1873–81); Juwainī, d. 1283 (*Ta'rīkh-i jihāngushāy*, a fundamental source for the history of the first Mongols in Iran, ed. Qazvīnī, 3 vols., *Gibb Memorial Series*, London, 1912–37; Eng. trans. Boyle, London; It. trans. Scarcia, Milan); Nasīrū'd-Dīn Tūsī, d. 1277 (a brief treatise on the finances during the Mongol period, see M. Minovī and W. Minorsky, 'Nasīr ad-Dīn Tūsī on Finance', text and Eng. trans. in *Bulletin of the School of Oriental Studies*, vol. X, part 3, 1940); Rashīdu'd-Dīn Hamadānī, d. 1318 (*Jāmi' at-Tavārīkh*, basic source for the history of the Il-khānids, Mongols, and other peoples, partial ed. Quatremère, Paris, 1836; E. Blochet, London, 1910–14; K. Jahn, Leiden, 1951; complete text and trans. in course of pub. by the Soviet Academy of Sciences under the title *Sbornik letopisei*, 1946; *Mukātibāt-i Rashīdī*, ed. M. Shafi', Lahore, 1947, is a collection of the author's invaluable correspondence; further correspondence and official documents remain unpublished); Wassāf, continued up to 1312 by Rashīdu'd-Dīn (*Ta'rīkh-i Vassāf*, Bombay, 1853; ed. with partial trans. Hammer Purgstall, Vienna, 1856); Hamdullāh Mustaufī Qazwīnī, d. after 1340 (*Ta'rīkh-i guzīdè*, ed. Browne, *Gibb Memorial Series*, London, 1910; *Nuzhat al-qulūb*, ed. with partial trans. G. Le Strange, *Gibb Memorial Series*, London, 1915; complete but unsatisfactory edn, Bombay, 1894); Saifī Harawī, first quarter of the 14th century, wrote an important regional history of Herāt (*Ta'rīkh-nāmè-vi Herāt*, ed. M. Zubeir Siddiqi, Calcutta, 1944); Mahmūd Kutubī, early 15th century (*Ta'rīkh-i muzaffarī*, ed. Browne with an abridged Eng. trans. in his edn of *Ta'rīkh-i guzīdè* mentioned above, important for the history of the Muzaffarids and southern Iran).

Standard works on the period by European scholars:

B. Spuler, *Die Mongolen in Iran*, 2nd edn, Berlin, 1955.

I. P. Petrushevskii, *Zemledelie i agrarnie otnosheniya v Irane XIII–XIV vekov*, Moscow, 1960.

Both the above works contain very full critical bibliographies of the sources, including the important Mongolian sources, as well as those in Chinese, Syriac, Armenian, etc.

On the Sarbedārī:

I. P. Petrushevskii, 'Dvizhenie Sarbedarov v Horasane' in *Uchenie Zapiski Inst. Vost. Ak. Nauk SSSR*, vol. XIV, Moscow, 1956.

Chapter 7 : Tamerlane and the Timurids

Primary sources. The earliest biography of Tamerlane is the *Zafar-nāmè* of Nizāmuddīn Shāmī, written in 1401–4 (ed. Tauer, Prague, 1937), re-written by Alī Yazdī in 1424 (inaccurate edn by M. Ilahdad, Calcutta, 1887–88; antiquated trans. by Petit de la Croix, Paris, 1722). A most important Timurid historian is Hāfiz-i Abru, d. 1430 (*Majma' at-tavārīkh*, a universal history in four volumes, the last of which, on the Timurids, is particularly important and bears the title *Zubdat at-tavārīkh*, ed. and trans. Khānbābā Bāyānī, 2 vols., Paris and Teheran, 1936–38); Abd ar-Razzāq Samarqandī, d. 1482, wrote a continuation of this last work (*Matla' as-sa 'dain*, Lahore, 1941–49; partial Fr. trans. by Quatremère in *Notices et Extraits de la Bibliothèque du Roi*, vol. XIV, Paris, 1841). Mīrkhwānd, d. 1498 (*Rauzat as-safā*, an immense universal history in 7 books, ed. Rizā Qulī Khān, 2 vols., Teheran, 1853–54; trans, Rehatzek, 5 vols., London, 1891–94); continuation of Mīrkhwānd by Khāndamīr, d. 1536 (*Habīb as-siyar*, ed. Humā'ī, 4 vols., Teheran, 1954); Daulatshāh, fl. 1490, produced a collection of poets' lives (*Tazkirat ash-shu'arā'*, ed. Browne, London, 1901) which contains important information on the life of the Timurid period.

An important source for the study of the last Aq-qoyunlu and the first Safavids is Fazlullāh ibn Rūzbihān of Khunjī, d. 1521 at Bukhārā, who was a fierce anti-Shi'ite and anti-Safavid (*Ta'rīkh-i 'ālam-ārāy-i amīnī*; trans. and summarized in V. Minorsky, *Persia in A.D. 1478–1490*, London, 1957).

Local histories include:

Zahīru'd-Dīn Mar'ashī, *Ta'rīkh-i Tabaristān*, ed. Dorn in *Muhammedanische Quellen zur Geschichte der südlichen Küstländer des Kaspischen Meeres*, vol. I, St. Petersburg, 1850; and *Ta'rīkh-i Gīlān i Deilamistān*, ed. Rabino, Resht, 1912. Important for the history of Herāt and of the Shaibanids are the memoirs of Zainu'd-Dīn Vāsifī, d. *ca.* 1551–66 (*Badā'i' al-waqā'i'*, ed. Bolduirev, Moscow, 1961).

There is only one important source in Arabic: Ahmad ibn 'Arabshāh, d. *ca.* 1450 ('*Ajā'ib al-maqdūr fī akhbār Tīmūr*, Cairo, 1868–69; Eng. trans. Sanders, London, 1936).

Interesting contemporary European sources are the account of the journey of the Spanish envoy Clavijo in 1403–5 to the court of Tamerlane (various edns and trans., especially Eng. trans. Le Strange, 1928), and the famous accounts of the Venetian ambassadors to the court of the Aq-qoyunlu - Caterino Zeno (1471-73), Iosafat Barbaro (1471-78, and Ambrogio Contarini (1474-76)—published in Ramusio's great collection (*Delle navigazioni e viaggi*, Venice), and of the Russian merchant from Tver, Atanasio Nikitin, who was in Iran in the years 1467-69 and again in 1472 (*Khozhdeniya za tri morya*, ed. B. D. Grekov and V. P. Adrianova-Perets, Moscow, 1948).

Works by European scholars:

W. Barthold, *Zwölf Vorlesungen über die Geschichte der Türken Mittelasiens*, trans. T. Menzel, Berlin, 1925.

W. Barthold, *Herat unter Husein Baiqara*, trans. W. Hinz, Leipzig, 1937.

W. Barthold, *Ulugh Beg und seine Zeit*, trans. W. Hinz, Leipzig, 1935.

L. Bouvat, *L'empire mongol: 2e phase, Timour et les timourides*, Paris, 1927.

L. Bouvat, *Essai sur la civilisation timouride*, Paris, 1926.

H. Melzig, *Timur*, New York, 1940.

Harold Lamb, *Tamerlane the Earth-Shaker*, London, 1932.

A. Y. Yakubovskii, 'Timur. Opuit kratkoi harakteristiki' in *Voprosui Istorii*, nos. 8-9, 1946.

V. A. Gordevskii, *Kara-Koyunlu*, Baku, 1927.

W. Minorsky, *La Perse au XVe siècle entre la Turquie et Venise*, Paris, 1933.

Chapter 8: The Safavids

Primary sources. For the early period of the Safavid dynasty, see the anonymous *Ta'rīkh-i shāh Ismā'īl-i Safavī* (ed. with partial trans. in Denison Ross, *Early Years of Shah Ismail I*, London, 1896), and part IV of Book III of Khāndamīr, listed above. The poems of Shāh Ismā'īl in Azeri have been published by T. O. Gandjei (*Il Canzoniere di Shāh Ismā'īl*, Naples, 1959). See also: Yahyā Qazvīnī, 1555 (*Lubb at-tavārīkh*; It. trans. Pietro della Valle, 1623; two Latin trans., Paris, 1690, and Halle, 1783); Khūrshāh al-Husainī, ambassador to the Indian Muslim court of Ahmednagar in Iran in 1546, d. 1565 (*Ta'rīkh-i ilchī-yi Nizāmshāh*, extracts in Schefer, *Chrestomathie Persane*, vol. II, pp. 55-104, Paris, 1883); the *Tazkirè-yi Shāh Tahmāsp*, first believed to be the memoirs of Shāh Tahmāsp I but later shown to be the record of conversations held in 1561 between the Shāh and a Turkish embassy (ed. Horn in *Zeitschr. d. Deut. Morg. Ges.*, vols. 44-45, 1890); Hasan Bek Rūmlū, who belonged to the qizilbāsh tribe of the Rūmlū (*Ahsan at-tavārīkh* in twelve large books, of which one only, Book XII, concerning events between 1494 and 1578, has been published by C. N. Seddon in *Gaekwad Oriental Series*, LVII, Text, and LXIX, abridged trans., Baroda, 1931-34); Sharaf Khān Bidlīsī, a Sunnite Kurd emir who was a vassal of the Safavids and wrote a work in two volumes in 1596 which is also important for the mediaeval history of the Kurds (*Sharaf-nāmè*, ed. Vel'yaminov-Zernov, 2 vols., St Petersburg, 1860-62; new edn, Cairo, 1931; Fr. trans. Charmois, 2 vols., St Petersburg, 1868-75); Iskandar beg Munshī, the most important Safavid historian, who lived at the court of Shāh 'Abbās I and died in 1633 (*Ta'rīkh-i 'ālam-ārāy-i abbasī*, 2 vols., Teheran, 1955-56; continued by the author himself up to his death as *Zeil-i ta'rīkh-i 'ālam-ārāy-i abbasī*, ed. S. Khānsārī, Teheran, 1938);

Muhammad Yūsuf Qazvīnī Vālih (*Khuld-i barrīn*, which records events up to 1667–68, partial edn covering the reign of Shāh Safi, 1634–42, by S. Khansari in his edn of the *Ƶeil* of Iskandar Beg listed above); Shaikh Husain ibn Shaikh Abdāl Zāhidī, descended from an old *shaikh* of the Safavid brotherhood, wrote during the reign of Shāh Sulaiman (1666–94) a genealogy of the Safavids (*Silsilat an-nasab-i safaviyyè*, critical edn in *Publications Iranshahr*, no. 6, Berlin, 1924–25); 'Abd al-Fattāh Fūminī, author of a local history of Gīlān from 1517 to 1629 (*Ta'rīkh-i Gīlān*, ed. Dorn in *Quellen zur Geschichte der südlichen Küstländer*, pt. III, St Petersburg, 1858); an important source for the Safavid administration is the anonymous *Tazkirat al-mulūk* (ed. and trans. Minorsky in the *Gibb Memorial Series*, N.S., vol. XVI, London, 1943); and numerous unpublished documents, firmans, letters, etc., are also to be found in European libraries. Some of the documents in Florence have been published and translated into Italian by V. Pontecorvo ('Relazioni tra lo scià 'Abbās e i Granduchi di Toscana Ferdinando I e Cosimo II', in *Rendic. Lincei. Sc. Mor.*, 8° series, IV, 1949, pp. 157 *et seq.*). some of those in the Museum of the Armenian SSR have been published by M. N. Hubua (Tbilisi, 1953).

Of particular interest for this period are the diaries and accounts of European travellers, including Marin Sanuto (*Diarii*, 30 folio vols., Venice, 1879–1902), who recorded events between the years 1496 and 1533; an anonymous Venetian (1514); the Venetians M. Membré (1542), *Relazione di Persia*, Naples, 1969, G. Minadoi (1558) and V. D'Alessandri (1571); the merchants Anthony Jenkinson (1561), Richard Johnson (1561), and Arthur Edwards (1568–69); the Roman nobleman Pietro Della Valle (1617–27; his *Lettere*, 2 vols., Turin, 1843, are most important); Sir Thomas Herbert (1627–29); the Germans, Adam Olearius (1635–38) and Engelbert Kämpfer (1684 onwards); the French merchant Tavernier (*ca.* 1640–60); Sir John Chardin (1664–77); the Catholic missionaries R. Du Mans, who spent fifty years in Iran (1645–96), and P. Sanson (1683–91); and the Russian merchant A. F. Kotov (1623). Don Juan of Persia—despite his name —is none other than the Azerbaijāni *qizilbāsh* Uruj Bek, who went to Spain in 1599 as secretary of a Safavid embassy, was converted to Christianity, and wrote a description of Persia under his new name, which was first published in Valladolid in 1604, followed by later editions.

Works by European scholars include:

W. Hinz, *Irans Aufstieg zum Nationalstaat*, Berlin, 1936.

L. Bellan, *Chah Abbas I*, Paris, 1932.

H. R. Roemer, *Der Niedergang Irans nach dem Tode Isma'ils des Grausamen 1577–1581*, Würzburg, 1939.

W. Minorsky, *La domination des Dailamites*, Paris, 1932.

H. R. Roemer, *Shah Ismail II*, Leipzig, 1940.

F. Babinger, 'Marino Sanuto's Tagebücher als Quellen zur Geschichte der Safawiya', in *Oriental Studies Presented to Edward Granville Browne*, 1922.

Sir E. Denison Ross, *Sir Anthony Sherley and his Persian Adventure*, London, 1933.

N. Falsafi, *Ƶindagānī-yi Shāh 'Abbās-i Avval* (a life of Shāh 'Abbās I), 2 vols., Teheran, 1332–35/1953–56.

Ghulam Sarwar, *History of Shāh Ismā'īl Safawi*, Aligarh, 1939.

J. Aubin, 'Etudes Safavides I: Shah Ismail et les notables de l'Iraq persan', in *Journal of Economic and Social History of the Orient*, II, 1, 1959, pp. 37–81.

H. Horst, *Tīmūr und Hōga 'Alī. Beitrag zur Geschichte der Safawiden*, Wiesbaden, 1958.

B. von Palombini, *Bündniswerben abendländischer Mächte um Persien*, 1453–1600, Wiesbaden, 1968.

K. M. Röhrborn, *Provinzen und Zentralgewalt Persiens im 16. und 17. Jahrhundert*, Berlin, 1966.

Chapter 9: The Afghans, Nādir Shāh, and Zands

Primary sources. Important for the period of Safavid decadence and the early years of Nādir Shāh are the unpublished *Zubdat at-Tavārīkh* of Muhammad Muhsin (1741–42), grand *mustaufī* of Nādir Shāh, and the autobiography of the Persian poet who wrote in the 'Indian style', 'Alī Hazīn, d. 1766 (*Tazkirat al-ahvāl*, ed. Balfour, London, 1831; trans. Balfour, London, 1836). There are at least ten chronicles devoted to Nādir's government and military campaigns. The most important are the works of Nādir's private secretary, Mīrzā Mahdī Khān (*Ta'rīkh-i Nādirī*, various editions published in Persia and India; Fr. trans., London, 1770, and Eng. trans., London, 1773, both by Sir William Jones; new Eng. trans. Guffar Syed, Ahmedabad, 1908); another important work is his collection of documents considered models of literary style but also of considerable historical interest (*Inshā*, Tabriz, 1294/1877); and the fundamental but still unpublished work of Muhammad Kāzim ('*Ālam-ārāy-i Nādirī* in three large volumes, for which see N. D. Miklukho-Maklal, 'Rukopis Alamara-i Nadiri' in *Uch. Zap. Inst. Vost. Ak. Nauk SSSR*, vol. VI, 1953.

Important for its account of the troubles following Nādir's death is the work of Abu 'l-Hasan ibn Muhammad Amīn Gulistānè (*Mujmal-i ta'rīkh-i ba'd-Nādiriyyè*, ed. O. Mann, Leiden, 1891, and M. Rizavī, Teheran, 1941–42).

There are two basic sources for the history of the Zands:
Muhammad Sadīq Mūsavi Nāmī, d. 1790 (*Ta'rīkh-i gītī-gushāi*, or *Ta'rīkh-i Zandiyyè*), continuation by Mirzā 'Abd al-Karīm and Muhammad Riza Shīrāzī up to 1794 (both ed. S. Nafīsī, Teheran, 1938); and 'Alī Riza Shīrāzī, for the years 1779–94 (his work is also entitled *Ta'rīkh-i Zandiyyè*, ed. Beer, Leiden, 1888).

The non-Persian sources include the interesting diary in Armenian of Sargis Gilianenc of New Julfa, describing the siege of Isfahān by the Afghans in 1722 (Russian trans. K. P. Patkanov, St Petersburg, 1870); and the autobiography of the *katholikos* of Echmiadzin, Abraam Kretaci, who attended the Mughān 'congress' to elect Nādir (Fr. trans. M. Brosset in *Collection des historiens arméniens*, vol. II); and the travel diaries of A. Voluinskii (1715–17), and of the Polish Jesuit, I. T. Krusinski, relating to the events of 1711–28 (*Tragica vertensis belli persici historia*, Fr. trans., Paris, 1736–39; Eng. trans. Du Cerceau, 2 vols., London, 1728); the travels of Le Brun (Amsterdam, 1718); and the important work of Jonas Hanway

(*An historical Account of the British trade over the Caspian Sea*, 4 vols., London, 1753); and H. Chick, *A Chronicle of the Carmelites in Persia*, London, 2 vols., 1939.

Works by European scholars include:

M. R. Arunova and K. Z. Ashrafyan, *Gosudarstvo Nadir-shaha Afshara*, Moscow, 1958. Contains a good bibliography.

L. Lockhart, *Nadir Shah*, London, 1938.

L. Lockhart, *The Fall of the Safavi Dynasty and the Afghan Occupation of Persia*, Cambridge, 1958.

W. Minorsky, *Esquisse d'une histoire de Nādir Shāh*, Paris, 1934.

Kishmishev, *Pokhodui Nadir Shaha v Gerat, Kandagar, Indiyu i sobuitiya v Persii posle ego smerti*, Tiflis, 1889.

N. D. Miklukho-Maklai, 'Iz istorii afganskogo vladychestva v Irane' in *Uch. Zap. Leningr. Gos. Univ.*, 179 (SVN vuip. 4), Leningrad, 1954.

Chapter 10: The Qājār dynasty to modern times

An important source for the early years of the Qājār dynasty is 'Abd ar-Razzāq Bek Dumbulī (1762–1827), a Kurd in the service of 'Abbās Mīrzā (*Ma'āthir-i Sultāniyyè*, which goes up to 1814, Tabrīz, 1825—one of the first books to be printed in Persia; Eng. trans. H. H. Brydges and D. Shea, London, 1833). Also important is the autobiography, with a long introduction on the history of the early Qājārs, of 'Abd Allāh Mustauf ī, late nineteenth century to early twentieth century (*Sharh-i zindagani-i man yā ta'rīkh-i ijtimā'ī va idārī-i doure-yi Qājār*, 3 vols., Teheran, 1324/1944).

The main sources for this period are listed in the standard works of S. Naf īsī, *Ta'rīkh-i ijtimā'ī va siyāsī-yi Irān der daure-yi mu'āsir*, Teheran, 1956; and A. K. Lambton, *Landlord and Peasant in Persia*, Oxford, 1953. This last work, though it does claim to cover political events, contains a very full general bibliography.

For the revolutionary period, the standard works are:

E. G. Browne, *A Brief Narrative of Recent Events in Persia*, London, 1909.

E. G. Browne, *The Persian Revolution of 1905–1909*, Cambridge, 1910.

E. G. Browne, *Prose and Poetry in Modern Persia*, Cambridge, 1914.

E. G. Browne, *A Year amongst the Persians* (1893; with a memoir, 1927).

M. S. Ivanov, *Iranskaia revolutsiia 1905–1911 govor*, Moscow, 1957.

On the Babis:

M. S. Ivanov, *Babidskie vosstaniya v Irane: 1848–52*, Moscow, 1939.

E. G. Browne, *Materials for the Study of the Bábí Religion*, Cambridge, 1918.

Further bibliographies are to be found in the articles on *Bāb, Bābīs, Bahā'ullāh*, and *Bahā'īs* by A. Bausani in the new edition of the *Encyclopaedia of Islam*.

There are many works of varying importance on modern Persia, the Persian re-awakening, etc. Mention may be made of the following:

Lord Curzon, *Persia and the Persian Question*, London, 1892.

F. Hesse, *Persien, Entwicklung und Gegenwart*, Berlin, 1932.

A. Akbar Siassi, *La Perse au contact de l'Occident, Etude historique et sociale*, Paris, 1931.

M. Nakhai, *L'évolution politique de l'Iran*, Paris, 1938.

W. Morgan Shuster, *The Strangling of Persia*, London, 1912.

H. Melzig, *Resa Schah*, Stuttgart, 1936.

D. N. Wilber, *Iran, Past and Present*, London, 6th edn, 1967.

A. C. Millspaugh, *Americans in Persia*, Washington, 1946.

Ellwell-Sutton, *Modern Iran*, London, 1941.

W. S. Haas, *Iran*, New York, 1946.

F. Steppat, *Iran zwischen den Weltmächten 1941–48*, Oberursel, 1948.

Amin Banani, *The Modernization of Iran 1921–1941*, Stanford, 1961. Contains an excellent, full bibliography, including the many essential works by Persian historians trained in modern methods of scholarship.

D. N. Wilber, *Contemporary Iran*, London, 1963.

R. W. Cottam, *Nationalism in Iran*, Pittsburgh, 1964.

M. L. Entner, *Russo-Persian Commercial Relations, 1828–1914*, Gainesville (Flo.), 1965.

S. Zabih, *The Communist Movement in Iran*, Berkeley-Los Angeles, 1966.

G. Scarcia, *La Persia durante la seconda guerra mondiale. Materiali e documenti*, in 'Oriente Moderno', XLVI, 1966, pp. 269–343.

N. R. Keddie, *Religion and Rebellion in Iran. The Iranian Tobacco Protest of 1891–1892*, London, 1966.

K. Asadulaev, *Sverzhenie dinastii Kadzharov v Irane (1920–1925)*. Dushamba, 1966.

P. Avery, *Modern Iran*, London, 1965

G. B. Baldwin, *Planning and Development in Iran*, Baltimore, 1967.

F. Kazemzadeh, *Russia and Britain in Persia, 1864–1914*, London, 1968.

H. Algar, *Religion and State in Iran 1785–1906. The Role of the Ulama in the Qajar Period*, Berkeley-Los Angeles, 1969.

A. K. S. Lambton, *The Persian Land Reform 1962–1966*, Oxford, 1969.

B. Nirumand, *Iran. The New Imperialism in Action*, London, 1969.

For recent events one should consult the specialist journals, particularly *Oriente Moderno*, founded in 1921 and published in Rome, which gives every month a detailed account of political and cultural affairs in Iran, with original translations from the Persian and foreign press. See also *The Middle East Journal* (Washington), *Middle Eastern Affairs* (New York), *Cahiers de l'Orient Contemporain* (Paris), and *L'Orient* (Paris).

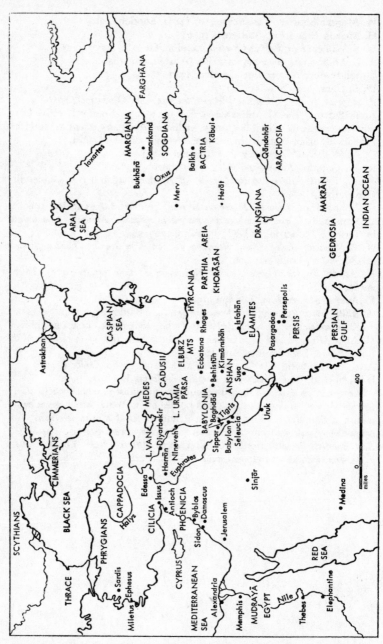

Ancient Iran under Darius (522–486 B.C.) and Alexander (359–336 B.C.)

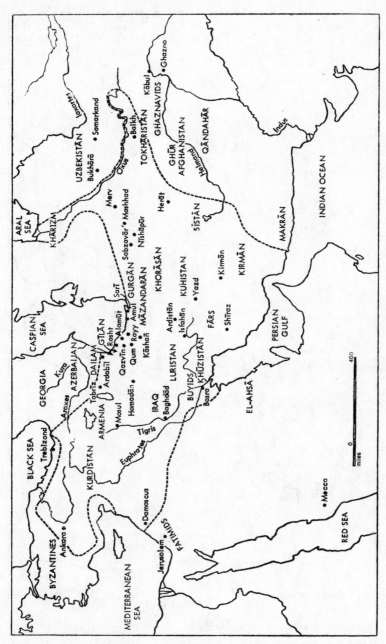

Persia under the Seljuks

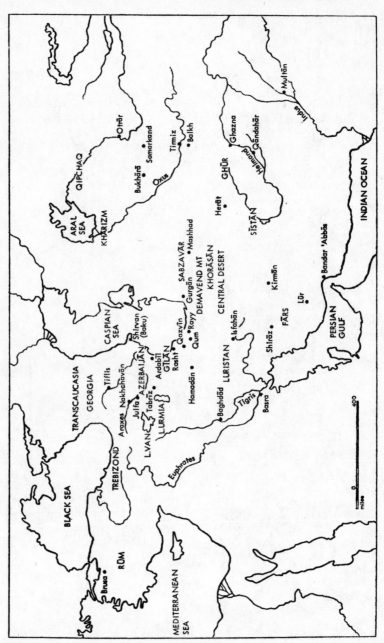

Persia under the Safavids and their successors

Index

Belisarius (Byzantine general), 65
Bihāfrīd movement, 77–8
Bihzād (miniature painter), 129
Buddhists, 108, 117
Bukhārā, 79–80, 106, 126
Burzōē (physician), 68
Buvaih or Būyè, founder of Buyid dynasty, 81
Buyid dynasty, 81, 83, 88
Byzantium. *See* Roman Empire

Cadusii tribe, 15, 28–9, 39
Cambyses I (600–599 BC), 15, 17, 36
Cambyses, son of Cyrus II, 18–19
Canals, 23, 84, 125
Cappadocia, 40, 47, 57
Caracalla, emperor, 43
Caravan routes. *See* Trade routes
Carina (Erzerum), 40
Carmathians, 96–7
Carpets, 152
Carus, emperor, 58
Caucasus, 12, 111, 155
Caucasian Iberia (Western Georgia), 41
Central Asia, 67, 87, 106, 108, 124, 138, 141
Chagrī-beg Dāūd, 95
Chang Ch'ien (traveller), 45–6
Characene, kingdom of, 38
Chess, introduction of, 67
China, 45–6, 56, 87, 108–9, 127, 152
Chīngīz Khān (d. 1227), 107–8, 124, 126
Chionite people, 59, 61
Chosroes. *See* Osrhoes
Chosroes I (531–579), 63–8, 89
Chosroes II (d. 628), 68–9
Christians, Christianity, 47, 59, 71, 74, 112, 114, 118; persecutions of, 56, 60–1; favourably regarded in early days, 58; pro-Roman intrigues, 59–60; Church of Iran made independent of Byzantium, 61; Nestorians, 62; and Mazdaeans, 64
Cilicia, 40, 47
Cimmerians, 14
Cities: development of, 34–5; life in, under the Arabs, 90–2;

under the Seljuks, 101; destroyed by the Mongols, 116; destroyed by Tīmūr, 125; life in, under the Safavids, 151–3
Cleopatra, 40
Coinage: introduction of, 22; Greek-influenced, 36; Safavid, 147
See also Paper money
Commagena, 47
Communications, 35
Confucius, 11
Conon (Athenian general), 28
Constantine I, emperor, 58–9
Constitution of 1906, 171
Cotton cultivation, 85
Crassus (consul of Syria), 39–40
Croesus, king of Lydia, 17–18
Ctesiphon (ancient Seleucia), 34, 43, 55, 58, 67, 70
Cyaxares I, 13
Cyaxares II, 14–15
Cyrus ('great king, king of Anshan', 640–615 BC), 14
Cyrus II (the Great; 558–528 BC), 16–19
Cyrus the Younger, 28

Dahae or Dai tribe, 37
Dailam, 73
Damascus, 69, 77
Daqīqī (poet), 80
Darius I (521–486 BC), 19–27, 32, 36
Darius II, 28
Darius III (335–330 BC), 29–30
Dating, system of, 46
Dayyaku (Medean chief), 13
Deioces (Medean chief), 13
Dervishes, 102
Diodotus, 37
Diyarbekir, 135
Drangiana (modern Sīstān), 18, 37–8
Dura, city of, 34, 47
Dura-Europos, 44–5, 47

Ecbatana (modern Hamadān, *q.v.*), 13, 17, 22, 35, 38, 44, 47, 70
Economy. *See* Agriculture; Coinage; Trade
Edessa, Syria, 35, 42, 55, 62, 69

Qandahār, 125, 135, 144, 158
Qara-qoyunlu dynasty (Turkoman), 130–1
Qazvīn, city of, 80, 103, 143, 144, 157
Qubilay Khān, 109–11
Qurratu'l-'Ain, known as Tāhirè (poetess), 166
Qutbu'd-Dīn Muhammad, king of Khārizm, 106

Racial purity (a foundation of Persian society), 62
Rashīdu'd-Dīn (physician and encyclopaedist), 115–16, 119–21
Rayy, city of (ancient Rhages, q.v.), 77, 79, 81, 85–6, 103
Rāzī (experimental scientist), 103
Rhages (later Rayy, q.v.), 15, 161
Rice cultivation, 85
Rizā Khān (Rizā Shāh), 176–9
Rizā Qulī Khān Hedāyat (1800–72), 167
Roads. See Communications
Roman Empire: and Parthia, 39–40, 42–3; conquers Armenia, 41; conflicts with Persia, 57–61, 65–9
Rūdagī (poet), 80
Ruknu'd-Dīn (Grand Master of Alamūt), 110
Rūm, sultanate of, 111
Russia, 162–3, 165, 168, 170–1, 176, 178
Rustam (Sassanid general), 32, 70

Sabzavār: city of, 100, 125; republic of, 121
Sa'dī (poet), 117, 161
Sadru'd-Dīn (Gaikhātū's minister), 112–13
Sa'du'd-Daula (vizier to Arghūn), 112
Safavids, 122, 127, 131, 135, 164; a dynastic and mystical brotherhood, 135–7; their conquests, 137–8; defeated at Chaldiran by the Ottomans, 138; their arrival, and Shi'ism in Iran, 138–40; culture, 141; economy, 142–3, 146–7, 148–53, 155; reign of 'Abbas the Great, 134–5;

decline, 145–6; social and political organization, 147–50; and the Afghan invasion, 154–6; campaigns of Nādir Shāh, and his harsh rule, 157–60; internecine strife, and end of the dynasty, 160–3
Saffarid dynasty of Khorāsān, 79
Saf īuddīn, Shaikh Ishāq, 136
Saka people, 38, 45
Sakastāna, 38–9
Samanid dynasty, 79–81
Sāmān-khudāt, founder of the Samanid dynasty, 79
Samarkand (ancient Marakanda, q.v.), 79, 106, 126–7
Sanjar, Seljuk ruler (d. 1157), 99–100
Sapor (Shāhpūr), 43
Sargon II (722–705 BC), 13
Sarī, port of, 86
Sarkash (musician), 69
Sāsān, 43, 48
Sassanid dynasty, 43; achievements of Ardashīr, 48–9; social and political organization, 49–51; trade, 51; religion, 51–7; conflicts and conquests, 57–62; and Mazdakism, 62–4; reforms of Chosroes I, 65–8; decline, 68–70
Satrapies, 21–2, 44
Sculpture, Parthian, 47
Scythians, 13
Seleucia, city of, 34–6, 38, 45, 49, 67; occupied by Mithridates, 37; capital of Parthia, 40; occupied by the Romans, 42–3; occupied by the Arabs, 70
Seleucia, state of, 36, 38
Seleucid dynasty, 36–43, 45
Seleucus I Nicator (d. 281 BC), 36
Seleucus II, 37
Selim the Grim, Ottoman sultan (1512–20), 138
Seljuks, 83, 94, 117; origins, and their conquests, 95; struggle with the Ismailis, 97–100; political system, 100–1; culture, 102–5; break up of their empire, 106
Semnān, 135, 137

under the Mongols, 108–9; Safavid period, 147–8, 151–3, 155
Trade routes, 41, 45, 51, 86
Trajan, emperor, 42
Transcaucasia, 86, 108, 111, 125, 138
Transoxiana, 76–7, 106–7, 125, 127
Trebizond, empire of, 111
Turfan, 46
Turkestan, 45
Turkomans, 128, 130, 159; their two dynasties, 130–5
Turks, 113, 179–80; invade Central Asia, 67; Tlek Khān Turks, 79–80; as slaves, 88
  See also Ottoman Turks; Safavids; Seljuks; Turkomans

Ugädäi, Great Khān (1229–41), 108
Ulugh Beg, Timurid ruler, 127
Universities: Islamic, 102–3; of Teheran, 177
'Unsurī (poet), 83
Uzbeks, 135, 137, 159
Uzun Hasan, Turkoman ruler, (d. 1478), 128, 130

Vahrām I (273–6), 55, 58
Vahrām II (276–93), 58
Vahrām III (d. 293), 58
Vahrām IV (388–99), 59
Vahrām V (421–ca 438), 60–1, 72
Vahrām, called Chōbēn (rebel general under Hormizd IV), 68–9
Valash, king of Persia (d. 488), 62
Valentinian, emperor, 59
Valerian, emperor, 57
Verus, Lucius, emperor, 42
Vologases I, king of Parthia (AD 51–77), 39, 42, 46

Vologases II, king of Parthia (128/9–147), 42
Vologases III, king of Parthia, 42
Vologases IV, king of Parthia, 42–3
Vologases V, king of Parthia (d. 222–3), 43
Vushmgīr, Ziyarid ruler, 81

White Huns. *See* Chionite people; Hephthalites
Writing, 25; adoption of Arabic script, 76
Wu Ti, emperor of China, 38, 45

Xenophon, 28

Xerxes I (486–465 BC), 27–8
Xerxes II, 28

Ya'qūb, Turkoman ruler, 131
Yazd, city of, 84, 135, 137, 157
Yazdagird I (399–421), 59–60
Yazdagird II (438/9–457), 61
Yazdagird III (632–51/2), 69–70, 73
Yazīd I, caliph (680–3), 75
Yemen, the, 67, 95

Zagros (Western Iran), 12
Zand dynasty, 160–2
Zarathustra. *See* Zoroaster
Zarmihr (Persian general), 62
Zeinab (Zenobia, queen of Palmyra), 57
Zeno the Isaurian, Byzantine emperor, 62
Zeugma, 40, 45
Zhāmāsp, king of Persia, 65
Ziyarid dynasty of Tabaristān, 80–1
Zoroaster, 11, 20, 25–6, 54; Zoroastrians and Zoroastrianism, 50, 52–4, 56, 61, 74, 77–8, 80, 114